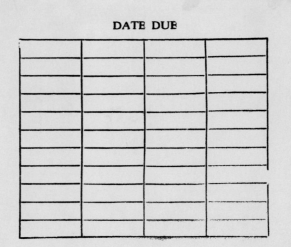

JANE AUSTEN

Modern Critical Views

Henry Adams
Edward Albee
A. R. Ammons
Matthew Arnold
John Ashbery
W. H. Auden
Jane Austen
James Baldwin
Charles Baudelaire
Samuel Beckett
Saul Bellow
The Bible
Elizabeth Bishop
William Blake
Jorge Luis Borges
Elizabeth Bowen
Bertolt Brecht
The Brontës
Robert Browning
Anthony Burgess
George Gordon, Lord
  Byron
Thomas Carlyle
Lewis Carroll
Willa Cather
Cervantes
Geoffrey Chaucer
Kate Chopin
Samuel Taylor Coleridge
Joseph Conrad
Contemporary Poets
Hart Crane
Stephen Crane
Dante
Charles Dickens
Emily Dickinson
John Donne & the Seven-
  teenth-Century Meta-
  physical Poets
Elizabethan Dramatists
Theodore Dreiser
John Dryden
George Eliot
T. S. Eliot
Ralph Ellison
Ralph Waldo Emerson
William Faulkner
Henry Fielding
F. Scott Fitzgerald
Gustave Flaubert
E. M. Forster
Sigmund Freud
Robert Frost

Robert Graves
Graham Greene
Thomas Hardy
Nathaniel Hawthorne
William Hazlitt
Seamus Heaney
Ernest Hemingway
Geoffrey Hill
Friedrich Hölderlin
Homer
Gerard Manley Hopkins
William Dean Howells
Zora Neale Hurston
Henry James
Samuel Johnson and
  James Boswell
Ben Jonson
James Joyce
Franz Kafka
John Keats
Rudyard Kipling
D. H. Lawrence
John Le Carré
Ursula K. Le Guin
Doris Lessing
Sinclair Lewis
Robert Lowell
Norman Mailer
Bernard Malamud
Thomas Mann
Christopher Marlowe
Carson McCullers
Herman Melville
James Merrill
Arthur Miller
John Milton
Eugenio Montale
Marianne Moore
Iris Murdoch
Vladimir Nabokov
Joyce Carol Oates
Sean O'Casey
Flannery O'Connor
Eugene O'Neill
George Orwell
Cynthia Ozick
Walter Pater
Walker Percy
Harold Pinter
Plato
Edgar Allan Poe
Poets of Sensibility & the
  Sublime

Alexander Pope
Katherine Ann Porter
Ezra Pound
Pre-Raphaelite Poets
Marcel Proust
Thomas Pynchon
Arthur Rimbaud
Theodore Roethke
Philip Roth
John Ruskin
J. D. Salinger
Gershom Scholem
William Shakespeare
  (3 vols.)
  Histories & Poems
  Comedies
  Tragedies
George Bernard Shaw
Mary Wollstonecraft
  Shelley
Percy Bysshe Shelley
Edmund Spenser
Gertrude Stein
John Steinbeck
Laurence Sterne
Wallace Stevens
Tom Stoppard
Jonathan Swift
Alfred, Lord Tennyson
William Makepeace
  Thackeray
Henry David Thoreau
Leo Tolstoi
Anthony Trollope
Mark Twain
John Updike
Gore Vidal
Virgil
Robert Penn Warren
Evelyn Waugh
Eudora Welty
Nathanael West
Edith Wharton
Walt Whitman
Oscar Wilde
Tennessee Williams
William Carlos Williams
Thomas Wolfe
Virginia Woolf
William Wordsworth
Richard Wright
William Butler Yeats

These and other titles in preparation

Modern Critical Views

JANE AUSTEN

Edited and with an introduction by
Harold Bloom
Sterling Professor of the Humanities
Yale University

CHELSEA HOUSE PUBLISHERS
New York ◊ Philadelphia

© 1986 by Chelsea House Publishers, a division of
Main Line Book Co.

Introduction © 1986 by Harold Bloom

Printed and bound in the United States of America

10 9 8 7 6 5 4 3 2

∞ The paper used in this publication meets the minimum
requirements of the American National Standard for Permanence
of Paper for Printed Library Materials, Z39.48–1984.

Library of Congress Cataloging-in-Publication Data
Jane Austen.
    (Modern critical views)
    Bibliography: p.
    Includes index.
Summary: A collection of critical essays on Austen
and her works. Also includes a chronology of events in
her life.
    1. Austen, Jane, 1775–1817—Criticism and interpreta-
tion. [1. Austen, Jane, 1775–1817—Criticism and
interpretation. 2. English literature—History and
criticism] I. Bloom, Harold. II. Series.
PR4037.J28 1986   823'.7   86–12974
ISBN 0–87754–682–7 (alk. paper)

Contents

Editor's Note

This book brings together a representative selection of the best literary criticism devoted to Jane Austen during recent years, arranged here in the chronological order of its original publication. I am grateful to Susan Laity for her erudition and judgment in helping to locate and select these essays.

The editor's introduction centers upon Austen's heroines as exemplars of the Protestant will, in imaginative descent from Richardson's Clarissa Harlowe. Joel Weinsheimer begins the chronological sequence with an essay that argues for choice as against chance in "the hierarchy of marriages" in *Pride and Prejudice*, insisting against critics solely addicted to irony that freedom in Austen is always mutual rather than solitary. Alice Chandler, considering the vision of sexuality in Austen, emphasizes how subtly the treatment of sexual selectivity works itself out in novels so overtly governed by custom and ceremony.

In a shrewd reading of *Sense and Sensibility*, Ruth apRoberts defends the early novel's aesthetic importance and its place in Austen's canon. Gene W. Ruoff, reflecting on the conclusion of the final novel, *Persuasion*, relates Austen to Wordsworth, in a way quite different from those attempted by the editor and by Ruth apRoberts. Austen's earliest writings are analyzed by our leading feminist critics, Sandra M. Gilbert and Susan Gubar, as instances of what will lead to her subversion of conventional expectations harbored towards a woman writer.

In an exegesis of *Emma*, Julia Prewitt Brown conveys a sense of the novel's deliberate self-absorption in its own heterocosm. Susan Morgan, writing upon *Northanger Abbey*, sees it as the book that establishes Austen's view of people as being fallible but redeemable, and so neither angels nor devils. *Mansfield Park* is read by Gary Kelly as a study of reading, and of the revelation of character by a reading aloud within the novel itself. Ann Molan's deft appraisal of "persuasion" in *Persuasion* sees it as a belief *in* one's self, rather than a conviction *that* one's self will win its agon with others, and with tradition.

In an intricate balance of manners and morals, Martin Price exalts Austen as a moral imagination rather than a mere asserter of morality, interestingly becoming the fourth critic in this volume who independently discovers Wordsworthian affinities where older criticism did not find them in the supposedly more Augustan than Romantic Austen. Robin Grove's reading of the ending of Austen's novels joins itself to Price's emphasis by praising Austen for the moral imagination that allows so much to be unsaid in the novelist's ambiguous conclusions.

Ian Watt, the eminent student of the historical rise of the novel as a genre, contributes a masterly grace note on *Sense and Sensibility, Emma,* and *Pride and Prejudice* that outlines Austen's modes of comic aggression. Finally, Deborah Kaplan considers Austen's feminine tropes of authority in *Sense and Sensibility,* finding in them a subtle means of the new writer coming to terms with a patriarchal tradition.

Introduction

The oddest yet by no means inapt analogy to Jane Austen's art of representation is Shakespeare's—oddest, because she is so careful of limits, as classical as Ben Jonson in that regard, and Shakespeare transcends all limits. Austen's humor, her mode of rhetorical irony, is not particularly Shakespearean, and yet her precision and accuracy of representation is. Like Shakespeare, she gives us figures, major and minor, utterly consistent each in her or his own mode of speech and being, and utterly different from one another. Her heroines have firm selves, each molded with an individuality that continues to suggest Austen's reserve of power, her potential for creating an endless diversity. To recur to the metaphor of oddness, the highly deliberate limitation of social scale in Austen seems a paradoxical theater of mind in which so fecund a humanity could be fostered. Irony, the concern of most critics of Austen, seems more than a trope in her work, seems indeed to be the condition of her language, yet hardly accounts for the effect of moral and spiritual power that she so constantly conveys, however implicitly or obliquely.

Ian Watt, in his permanently useful *The Rise of the Novel*, portrays Austen as Fanny Burney's direct heir in the difficult art of combining the rival modes of Samuel Richardson and Henry Fielding. Like Burney, Austen is thus seen as following the Richardson of *Sir Charles Grandison* in a "minute presentation of daily life," while emulating Fielding "in adopting a more detached attitude to her narrative material, and in evaluating it from a comic and objective point of view." Watt goes further when he points out that Austen tells her stories in a discreet variant of Fielding's manner "as a confessed author," though her ironical juxtapositions are made to appear not those of "an intrusive author but rather of some august and impersonal spirit of social and psychological understanding."

1

And yet, as Watt knows, Austen truly is the daughter of Richardson and not of Fielding, just as she is the ancestor of George Eliot and Henry James rather than of Dickens and Thackeray. Her inwardness is an ironic revision of Richardson's extraordinary conversion of English Protestant sensibility into the figure of Clarissa Harlowe, and her own moral and spiritual concerns fuse in the crucial need of her heroines to sustain their individual integrities, a need so intense that it compels them to fall into those errors about life that are necessary for life (to adopt a Nietzschean formulation). In this too they follow, though in a comic register, the pattern of their tragic precursor, the magnificent but sublimely flawed Clarissa Harlowe.

Richardson's *Clarissa,* perhaps still the longest novel in the language, seems to me also still the greatest, despite the achievements of Austen, Dickens, George Eliot, Henry James, and Joyce. Austen's Elizabeth Bennet and Emma Woodhouse, Eliot's Dorothea Brooke and Gwendolen Harleth, James's Isabel Archer and Milly Theale—though all these are Clarissa Harlowe's direct descendants, they are not proportioned to her more sublime scale. David Copperfield and Leopold Bloom have her completeness; indeed Joyce's Bloom may be the most complete representation of a human being in all of literature. But they belong to the secular age; Clarissa Harlowe is poised upon the threshold that leads from the Protestant religion to a purely secular sainthood.

C. S. Lewis, who read Milton as though that fiercest of Protestant temperaments had been an orthodox Anglican, also seems to have read Jane Austen by listening for her echoings of the New Testament. Quite explicitly, Lewis named Austen as the daughter of Dr. Samuel Johnson, greatest of literary critics and rigorous Christian moralist:

> I feel . . . sure that she is the daughter of Dr. Johnson: she inherits
> his commonsense, his morality, even much of his style.

The Johnson of *Rasselas* and *The Rambler,* surely the essential Johnson, is something of a classical ironist, but we do not read Johnson for his ironies, or for his dramatic representations of fictive selves. Rather, we read him as we read Koheleth; he writes wisdom literature. That Jane Austen is a wise writer is indisputable, but we do not read *Pride and Prejudice* as though it were Ecclesiastes. Doubtless, Austen's religious ideas were as profound as Samuel Richardson's were shallow, but *Emma* and *Clarissa* are Protestant novels without being in any way religious. What is most original about the representation of Clarissa Harlowe is the magnificent intensity of her slowly described dying, which goes on for about the last third of Richardson's vast novel, in a Puritan ritual that celebrates the preternatural strength of her will. For that is Richardson's sublime concern: the self-reliant apotheosis of the Protestant will. What is tragedy in *Clarissa* becomes serious or moral comedy in *Pride and Prejudice* and *Emma,* and something just the other side of comedy in *Mansfield Park* and *Persuasion.*

II

Rereading *Pride and Prejudice* gives one a sense of Proustian ballet beautifully working itself through in the novel's formal centerpiece, the deferred but progressive mutual enlightenment of Elizabeth and Darcy in regard to the other's true nature. "Proper pride" is what they learn to recognize in one another; propriety scarcely needs definition in that phrase, but precisely what is the pride that allows amiability to flourish? Whatever it is in Darcy, to what extent is it an art of the will in Elizabeth Bennet? Consider the superb scene of Darcy's first and failed marriage proposal:

> While settling this point, she was suddenly roused by the sound of the door-bell, and her spirits were a little fluttered by the idea of its being Colonel Fitzwilliam himself, who had once before called late in the evening, and might now come to inquire particularly after her. But this idea was soon banished, and her spirits were very differently affected, when, to her utter amazement, she saw Mr. Darcy walk into the room. In an hurried manner he immediately began an inquiry after her health, imputing his visit to a wish of hearing that she were better. She answered him with cold civility. He sat down for a few moments, and then getting up, walked about the room. Elizabeth was surprised, but said not a word. After a silence of several minutes, he came towards her in an agitated manner, and thus began:
> "In vain have I struggled. It will not do. My feelings will not be repressed. You must allow me to tell you how ardently I admire and love you."
> Elizabeth's astonishment was beyond expression. She stared, coloured, doubted, and was silent. This he considered sufficient encouragement; and the avowal of all that he felt, and had long felt for her, immediately followed. He spoke well; but there were feelings besides those of the heart to be detailed, and he was not more eloquent on the subject of tenderness than of pride. His sense of her inferiority—of its being a degradation—of the family obstacles which judgment had always opposed to inclination,

were dwelt on with a warmth which seemed due to the consequence he was wounding, but was very unlikely to recommend
his suit.

In spite of her deeply-rooted dislike, she could not be insensible
to the compliment of such a man's affection, and though her
intentions did not vary for an instant, she was at first sorry for
the pain he was to receive; till, roused to resentment by his subsequent language, she lost all compassion in anger. She tried,
however, to compose herself to answer him with patience, when
he should have done. He concluded with representing to her the
strength of that attachment which, in spite of all his endeavours,
he had found impossible to conquer; and with expressing his hope
that it would now be rewarded by her acceptance of his hand. As
he said this, she could easily see that he had no doubt of a fa-
vourable answer. He *spoke* of apprehension and anxiety, but his
countenance expressed real security. Such a circumstance could
only exasperate farther, and, when he ceased, the colour rose into
her cheeks, and she said:

"In such cases as this, it is, I believe, the established mode to
express a sense of obligation for the sentiments avowed, however
unequally they may be returned. It is natural that obligation
should be felt, and if I could *feel* gratitude, I would now thank
you. But I cannot—I have never desired your good opinion, and
you have certainly bestowed it most unwillingly. I am sorry to
have occasioned pain to anyone. It has been most unconsciously
done, however, and I hope will be of short duration. The feelings
which, you tell me, have long prevented the acknowledgment of
your regard, can have little difficulty in overcoming it after this
explanation."

Mr. Darcy, who was leaning against the mantelpiece with his
eyes fixed on her face, seemed to catch her words with no less
resentment than surprise. His complexion became pale with anger, and the disturbance of his mind was visible in every feature.
He was struggling for the appearance of composure, and would
not open his lips till he believed himself to have attained it. The
pause was to Elizabeth's feelings dreadful. At length, in a voice
of forced calmness, he said:

"And this is all the reply which I am to have the honour of
expecting! I might, perhaps, wish to be informed why, with so

little *endeavour* at civility, I am thus rejected. But it is of small importance."

Stuart M. Tave believes that both Darcy and Elizabeth become so changed by one another that their "happiness is deserved by a process of mortification begun early and ended late," mortification here being the wounding of pride. Tave's learning and insight are impressive, but I favor the judgment that Elizabeth and Darcy scarcely change, and learn rather that they complement each other's not wholly illegitimate pride. They come to see that their wills are naturally allied, since they have no differences upon the will. The will to what? Their will, Austen's, is neither the will to live nor the will to power. They wish to be esteemed precisely where they estimate value to be high, and neither can afford to make a fundamental error, which is both the anxiety and the comedy of the first proposal scene. Why after all does Darcy allow himself to be eloquent on the subject of his pride, to the extraordinary extent of conveying "with a warmth" what Austen grimly names as "his sense of her inferiority"?

As readers, we have learned already that Elizabeth is inferior to no one, whoever he is. Indeed, I sense as the novel closes (though nearly all Austen critics, and doubtless Austen herself, would disagree with me) that Darcy is her inferior, amiable and properly prideful as he is. I do not mean by this that Elizabeth is a clearer representation of Austenian values than Darcy ever could be; that is made finely obvious by Austen, and her critics have developed her ironic apprehension, which is that Elizabeth incarnates the standard of measurement in her cosmos. There is also a transcendent strength to Elizabeth's will that raises her above that cosmos, in a mode that returns us to Clarissa Harlowe's transcendence of her society, of Lovelace, and even of everything in herself that is not the will to a self-esteem that has also made an accurate estimate of every other will to pride it ever has encountered.

I am suggesting that Ralph Waldo Emerson (who to me is sacred) was mistaken when he rejected Austen as a "sterile" upholder of social conformities and social ironies, as an author who could not celebrate the soul's freedom from societal conventions. Austen's ultimate irony is that Elizabeth Bennet is inwardly so free that convention performs for her the ideal function it cannot perform for us: it liberates her will without tending to stifle her high individuality. But we ought to be wary of even the most distinguished of Austen's moral celebrants, Lionel Trilling, who in effect defended her against Emerson by seeing *Pride and Prejudice* as a triumph "of morality as style." If Emerson wanted to see a touch more Margaret Fuller in Elizabeth

Bennet (sublimely ghastly notion!), Trilling wanted to forget the Emersonian law of Compensation, which is that nothing is got for nothing:

> The relation of Elizabeth Bennet to Darcy is real, is intense, but it expresses itself as a conflict and reconciliation of styles: a formal rhetoric, traditional and rigorous, must find a way to accommodate a female vivacity, which in turn must recognize the principled demands of the strict male syntax. The high moral import of the novel lies in the fact that the union of styles is accomplished without injury to either lover.

Yes and no, I would say. Yes, because the wills of both lovers work by similar dialectics, but also no, because Elizabeth's will is more intense and purer, and inevitably must be dimmed by her dwindling into a wife, even though Darcy may well be the best man that society could offer to her. Her pride has playfulness in it, a touch even of the Quixotic. Uncannily, she is both her father's daughter, and Samuel Richardson's daughter as well. Her wit is Mr. Bennet's, refined and elaborated, but her will, and her pride in her will, returns us to Clarissa's Puritan passion to maintain the power of the self to confer esteem, and to accept esteem only in response to its bestowal.

III

John Locke argues against personifying the will: persons can be free, but not the will, since the will cannot be constrained, except externally. While one sleeps, if someone moved one into another room and locked the door, and there one found a friend one wished to see, still one could not say that one was free thus to see whom one wished. And yet Locke implies that the process of association does work as though the will were internally constrained. Association, in Locke's sense, is a blind substitution for reasoning, yet is within a reasoning process, though also imbued with affect. The mind, in association, is carried unwillingly from one thought to another, by accident as it were. Each thought appears, and carries along with it a crowd of unwanted guests, inhabitants of a room where the thought would rather be alone. Association, on this view, is what the will most needs to be defended against.

Fanny Price, in *Mansfield Park*, might be considered a co-descendant, together with Locke's association-menaced will, of the English Protestant emphasis upon the will's autonomy. Fanny, another precursor of the Virginia Woolf of *A Room of One's Own*, was shrewdly described by Lionel Trilling as "overtly virtuous and consciously virtuous," and therefore almost impossible to like, though Trilling (like Austen) liked Fanny very much. C. S. Lewis, though an orthodox moralist, thought Fanny insipid: "But into Fanny, Jane Austen, to counterbalance her apparent insignificance, has put really nothing except rectitude of mind; neither passion, nor physical courage, nor wit, nor resource." Nothing, I would say, except the Protestant will, resisting the powers of association and asserting its very own persistence, its own sincere intensity, and its own isolate sanctions. Trilling secularized these as "the sanctions of principle" and saw *Mansfield Park* as a novel that "discovers in principle the path to the wholeness of the self which is peace." That is movingly said, but secularization, in literature, is always a failed trope, since the distinction between sacred and secular is not actually a literary but rather a societal or political distinction. *Mansfield Park* is not less Protestant than *Paradise Lost,* even though Austen, *as a writer,* was as much a sect of one as John Milton was.

Fanny Price, like the Lockean will, fights against accident, against the crowding out of life by associations that are pragmatically insincere not because they are random, but because they are irrelevant, since whatever is not the will's own is irrelevant to it. If Fanny herself is an irony it is as Austen's allegory of her own defense against influences, human and literary, whether in her family circle or in the literary family of Fanny Burney, Fielding, and Richardson. Stuart Tave shrewdly remarks that: "*Mansfield Park* is a novel in which many characters are engaged in trying to establish influence over the minds and lives of others, often in a contest or struggle for control." Fanny, as a will struggling only to be itself, becomes at last the spiritual center of Mansfield Park precisely because she has never sought power over any other will. It is the lesson of the Protestant will, whether in Locke or Austen, Richardson or George Eliot, that the refusal to seek power over other wills is what opens the inward eye of vision. Such a lesson, which, we seek in Wordsworth and in Ruskin, is offered more subtly (though less sublimely) by Austen. Fanny, Austen's truest surrogate, has a vision of what Mansfield Park is and ought to be, which means a vision also of what Sir Thomas Bertram is or ought to be. Her vision is necessarily moral, but could as truly be called spiritual, or even aesthetic.

Perhaps that is why Fanny is not only redeemed but can redeem others. The quietest and most mundane of visionaries, she remains also one of the firmest: her dedication is to the future of Mansfield Park as the idea of order it once seemed to her. Jane Austen may not be a Romantic in the high Shelleyan mode, but Fanny Price has profound affinities with Wordsworth, so that it is no accident that *Mansfield Park* is exactly contemporary with

The Excursion. Wordsworthian continuity, the strength that carries the past alive into the present, is the program of renovation that Fanny's pure will brings to Mansfield Park, and it is a program more Romantic than Augustan, so that Fanny's will begins to shade into the Wordsworthian account of the imagination. Fanny's exile to Portsmouth is so painful to her not for reasons turning upon social distinctions, but for causes related to the quiet that Wordsworth located in the bliss of solitude, or Virginia Woolf in a room of one's own:

> Such was the home which was to put Mansfield out of her head, and teach her to think of her cousin Edmund with moderated feelings. On the contrary, she could think of nothing but Mansfield, its beloved inmates, its happy ways. Everything where she now was was in full contrast to it. The elegance, propriety, regularity, harmony, and perhaps, above all, the peace and tranquillity of Mansfield, were brought to her remembrance every hour of the day, by the prevalence of everything opposite to them *here*.
>
> The living in incessant noise was, to a frame and temper delicate and nervous like Fanny's, an evil which no super-added elegance or harmony could have entirely atoned for. It was the greatest misery of all. At Mansfield, no sounds of contention, no raised voice, no abrupt bursts, no tread of violence, was ever heard; all proceeded in a regular course of cheerful orderliness; everybody had their due importance; everybody's feelings were consulted. If tenderness could be ever supposed wanting, good sense and good breeding supplied its place; and as to the little irritations, sometimes introduced by Aunt Norris, they were short, they were trifling, they were as a drop of water to the ocean, compared with the ceaseless tumult of her present abode. Here, everybody was noisy, every voice was loud (excepting, perhaps, her mother's, which resembled the soft monotony of Lady Bertram's, only worn into fretfulness). Whatever was wanted was halloo'd for, and the servants halloo'd out their excuses from the kitchen. The doors were in constant banging, the stairs were never at rest, nothing was done without a clatter, nobody sat still, and nobody could command attention when they spoke.
>
> In a review of the two houses, as they appeared to her before the end of a week, Fanny was tempted to apply to them Dr. Johnson's celebrated judgment as to matrimony and celibacy, and say, that though Mansfield Park might have some pains, Portsmouth could have no pleasures.

The citation of Dr. Johnson's aphorism, though placed here with superb wit, transcends irony. Austen rather seeks to confirm, however implicitly, Johnson's powerful warning, in *The Rambler,* number 4, against the over-whelming realism of Fielding and Smollett (though their popular prevalence is merely hinted):

> But if the power of example is so great, as to take possession of
> the memory by a kind of violence, and produce effects almost
> without the intervention of the will, care ought to be taken, that,
> when the choice is unrestrained, the best examples only should
> be exhibited; and that which is likely to operate so strongly,
> should not be mischievous or uncertain in its effects.

Fanny Price, rather more than Jane Austen perhaps, really does favor a Johnsonian aesthetic, in life as in literature. Portsmouth belongs to representation as practiced by Smollett, belongs to the cosmos of *Roderick Random.* Fanny, in willing to get back to Mansfield Park, and to get Mansfield Park back to itself, is willing herself also to renovate the world of her creator, the vision of Jane Austen that is *Mansfield Park.*

IV

Sir Walter Scott, reviewing *Emma* in 1815, rather strangely compared Jane Austen to the masters of the Flemish school of painting, presumably because of her precision in representing her characters. The strangeness results from Scott's not seeing how English Austen was, though the Scots perspective may have entered into his estimate. To me, as an American critic, *Emma* seems the most English of English novels, and beyond question one of the very best. More than *Pride and Prejudice,* it is Austen's masterpiece, the largest triumph of her vigorous art. Her least accurate prophecy as to the fate of her fictions concerned *Emma,* whose heroine, she thought, "no one but myself will much like."

Aside from much else, Emma is immensely likable, because she is so extraordinarily imaginative, dangerous and misguided as her imagination frequently must appear to others and finally to herself. On the scale of being, Emma constitutes an answer to the immemorial questions of the Sublime: More? Equal to? Or less than? Like Clarissa Harlowe before her, and the strongest heroines of George Eliot and Henry James after her, Emma Woodhouse has a heroic will, and like them she risks identifying her will with her imagination. Socially considered, such identification is catastrophic, since the Protestant will has a tendency to bestow a ranking upon other selves, and such ranking may turn out to be a personal phantasmagoria. G. Armour Craig rather finely remarked that: "society in *Emma* is not a ladder. It is a web of imputations that link feelings and conduct." Yet Emma herself, expansionist rather than reductionist in temperament, imputes more fiercely and freely than the web can sustain, and she threatens always, until she is enlightened, to dissolve the societal links, in and for others, that might allow some stability between feelings and conduct.

Armour Craig usefully added that: "*Emma* does not justify its heroine nor does it deride her." Rather it treats her with ironic love (not loving irony). Emma Woodhouse is dear to Jane Austen, because her errors are profoundly imaginative, and rise from the will's passion for autonomy of vision. The splendid Jane Fairfax is easier to admire, but I cannot agree with Wayne Booth's awarding the honors to her over Emma, though I admire the subtle balance of his formulation:

> Jane is superior to Emma in most respects except the stroke of
> good fortune that made Emma the heroine of the book. In matters
> of taste and ability, of head and of heart, she is Emma's superior.

Taste, ability, head, and heart are a formidable fourfold; the imagination and the will, working together, are an even more formidable twofold, and clearly may have their energies diverted to error and to mischief. Jane Fairfax is certainly more *amiable* even than Emma Woodhouse, but she is considerably less interesting. It is Emma who is meant to charm us, and who does charm us. Austen is not writing a tragedy of the will, like *Paradise Lost,* but a great comedy of the will, and her heroine must incarnate the full potential of the will, however misused for a time. Having rather too much her own way is certainly one of Emma's powers, and she does have a disposition to think a little too well of herself. When Austen says that these were "the real evils indeed of Emma's situation," we read "evils" as lightly as the author will let us, which is lightly enough.

Can we account for the qualities in Emma Woodhouse that make her worthy of comparison with George Eliot's Gwendolen Harleth and Henry James's Isabel Archer? The pure comedy of her context seems world enough for her; she evidently is not the heiress of all the ages. We are persuaded, by Austen's superb craft, that marriage to Mr. Knightley will more than suffice to fulfill totally the now perfectly amiable Emma. Or are we? It is James's genius to suggest that while Osmond's "beautiful mind" was a prison of the spirit for Isabel, no proper husband could exist anyway, since neither Touchett nor Goodwood is exactly a true match for her. Do we, presumably against

Austen's promptings, not find Mr. Knightley something of a confinement also, benign and wise though he be?

I suspect that the heroine of the Protestant will, from Richardson's Clarissa Harlowe through to Virginia Woolf's Clarissa Dalloway, can never find fit match because wills do not marry. The allegory or tragic irony of this dilemma is written large in *Clarissa,* since Lovelace, in strength of will and splendor of being, actually would have been the true husband for Clarissa (as he well knows) had he not been a moral squalor. His death-cry ("Let this expiate!") expiates nothing, and helps establish the long tradition of the Anglo-American novel in which the heroines of the will are fated to suffer either overt calamities or else happy unions with such good if unexciting men as Mr. Knightley or Will Ladislaw in *Middlemarch.* When George Eliot is reduced to having the fascinating Gwendolen Harleth fall hopelessly in love with the prince of prigs, Daniel Deronda, we sigh and resign ourselves to the sorrows of fictive overdetermination. Lovelace or Daniel Deronda? I myself do not know a high-spirited woman who would not prefer the first, though not for a husband!

Emma is replete with grand comic epiphanies, of which my favorite comes in volume 3, chapter 11, when Emma receives the grave shock of Harriet's disclosure that Mr. Knightley is the object of Harriet's hopeful affections:

> When Harriet had closed her evidence, she appealed to her dear Miss Woodhouse, to say whether she had not good ground for hope.
>
> "I never should have presumed to think of it at first," said she, "but for you. You told me to observe him carefully, and let his behavior be the rule of mine—and so I have. But now I seem to feel that I may deserve him; and that if he does choose me, it will not be any thing so very wonderful."
>
> The bitter feelings occasioned by this speech, the many bitter feelings, made the utmost exertion necessary on Emma's side to enable her to say in reply,
>
> "Harriet, I will only venture to declare, that Mr. Knightley is the last man in the world, who would intentionally give any woman the idea of his feeling for her more than he really does."
>
> Harriet seemed ready to worship her friend for a sentence so satisfactory; and Emma was only saved from raptures and fondness, which at the moment would have been dreadful penance, by the sound of her father's footsteps. He was coming

through the hall. Harriet was too much agitated to encounter him. "She could not compose herself—Mr. Woodhouse would be alarmed—she had better go;"—with most ready encouragement from her friend, therefore, she passed off through another door—and the moment she was gone, this was the spontaneous burst of Emma's feelings: "Oh God! that I had never seen her!"

The rest of the day, the following night, were hardly enough for her thoughts.—She was bewildered amidst the confusion of all that had rushed on her within the last few hours. Every moment had brought a fresh surprise; and every surprise must be matter of humiliation to her.—How to understand it all! How to understand the deceptions she had been thus practising on herself, and living under!—The blunders, the blindness of her own head and heart!—she sat still, she walked about, she tried her own room, she tried the shrubbery—in every place, every posture, she perceived that she had acted most weakly; that she had been imposed on by others in a most mortifying degree; that she had been imposing on herself in a degree yet more mortifying; that she was wretched, and should probably find this day but the beginning of wretchedness.

The acute aesthetic pleasure of this turns on the counterpoint between Emma's spontaneous cry: "Oh God! that I had never seen her!" and the exquisite comic touch of: "She sat still, she walked about, she tried her own room, she tried the shrubbery—in every place, every posture, she perceived that she had acted most weakly." The acute humiliation of the will could not be better conveyed than by "she tried the shrubbery" and "every posture." Endlessly imaginative, Emma must now be compelled to endure the mortification of reducing herself to the postures and places of those driven into corners by the collapse of visions that have been exposed as delusions. Jane Austen, who seems to have identified herself with Emma, wisely chose to make this moment of ironic reversal a temporary purgatory, rather than an infernal discomfiture.

JOEL WEINSHEIMER

Chance and the Hierarchy
of Marriages in Pride and Prejudice

Chance is given significance in Jane Austen's novels by her insistence on the value of its opposite—rational and deliberate choice. And it is an important aspect of her realism that she does not divide choice and chance into two mutually exclusive forces. Ideal choice made in full awareness of motives and consequences is, after all, a rare occurrence in her novels. Few characters achieve it at all, and they more often reach it as a climax rather than as the norm of their moral life. In general decision and action are determined by a variously composed mixture of choice and chance, and only as a given character increases his knowledge of self and others does choice begin to predominate.

Little critical comment has been devoted to the operation of chance in Jane Austen's works, perhaps because it has been eclipsed by the tightness of her plots and the preeminently unchaotic sanity of her ideals. But Lionel Trilling has wisely observed that "Jane Austen's first or basic irony is the recognition that the spirit is not free, that it is conditioned, that it is limited by circumstance" and that "only by reason of this anomaly does spirit have virtue and meaning." Just as the spirit is morally dependent on and made meaningful by uncontrolled circumstance, so also is plot enriched by Jane Austen's consciousness of chance. W. J. Harvey, in discussing the plot of *Emma,* attributes the "solidity and openness of the novel" to the fact that "it allows for the contingent." Again, Lionel Trilling finds *Mansfield Park*

From *ELH* 39, no. 3 (September 1972). © 1972 by The Johns Hopkins University Press.

more unique than typical in its "need to find security, to establish, in fixity and enclosure, a refuge from the dangers of openness and chance."

Paul Zietlow presents by far the most extensive analysis of chance in Jane Austen's novels in his examination of *Persuasion*, which is the novel of her canon that most overtly invites this treatment. But the presence of chance in *Pride and Prejudice* is neither so striking nor obtrusive as in *Persuasion*, where, as Zietlow has pointed out, the reunion of Anne and Wentworth seems almost Providential. The "dark, menacing quality" which he and others sense in *Persuasion* is absent in the "light, and bright, and sparkling" *Pride and Prejudice*. Nor do the fortunes of Elizabeth Bennet undergo so complete a reversal as those of Anne Elliot. This comparative uniformity of happiness in *Pride and Prejudice* tends to conceal the operation of chance as a thematic motif and plot device in bringing the novel to a felicitous conclusion. But, like *Persuasion*, the fortuitous emerges in *Pride and Prejudice* as a force with which both its characters and its readers must contend.

As a working definition, we may suggest that all effects not voluntarily produced be considered, morally speaking, as the results of chance. Supplementing this definition, there are two distinct, but connected, phases of action in which chance can interpose. The first occurs in the process of decision when, through self-ignorance or self-deception, a character remains unaware of the actual motivation that brings him to a specific conclusion or plan of action. The second occurs simply when a given intention fails to produce the desired effect, when the consequences of an action are unforseen and unexpected. Chance then fills the gap left by the lapse of control either of one's self or one's circumstances. Both instances are caused by a more or less avoidable (and thus morally significant) ignorance, and both are imaged in Jane Austen's novels as a variety of "blindness."

With this definition of chance in mind, we may investigate, first, Jane Austen's method of establishing chance as a credible and effective plot device, and, second, her evaluation of the balance of chance and choice in the novel's several marriages. Critics have already suggested several perspectives on the hierarchy of marriages in *Pride and Prejudice*; each couple seems to be yoked because both partners achieve the same moral rank, and thus are fit mates. What has not yet been fully explored is the fact that the characters' responses to chance are significant criteria for the evaluation of their relative merits. Ranked by their reactions to the fortuitous, the characters range from partial self-determination to complete domination by chance, and each married couple illustrates a double view of one position in the novel's scale of imperfect responses to chance.

To assess the operation of chance in *Pride and Prejudice*, it may first be helpful to consider Jane Austen's method of making the most fortuitous incidents seem probable and natural. Dorothy Van Ghent replies to those readers who feel that *Pride and Prejudice* is so limited that its value is minimal by reminding them that "when we begin to look upon these limitations . . . as having the positive function of defining the form and meaning of the book, we begin also to understand that kind of value that can lie in artistic mastery over a restricted range." "The exclusions and limitations are deliberate," and as soon as we acknowledge them so, we also realize that the novel's restricted setting is defined by and thus implies the larger world which comprehends it. How this double awareness of part and whole can account for the credibility of chance events in *Pride and Prejudice* is best illustrated by examining the three incidents that appear most fortuitous.

The rerouting and rescheduling of the proposed trip to the Lake country, the early return of Darcy to Pemberley in time to meet Elizabeth there, and Elizabeth's failure to expose Wickham to Lydia or her parents all seem to be the result of chance. Yet the author assigns each a cause: Mr. Gardiner is "prevented by business" from his original plans; Darcy's "business with his steward had occasioned his coming forward a few hours before the rest of the party"; and Wickham is spared exposure because when Elizabeth "returned home [from the Collins's parsonage], the ——shire was to leave Meryton in a week or a fortnight's time." Here the duties of an active businessman, the concerns of the landed nobility, and the directives of the war office each signify a sphere of causation alien to the provincial setting of the novel. Yet precisely because of its provinciality, they achieve significance and probability. Jane Austen balances the surprise and the credibility of improbable events by imposing limitations that both suspend and maintain our awareness of the larger world. Thus whether chance occurrences will imply direction by Providence becomes a matter of choice for Jane Austen, since she suggests in the novel an alternative sphere of terrestrial causation intervening between the Providential and the immediate.

By establishing chance as a realistic technique of plot development, Jane Austen enables the reader to acknowledge its presence without apology for mystery or legerdemain. Consequently, we can understand that the operation of chance minimizes the danger (which Mary Lascelles warns is inherent in its "exactness of symmetry") of imposing a benumbing order on the material of the novel. Chance has its own symbology, and is employed in a pervasive thematic pattern paralleling that of choice.

Two significant symbols of chance underlying the affairs of the Longbourn circle are the entail by which Mr. Bennet's estate will devolve on Mr. Collins ("'such things . . . are all chance in this world'") and the lottery at the Phillips home, where Lydia "soon grew too much interested in the game, too eager in making bets and exclaiming after prizes, to have attention for anyone in particular." The entail typifies the financial insecurity of the middle-class woman, which participation in the marriage lottery is intended to remedy. As Mr. Collins remarks using an associated metaphor, "'When persons sit down to a card table, they must take their chance of these things.'" Here Jane Austen depicts the hope of chance solutions for chance ills. But the gamble of the marriage lottery also symbolizes design—even though we usually conceive of design as effort directed toward a particular end, thus limiting the operation of chance.

In *Pride and Prejudice* (as in *Emma*) design and its correlates—art, scheming, contrivance, and cunning—become associated with chance by the partial disjunction of intention and effect. In the cases of Mrs. Bennet's contrivances for Jane, Lady Catherine's frank condescension to Elizabeth at Longbourn, and Miss Bingley's arts of captivating Darcy, the existence of the design *per se* initiates its own frustration. The "quality of powerlessness" which Marvin Mudrick finds characteristic of the "simple" characters in the novel derives from their inability to conceive of an event as a somewhat unpredictable intersection of diverse causes. There are, for example, at least five forces operating in Jane's estrangement from Bingley: her reserve, her parent's impropriety, Darcy's interference, Miss Bingley's cooperation with Darcy, and Bingley's malleability—any one of which would have been insufficient to separate them. Without an awareness of this multiplicity, design is ineffectual, and its bafflement will seem attributable to the perversity of ill fortune.

If Charlotte Lucas is typical of the designers engaged in the marriage lottery, it becomes clear that those who most credit chance, most employ art. Her marriage, of the three we will center on, is the most pathetic. Charlotte demonstrates her intelligence, as does Elizabeth, by acknowledging that marriage does not always bring happiness. Marriage, Charlotte implies, can be contrived successfully: "'Bingley likes your sister undoubtedly; but he may never do more than like her, if she does not help him on.' '. . . Your plan is a good one,' replied Elizabeth, 'where nothing is in question but the desire of being well married; and if I were determined to get a rich husband, or any husband, I dare say I should adopt it.'" Conversely, from Charlotte's perspective, "'Happiness in marriage is entirely a matter of chance. . . . And it is better to know as little as possible of the defects of the person with whom you are to pass your life.'"

Charlotte's plan *is* a good one if she is to catch "any husband." She succeeds in the same way as Lydia, who is also too involved in the lottery "to have attention for anyone in particular." But the pathos of Charlotte's marriage is that, because of her intelligence, her ignorance must be a pretense. And thus she never arrives, as does Lydia, at the "sublime and refined point of felicity, called, the possession of being well deceived." Charlotte begins, as we have seen, by espousing the value of ignorance in courtship, since the knowledge of the partner's defects has no bearing on one's chance of happiness, and she follows her prescription unswervingly. After Elizabeth rejects Collins, Charlotte satisfies her curiosity by "walking toward the window and pretending not to hear" Mr. Collins rationalize his disappointment. When thus informed that Collins is, for the moment, unattached, she sets the pretended ignorance of her marriage scheme into motion: "Miss Lucas perceived him from an upper window as he walked toward the house, and instantly set out to meet him accidentally in the lane." And as is usual in Jane Austen's novels, the means justify the end. During Elizabeth's visit to the parsonage, she notices that "when Mr. Collins said anything of which his wife might reasonably be ashamed, . . . Charlotte wisely did not hear." Whatever modicum of happiness Charlotte enjoys in her marriage results not from chance, as she had predicted, but from her persistence in the same pretended self-deception that characterized her courtship. In this way she unwittingly becomes a fit mate for Collins, who is similarly defined by the "perseverence in willful self-deception" in his deafness to Elizabeth's rejection.

Collins himself remarks the perfection of this union at Elizabeth's departure: "'My dear Charlotte and I have but one mind and one way of thinking. There is in everything a most remarkable resemblance of character and ideas between us. We seem to have been designed for each other.'" Here is at least a triple irony. Since their compatibility is small, only a perverse design could have joined them. Nevertheless, Collins does design Charlotte for a wife, and at the same time, she designs him for a husband—though both are merely searching for any mate available. But, most important, they are attracted to each other by a force superior to them both—their mutual identity. Here again Jane Austen posits a new sphere of causation, non-Providential, yet extrinsic to the forces of which the characters are immediately aware. In *The Family Reunion* Agatha concisely describes this sphere and the folly of ignoring it:

> Thus with the most careful devotion
> Thus with precise attention
> To detail, interfering preparation
> Of that which is already prepared

Men tighten the knot of confusion
Into perfect misunderstanding.
Reflecting a pocket-torch of observation
Upon each other's opacity.

Although all the characters in the novel get what they want, their designs do
not effect their felicity. Contrivance is either the ignorant "preparation of
that which is already prepared," or else it is simply irrelevant to the outcome.
The most explicit instance of the folly of design occurs in Mrs. Bennet's self-
applause for keeping Jane and Bingley together at Netherfield: " 'This was a
lucky idea of mine, indeed!' said Mrs. Bennet, more than once, as if the
credit of making it rain were all her own." Design and chance are allied in
Pride and Prejudice because Jane's marriage and the rain are equally of Mrs.
Bennet's devising.

While Jane Austen validates Darcy's claim that "whatever bears affinity
to cunning is despicable," she does not conclude that its opposite is more
laudable. Mr. Bennet's indolent detachment from his wife and daughters
increases their vulnerability, and signals his moral deficiency. And Bingley,
though not at all cunning, is fit for no better than Jane. The marriage of Jane
and Bingley, like that of Charlotte and Collins, also discloses a dual perspective on a single position in the hierarchy of marriages, and, as we noticed
in the parson and his wife, their placement in this moral scale results in part
from their similar responses to chance.

It is the chance involved in Bingley's spontaneously picking Netherfield
as a home that initiates the novel's action. "Mr. Bingley had not been of age
two years, when he was tempted by an accidental recommendation to look
at Netherfield House. He did look at it and into it for half an hour, was
pleased with what the owner said in its praise, and took it immediately."
But his caprice is more estimable than that of Mr. Collins, since by this
method Bingley chooses a house, Collins a wife. Bingley's "needless precip-
itance" is further developed in his reply to Mrs. Bennet's inquiry whether
he will stay long at Netherfield: " 'Whatever I do is done in a hurry . . . and
therefore if I should resolve to quit Netherfield, I should probably be off in
five minutes.' " However, Darcy remains unconvinced of his friend's reso-
luteness; such decisiveness is mere fantasy. On the contrary, Darcy informs
him, " 'Your conduct would be quite as dependent on chance as that of any
man I know; and if, as you were mounting your horse, a friend were to say,
"Bingley, you had better stay till next week," you would probably do it, you
would probably not go—and, at another word, might stay a month.' " What
Darcy clarifies for us is that capricious choice is not the affirmation of in-

dividual power or of freedom from external restraint; rather it is the reliance on an immediate cause (the nearby friend, Darcy) whose presence is accidental. Caprice is no more than the unacknowledged determination of choice by chance.

Bingley's unconscious dependence on chance parallels that of Jane, and thereby prepares us for their marriage. Like Bingley, Jane is without design. Quite the opposite, she nearly fulfills Charlotte's prophecy that her reserve will not suffice to hold Bingley. The complement of Jane's restraint in the display of affection is her restraint in censure, and the basis of both is her response to that ignorance which produces the appearance of chance. Jane's recognition that she does not know the degree of Bingley's affection accounts for her unwillingness to entrap him. Because of the same self-acknowledged ignorance she suspends judgment when Elizabeth repeats Wickham's version of Darcy's duplicity. Nothing remained for Jane to do "but to think well of them both, to defend the conduct of each, and throw into the account of accident or mistake, what ever could not otherwise be explained." Jane's *sancta simplicitas* is thus preserved by her remaining in a cocoon of ignorance. In one sense, Jane is the personification of the comic hope of *Pride and Prejudice*. Of all the characters, she most consistently expects that all will end well. But this prognosis is undermined as the reader comes to realize that the "account of accident or mistake" will not sustain the new data continually being unfolded. And as chance yields to pattern, we understand more clearly that the "sanguine hope of good" which makes possible Jane's favorable interpretations of the presence of evil does not result from an accurate observation of her world, but is merely the projected "benevolence of her heart." Our reaction therefore is twofold: we reverence her benevolence, and deprecate her fixation in it.

Jane's "angelic" response to chance is initially adequate. She humbly presumes the possibility of ignorance and error. But her benign skepticism produces no knowledge, and thus becomes its own caricature—stultified and incapable of adapting to the flux of the sublunary world. Her control is diminished, her choice incapacitated, and in their absence Jane is governed by chance. Both Bingley and Jane are characterized by a perseverance in self-deception like that of Charlotte and Collins, but their unscheming good nature elevates them above the parson and his wife. Of Bingley's ductility and Jane's petrification, we are forced to say (as does Elizabeth describing Darcy and Wickham), "'There is but such a quantity of merit between them; just enough to make one good sort of man.'"

Jane's fixation is not unique within the Bennet family. In the marriage of Mr. and Mrs. Bennet the reader discovers that both "neglect and mistaken

indulgence," both detachment and design, are manifestations of internal necessity or fixation. Elizabeth upbraids her father's indolence by illustrating
its effect on his children: if he will not bestir himself, she says, "'Lydia's
character will be fixed, and she will, at sixteen, be the most determined flirt
that ever made herself and her family ridiculous.'" Nor is even Lydia's flirtation free; it is fixed on a scarlet coat. That the parents' fixation will contribute to the child's fixation is probable and natural. What is surprising is
that any of the Bennet daughters escape "the disadvantages of so unsuitable
a marriage" as that of their parents. How Elizabeth does so is the central
concern of *Pride and Prejudice*. And her liberation involves a response to
chance that raises the moral value of her marriage above that of the others.

A significant form of verbal irony in the first half of the novel is Elizabeth's perversion of metaphors of chance: "'Mr. Bingley's defence of his
friend was a very able one I *dare* say, but since he is unacquainted with
several parts of the story, and has learnt the rest from that friend himself, I
shall *venture* still to think of both gentlemen as I did before'" (my italics).
Ironically, the limitations of Bingley's defence of Darcy are identical to the
defects in Elizabeth's defence of Wickham. Yet Elizabeth is unaware that her
evaluation of Wickham is a "venture," not a certainty. Similarly, while trying
to penetrate Mr. Collins's deafness, Elizabeth assures him, "'I am not one
of those young ladies (if such young ladies there are) who are so *daring* as
to *risk* their happiness on the *chance* of being asked a second time'" (my
italics). Elizabeth knows that to refuse Collins's offer does not "risk" her
happiness since the chance of any is nil: "'You could not make *me* happy,
and I am convinced that I am the last woman in the world who could make
you so.'" The similarity of this rebuff of Collins to Elizabeth's rejection of
Darcy is striking: "'I had not known you a month before I felt that you
were the last man in the world whom I could ever be prevailed on to marry.'"
This parallel phrasing in Elizabeth's two refusals of marriage suggests one
facet of her fixation. To refuse Darcy does risk her happiness, but Elizabeth
denies the gambling metaphor by presuming an omniscience of Darcy like
that she possessed of Collins. In the first half of the novel Elizabeth's continual repetition of the metaphors associated with the marriage lottery indicates that while she seems unaffected by it, her attempt to deny chance
proves it real and threatening.

If Collins is often impenetrably deaf to Elizabeth, the reverse is also
true. "'My dear Miss Elizabeth,'" he remarks to her at the Netherfield ball,
"'I have the highest opinion in the world of your excellent judgment in all
matters within the scope of your understanding, but permit me to say. . . .'"
Disguised in Mr. Collins's flatulence is Elizabeth's unawareness that the

scope of her understanding is too small, that it has gathered too little data, to evaluate circumstances accurately. These limitations of self-knowledge must become conscious if she is to escape entrapment in her own illusory omniscience. What Elizabeth must learn, among other things, is that chance is predicated on ignorance, and insofar as ignorance can be under one's control, to that extent is chance capable of regulation. The paradigm of her awakening occurs in Rosings Park. "More than once did Elizabeth in her ramble within the Park, unexpectedly meet Mr. Darcy.—She felt all the perverseness of the mischance that should bring him where no one else was brought; and to prevent its ever happening again, took care to inform him at first that it was a favorite haunt of hers.—How it could occur a second time was very odd!—Yet it did, even a third." At least one critic has noted that it is a "series of incidents over which Elizabeth has no control that reunites" her with Darcy. And in Rosings Park only by an involuntary empiricism does Elizabeth discover a pattern emerging from what seemed to be fortuitous in his actions.

On the possibility of Darcy's knavery Jane is in a quandary: "'It is difficult indeed—it is distressing.—One does not know what to think.'" But Elizabeth retorts, "'I beg your pardon;—one knows exactly what to think.'" Throughout the novel Elizabeth recognizes, as Jane does not, the necessity of judgment in the presence of evil. But Elizabeth here manifests the same needless precipitancy in decision that characterizes Bingley, and is thus to a similar extent directed by chance. Her prejudice originates in the coincidence of her being near enough to overhear Darcy's snub. And only when Elizabeth comes to understand that she has persevered in willful self-deception, has "'courted prepossession and ignorance, and driven reason away,'" is she released from the dominion of chance. Her perspective is then broadened, and she becomes capable of "giving way to every variety of thought," of "reconsidering events," and, most significantly, of "determining probabilities."

Although Reuben Brower finds it "an odd, rather legalistic process," "determining probabilities" is, nevertheless, the most appropriate of the responses to chance dramatized in *Pride and Prejudice,* and Elizabeth's capacity to determine the probabilities of possible events validates the novel's placement of her marriage above that of Jane in the moral hierarchy. If one must have a fixation, Jane's fixation in the suspension of censure is more praiseworthy than Elizabeth's in prejudice. But because Elizabeth escapes herself, she achieves the higher moral status. If Jane superficially affirms chance but ultimately denies it, the reverse is true of Elizabeth. She finally credits chance and attempts to cope with it.

For a gambler, determining probabilities is relatively easy. He knows the dice and how they are marked. But Elizabeth and Darcy must discover while blindfolded how the dice are constructed. They are forced to define their world inductively before deciding the probability of a given outcome. The possibility of error in this process destroys the self-assurance with which Elizabeth had judged Darcy and Wickham. And had Darcy known the difficulty of determining probabilities when he first proposed, his countenance would not have "expressed real security" while "he *spoke* of apprehension and anxiety." Such security only causes vexation. As Jane comments, "'His being so sure of succeeding, was wrong . . . and certainly ought not to have appeared; but consider how much it must increase his disappointment.'" That by the time of his second proposal Darcy has been educated in the vagaries of mischance is shown by the "more than common awkwardness and anxiety of his situation." And here his humility is rewarded with success because it presumes that Elizabeth is free either to accept or reject him. Likewise, when Darcy returns at last to the Bennet home, Elizabeth acknowledges the possibility of a variety of motives and distrusts what appears to be simple cause and effect relationship. She hopes that his return means "that his affection and wishes must still be unshaken. But she would not be secure."

The anxiety of Elizabeth and Darcy demonstrates that their reappraisal of the operation of chance does not make them capable of molding the world to their satisfaction. Whatever additional control the recognition of chance gives them is dwarfed by their glimpse of the far greater chaos beyond their direction. Nor does Jane Austen lead us toward the pride of Stoicism. The inner world, like the outer, is susceptible of only small (though significant) control. "Health and temper to bear inconveniences—cheerfulness to enhance every pleasure—and affection and intelligence, which might supply it among themselves if there were disappointments abroad" characterize the Gardiners as a couple high in the moral scale; but these qualities are rare and can be generated only in a naturally fertile soil of which there is very little on this earth.

It is true that for Jane Austen self-knowledge and self-control crown the moral hierarchy, and where her characters fail in these respects they fall under the lash of her wit. The art of self-manipulation to prevent the deception of others is laudable and difficult of mastery. But the qualms one has about the value of complete self-consciousness result from its persistent tendency toward knavery; or from a more Romantic perspective, self-consciousness might be imaged as the wearing of a true mask, a persona identical to the person behind it. But what the viewer of such a mask always realizes is that this duality is perilously close to the duplicity of such as Wickham.

Jane Austen circumvents the problems involved in over-rationalizing behavior by reminding us of the operation of the unconscious even in the most consequential choices. Reason is parodied in Mary's windy moralizing and in Mr. Collins's formulaic proposal to Elizabeth. But, more important, the central marriage of *Pride and Prejudice* is based not alone on reason and the growing mutual understanding between Darcy and Elizabeth, but also on a thoroughly spontaneous affection—one which flowers entirely contrary to the efforts and expectations of the characters. Bingley and Jane "considered it, we talked of it as impossible." One reason why the marriage of Darcy and Elizabeth seems impossible is that "it has been most unconsciously done." Elizabeth can take no credit for having knowingly elicited Darcy's addresses, yet "it was gratifying to have inspired unconsciously so strong an affection." Elizabeth cannot say how long she has loved Darcy: "'It has been coming on so gradually, that I hardly know when it began.'" And similarly Darcy, when Elizabeth asks him to describe the origin of his love, replies, "'I cannot fix on the hour, or the spot, or the look, or the words, which laid the foundation. It is too long ago. I was in the middle before I knew that I *had* begun.'" Finally, there is no immediate cause—not even conscious will—for the affection of Darcy and Elizabeth, and this freedom constitutes their peculiar felicity.

Elizabeth wonders at one point "how far it would be for the happiness of both that she should employ the power, which her fancy told her she still possessed, of bringing on the renewal of [Darcy's] addresses." Luckily she never has the opportunity to do so, for this would bring her to the level of Miss Bingley. As we have seen, it is superfluous or worse to arrange what is already arranged. This inefficacy of the will in matters of affection is found not only in the "simple" characters, as Mudrick contends, but in "complex" characters as well. Rather than attempting to snare Darcy, Elizabeth acts toward him as she resolves to act toward Bingley. It is hard, she thought, "'that this poor man cannot come to a house, which he has legally hired, without raising all this speculation! I *will* leave him to himself.'" Such is Elizabeth's response to the "truth universally acknowledged" that governs the novel. What she here clarifies for us is that when left alone by the Mrs. Bennets of this world, the individual's self emerges lucidly, without being falsified by the pattern imposed by others' wishes.

The unpredictability of events in *Pride and Prejudice* results from the fact that, from the characters' point of view, all manner of improbability is discovered. Wickham's knavery teaches Elizabeth to "draw no limits in the future to the impudence of an impudent man." And at the other extreme, she finds in Darcy's assistance of Lydia "an exertion of goodness too great to be probable." Even determining probabilities is inadequate if we are not prepared for the unlikely.

On the other hand, when probability of action or motivation is too easily calculated, Jane Austen puts us on our guard. Just as she portrays the improbable, so also do we find the over-probable, and sometimes both simultaneously:

> Never, since reading Jane's second letter, had [Elizabeth] entertained a hope of Wickham's meaning to marry [Lydia]. No one but Jane, she thought, could flatter herself with such an expectation. *Surprise was the least of her feelings* on this development. . . . But now *it was all too natural*. For such an attachment as this, she might have sufficient charms; and though she did not suppose Lydia to be deliberately engaging in an elopement, without the intention of marriage, *she had no difficulty in believing* that neither her virtue nor her understanding would preserve her from falling an easy prey (my italics).

Here the over-probable becomes a source of pity or aversion because it implies an involuntary entrapment by an exterior and mechanical cause. Lydia falls an "easy prey" to Wickham because he is thoroughly self-conscious, and she is not. And she is a prey to herself by her self-will and carelessness. Here, as elsewhere, Wickham falls victim to his own contrivance. Nevertheless, they do surprisingly marry, contrary to Elizabeth's expectations, and at the same time fulfill her suspicion that little "permanent happiness could belong to a couple who were only brought together because their passions were stronger than their virtue." Likewise, the over-probable and improbable are combined when Miss Bingley teases Darcy about his pleasure from Elizabeth's fine eyes: "'I am all astonishment. How long has she been such a favorite?—and pray when am I to wish you joy?'" To which Darcy replies, "'That is exactly the question I expected you to ask.'" Miss Bingley's comment is completely predictable and therefore inane; yet ultimately it is justified.

Samuel Kliger has observed that in *Pride and Prejudice* the eighteenth century's "rationalistic quest of the mean between two extremes requires that the probabilities for the heroine's behavior be set up between two alternatives, neither of which is acceptable alone." Just such a quest for the mean is completed in Jane Austen's reconciliation of the over-probable and the improbable, the inevitable and the impossible. Indeed this union informs the whole of *Pride and Prejudice* since it is the basis of the "truth universally acknowledged, that a single man in possession of a good fortune, must be in want of a wife." We would assume any truth universally acknowledged in a Jane Austen novel to be either false or trite; yet, as one critic concedes, "by the end of the novel we are willing to acknowledge that both Bingley and Darcy were 'in want of a wife.'"

The ignorance of this truth occasions the most significant illusion of chance in *Pride and Prejudice* and, perhaps, in all Jane Austen's novels. It is an illusion that appears in the frequent, but repressed, response that the impossibly happy conclusion of the novel is, after all, fortuitous. This response springs from the only partial awareness of a cause neither Providential nor physical, but rather moral. *Pride and Prejudice,* taken as a whole, enforces our recognition that an unmarried man or woman is incomplete. Not only is the urge to mate a physical drive, but it is a moral necessity if one is to become more than the sum of the multiple idiosyncrasies that compose the individual personality. Jane Austen sees the individual "not as a solitary being completed in himself, but only as completed in society." The "complex" individual is not isolated by his freedom, as Mudrick contends, quite the opposite. If anyone, only the "simple," myopic, and fixated individuals are isolated, since for them other people never become real. Darcy increases the scope of his freedom by enlarging his society to include not only Elizabeth, but her family as well. And in Wickham he creates a brother. By his freedom Darcy establishes and vindicates his position in society.

The truth universally acknowledged that *humanitas* cannot be achieved alone is sometimes lost among the welter of socioeconomic interpretations of the novel's marriages, but the driving force of *Pride and Prejudice* cannot be explained by reference to the pocketbook. Rather, Jane Austen invites us to examine the possibility that an individual can merit and achieve happiness in a community that becomes valuable by his joining it. "'Without scheming to do wrong, or to make others unhappy, there may be error, and there may be misery. Thoughtlessness, and want of attention to other people's feelings, and want of resolution, will do the business.'" The sources of misery are various; but when informed by thoughtfulness, sympathy, and commitment, fulfillment in marriage is not a matter of chance.

ALICE CHANDLER

"A Pair of Fine Eyes": Jane Austen's Treatment of Sex

It is a truth universally acknowledged that Jane Austen's novels are about courtship and marriage. But it is a truth almost as universally ignored that they are also very much about sex. As a social force, as an embodiment of value systems, as an index of personal maturity, the role of marriage in Jane Austen's work has been ably and extensively examined. But as the consummation of sexual attraction between a man and a woman and as the reconciliation of "maleness" and "femaleness," her conception of marriage has seldom been discussed.

One reason for the imbalance of emphasis lies in our preconceptions about her personality. Few critics consciously share Marvin Mudrick's view of a Jane Austen armored in impenetrable wit and muslin against the "personally involving aspects of sex" and the "unknown adult commitment of sexual love." But his vision of her as a defensively ironic "genteel spinster" does represent a popular and subtly pervasive stereotype. The phrases he uses about her—"routed by the sexual question," "fogged in bourgeois morality," opposed to "sexual vitality," and in favor of "frigidity as a standard of sexual conduct"—while inaccurate in themselves, serve to suggest the kinds of presuppositions to which Jane Austen has been subject and which have rendered the sexual aspects of her work less visible than they should be.

A second reason that the sexual element in Jane Austen's fiction has

From *Studies in the Novel* 7, no. 1 (Spring 1975). © 1975 by North Texas State University.

tended to be ignored lies in her art itself. The coolness and deftness of her surface and the interplay of irony and wit have made her novels seem more purely cerebral than they are and have reinforced the presumptions about her temperament. A merciless satirist of false or excessive feeling, she has wrongly been seen as suspicious of all feeling; and her very desire to subsume sex within marriage has somehow made her seem to be endorsing marriage without sex. Because the conventions of nineteenth-century fiction make it almost impossible for the hero and heroine to touch and even, at a certain level of frankness, to speak, the tendency has been to see the overt levels of plot and dialogue as reflecting her total vision of sex and marriage. And yet her novels are no less subtle and realistic here than in their depiction of any other forms of human relationship.

I shall try in this essay to redress the balance and, particularly in the first portion, to single out and emphasize Jane Austen's handling of physical sexuality. Jane Austen's books treat many other serious themes as well: art and nature, feeling and reason, freedom and order, the individual and society. It is precisely because all these issues come to a focus in marriage and are dramatized in her novels through the incidents of wooing and wedding that we cannot leave sex out. If marriage is the ultimate source of social order and the very soul of the status quo, it achieves this harmony only through the disruptive and disorderly force of sex. The predominant novelist of social stability, Jane Austen is also the chronicler of the sexual selectivity that creates it. As a writer whose books all end with marriages, her problem was not that she failed to recognize the foreplay of attraction and repulsion, of looking and liking, of teasing and touching that can lead to matrimony, but that she could not express her views directly. Her indirections, however, are surprisingly subtle and frank.

In studying Jane Austen's "indirections" we must be aware of the limited range of explicit statement allowed to a novelist of her generation. Although the easy eighteenth-century conventions of her youth allowed her to read what she later termed the "impassioned and most exceptionable parts of Richardson," and, as we shall see, the more indelicate portions of Shakespeare, even male authors by the turn of the century could no longer speak freely of plackets and bosoms. We have only to look at Scott—by all accounts a clubbish man in company—to see how pervasively these taboos affected fiction. For a woman, of course, the problem was compounded; and though Jane Austen was closer than Scott in some ways to her eighteenth-century fictional forebears, she, too, was bound by pre-Victorian limitations of subject matter which had already turned physical sex into a topic for covert implication rather than overt description.

The trouble with covert implication is that we cannot be sure if the implication is really there or if we have simply imagined it. It is therefore useful to begin by examining Jane Austen's use of literary allusion, since it involves the kind of deliberate and conscious choice of materials that assures not only that *we* know what she is doing but that *she* does, too. The most familiar use of another literary work to expand a situation in her novels is the sustained use of the play *Lovers' Vows* in *Mansfield Park*. The explicit and immodest relationship between Anhalt and Amelia in the play foreshadows the relationship that will develop between Edmund Bertram and Mary Crawford as the actors of these parts, just as the role of Agatha, which Maria Bertram wants to play, is prophetic of her final condition as an abandoned mistress. Henry Crawford's protean nature is suggested by his willingness to take any male part in *Lovers' Vows*. His moral instability is further elucidated by his almost ventriloquistic reading of all the voices in Shakespeare's *Henry VIII*, a play about a great misuser of women, from which words like "maidenhead" and "emballing" had not been bowdlerized in Jane Austen's lifetime. Fanny's story, too, involves a literary allusion, since her name, Fanny Price (though not, as we shall see, without a possible cant interpretation) comes from Crabbe's *Parish Register,* where Fanny Price is a chaste and lovely maiden, who resists a sexually eager young squire to marry the pure youth of her choice.

A more daring use of literary allusion to express the inexpressible occurs in *Sense and Sensibility,* very much a book about sexual wiles and entanglements, with its highly charged seducer, Willoughby, and his willing victim, Marianne. What Jane Austen is trying to imply about the lovers, though she cannot directly say it, comes out in an early episode regarding Willoughby's offer of a horse. Marianne, though eager to go galloping with him, is obliged for reasons of economy and prudence to reject the animal he has offered her. He, however, will not accept her refusal and, bending closely over her, whispers an ardent plea that she continue to call it hers. "The horse is still yours," he says, "though you cannot use it now. I shall only keep it till you can claim it. When you leave Barton to form your own establishment, Queen Mab shall receive you." Willoughby's statement, with its breathy intimacy, seems merely another example of Jane Austen's skillfully handled characterizations until we remember the actual Queen Mab passage:

> This is the hag when maids lie on their backs
> That presses them and learns them first to bear,

and recognize its applicability to their relationship. Willoughby later confesses that his motive was never wholly honorable. But this early allusion tells us precisely what his intentions are, what he is really offering Marianne, and what will be her fate if she leaves the protection of her mother's home. It defines Marianne for us, too, since she seems almost as eager to ride Queen Mab—to gallop on the "fairies' midwife"—as Willoughby is to ride with her. While not as plainly sexual a character as the hot little Lucy Steele, Marianne is far from the naively sentimental dreamer that she is often said to be and far more than an exemplar of romantic sensibility. As her later attack of old-fashioned "hysteria" shows, she is very much a creature of flesh and blood, who becomes psychosomatically and then physically ill when her desires are thwarted.

Another literary allusion, following closely on the Queen Mab passage, reaffirms Jane Austen's intention to underscore Willoughby's and Marianne's relationship. We are told that Willoughby "presently took up her scissors and cut off a long lock of her hair, for it was all tumbled down her back; and he kissed it, and folded it up in a piece of white paper and put it into his pocketbook." Willoughby is not quite Pope's baron and Marianne is hardly Belinda—but the ravishing of the hair, which meets with no resistance from the lady, carries the same unvarnished sexual connotation.

Puns and riddles, too, suggest that Jane Austen was rather more knowing than has been realized. Perhaps Mary Crawford's allusion to the "*Rears* and *Vices* of admirals" is only an accident, but its cynical sexuality seems very much in character. However, when Mr. Woodhouse—dear, valetudinarian, fussy Mr. Woodhouse—makes an improper allusion, we must begin to wonder about his creator's intentions. And yet, the seemingly innocuous riddle about "Kitty, a fair but frozen maid" that Mr. Woodhouse keeps trying to recall and that Emma actually transcribes into her album is a naughty one, indeed:

> Kitty, a fair but frozen maid,
>   Kindled a flame I still deplore;
> The hood-wink'd boy I call'd in aid,
> Much of his near approach afraid,
>   So fatal to my suit before.
>
> . . . .
>
> To Kitty, Fanny now succeeds,
>   She kindles slow but lasting fires;
> With care my appetite she feeds;
> Each day some willing victim bleeds,
>   To satisfy my strange desires.

> Say, by what title, or what name,
>   Must I this youth address?
> Cupid and he are not the same
> Tho' both can raise or quench a flame—
>   I'll kiss you if you guess.

The riddle is taken from John Almon's *New Foundling Hospital for Wit,*
a late eighteenth-century melange of odes on Johnson's dictionary and verses
on a three-seated privy, and is said to have been written by Garrick. It
involves a series of sly allusions. Read with a knowledge of eighteenth-century
slang, the first stanza reveals itself to be about a man who has contracted
venereal disease ("a flame I yet deplore") from patronizing "frozen Kitty."
(A "forward Kittie," as in some versions, would be a bold prostitute.) Having
cured himself in the omitted second stanza, he relates how he now derives
pleasures from frequenting only the virginal Fanny. ("Fanny" in eighteenth-
century and in modern British slang = female pudendum.) The reference in
the last three lines—"some willing victim bleeds"—is literally hymeneal. The
solution to the final stanza, "a chimney sweep," must have been productive
of much drawing-room mirth, not simply because it so cleverly catches up
all the fire similes that run through the poem but because "chimney sweep-
ing" was a well-known cant term for sexual intercourse.

Precisely what kind of game Jane Austen is playing with Mr. Woodhouse
and her readers is hard to tell. Given the obviousness of the language, it
seems unlikely she did not understand it, but it is hard to know whether to
take Mr. Woodhouse's repeated references to the riddle as a sign of his
naiveté or simply as one of the many ways in which he is made to embody
the tastes and manners of an earlier age. But his recollected pun should
remind us that the England of Mr. Woodhouse's youth—and of Jane Austen's, too—was far from prudish. Although the printed riddle books of the
early nineteenth century tended to be chaste, those of the 1740s and 1750s
were frequently improper. In fact, one could probably trace the rise of post-
Evangelical propriety with considerable accuracy simply by seeing when the
word "pen" in the riddle books ceased to mean a sexual tool and became a
mere instrument of writing.

Born in 1775, although she did not publish her first novel until 1811,
Jane Austen must have known both worlds. Her complicity with regard to
Mr. Woodhouse raises questions about her intentions elsewhere. What, for
example, were she and Crabbe thinking about when they named their virginal
heroine "Fanny Price"? Is it simply an accident that the broad-humored
Middletons in *Sense and Sensibility* find the first initial of Elinor's lover so

conducive to constant hilarity: "The letter F——— had likewise been brought forward, and found productive of such countless jokes that its character as the wittiest letter in the alphabet had long been established." Does F——— really stand for Ferrars? Or does it stand for that four-letter verb, omitted by Johnson and most subsequent lexicographers, but given with the definition "foeminam subagitare" in Nathaniel Bailey's highly popular octavo volume, *An Universal Etymological Dictionary,* first published in 1721 and reprinted several times thereafter.

Although we cannot have the same degree of certainty that Jane Austen's use of what the twentieth century calls sex symbolism was as deliberate as her use of allusions, puns, and riddles, her referents are so obvious at times that it is hard to believe they are unconscious. *Mansfield Park,* Marvin Mudrick's shrine of the sexual taboo and Kingsley Amis's palace of prudery, is curiously rich in sex symbols—perhaps because it is more a hothouse than a refrigerator. It nurtures not only the blooming Bertram girls and the sexually dynamic Mary Crawford but also the nubile Fanny Price, whose growth to womanhood, in both the moral and physical sense, forms the mainspring of the novel. It is an interesting comment on nineteenth-century social values that nobody really notices Fanny until she reaches puberty. In a recent article, Ann Banfield rightly points out that the "notice others begin to take of Fanny is a measure of their increasing (or decreasing) vision and judgment." But, like other critics, she has not observed that Fanny's importance also depends on her being "in" or "out"—ripe for the marriage market or not yet sufficiently matured to warrant interest.

In a scene full of subtle undercurrents, Edmund Bertram reports that his father has noticed Fanny's maturation immediately upon his return from Antigua. "'Your complexion is so improved!—and you have gained so much countenance!—and your figure—Nay, Fanny, do not turn away about it—it is but an uncle. If you cannot bear an uncle's admiration, what is to become of you? You must really begin to harden yourself to the idea of being worth looking at.—You must try not to mind growing up into a pretty woman.'" But Fanny must blush, for it is her newfound womanliness (here signified by her figure) that she cannot handle, either as it makes her conscious of her attraction toward Edmund or as it attracts Henry Crawford toward her. Her problem is not that she is a prude, but that she must pretend to be one. (In her inability to express her feelings because of her subordinate role in the family, she is a forerunner of such frustrated Brontë heroines as Jane Eyre and Lucy Snowe—women who must conceal their emotions no matter what they feel.)

Given the theme of maturation, it is no wonder that sexual implications abound in *Mansfield Park*. Tony Tanner has pointed out the sexual significance of the locked garden at Sotherton, and Gerald Gould has explored the gate scene further and showed how the various sexual relationships among the characters are foreshadowed by the symbolic use of gates, keys, gardens, wilderness, and pointed spikes. However, no one to my knowledge has pointed out that the rakish Henry Crawford's chain is too big to fit through the hole in Fanny's cross but that her beloved Edmund's chain slips through quite nicely. Nor has anything been made of Fanny's horseback riding. She is frightened of riding, as we imagine she would be at first, but riding Edmund's mare gives her great pleasure. When Mary Crawford, a born horsewoman, takes it away from her and starts riding with Edmund herself, Fanny, with almost clinical accuracy, develops a headache.

Jane Austen, then, is not so innocent as we have imagined her, nor devoid of resources for expressing what she knows. But while I think it important to demonstrate the exclusively sexual element in her novels, I have isolated these examples from their context only to prove the point that she is neither ignorant nor fearful, and certainly not prim. What is more important about Jane Austen's art, however, is the way in which she fuses the physical with the emotional and the intellectual to create a sense of total human relationships. It is a restrained art that limits its subject matter and finds its material in the commonplaces of daily activity—in speaking and smiling, in walking and dancing. But it is a translucent surface that reveals the emotions underneath. The techniques she uses and the values she prescribes can best be seen in *Pride and Prejudice,* her fullest study of male-female relationships.

In attempting to trace the course of a love affair, the French romancers of the seventeenth century had recourse to a device called the *carte du tendre*—a map which treated the progress of affection through all the pleasant territories of Inclination, Complaisance, Tenderness, and Respect and all the hostile areas of Pride, Negligence, Indiscretion, and Mischance. *Pride and Prejudice* explores much the same geography of the feelings, but never abstractly and always against the familiar background of the English landscape. Because its hero and heroine are Elizabeth and Darcy, the most articulate of all Jane Austen's protagonists, these conscious and unconscious attractions and repulsions are usually turned into language, into a surface structure of wit and epigram. But body language is also speech and, like purely verbal communication, reveals attitudes of aversion and attraction. Exemplified by gestures and actions that are at once realistic and metaphoric, the method is brilliantly revealing.

Nowhere is the combination of realism and metaphor more clearly shown than in her use of the dance. It is possible to reconstruct many of the

social customs of the age simply by studying the descriptions of balls and
dances in *Emma,* in *Mansfield Park,* in *Pride and Prejudice,* and even in
Northanger Abbey; but it is also possible to see the ritualized encounters of
the ballrooms as indicators of social and sexual definition. What partners
may dance with one another, what partners *do* dance with one another—
what woman the man chooses, what man the woman entices or resists—the
pairings and nonpairings involved all provide dramatizations of the mating
process that are seldom as visible elsewhere. Given the inhibitions of early
nineteenth-century customs, the dance is one of the few places where choosing is apparent and touching is allowed. Jane Austen knew precisely what
she meant when she says that "to be fond of dancing [is] the first step toward
falling in love."

It is not surprising, then, that the first dance at Netherfield serves to
define the male protagonists. Bingley, the normative man in this novel, enjoys
dancing. Lively and unreserved, he dances every dance, moving from woman
to woman until he fixes his feelings on Jane. The sense of flow and ease that
we associate with Bingley throughout the novel appears here very plainly;
he is both socially and sexually relaxed, lacking depth and firmness perhaps,
but free to give and receive affection. Darcy, by contrast, is restrained. Although he has all the attributes of an attractive male—a fine, tall person,
good features, and noble bearing—he is constrained and solitary. While the
others pair off in dancing couples, he walks about the room alone. He is not
insensible to female beauty, as his comments about Jane Bennet prove, but
he is too constricted within himself—too "fastidious" Bingley calls him—
to seek a partner. Ironically, proud and intolerant as he may be, his very
inaccessibility enhances his worth.

At the second ball, even more than on the first occasion, Jane Austen
makes clear the role of the dance as part of the courtship ritual and begins
to use it, as she will continue to do, to define the sexual relationships of her
protagonists. When Sir William Lucas calls dancing "one of the first refine-
ments of polished societies," he provokes Mr. Darcy to the startling rejoinder
that "it has the advantage of being in vogue amongst the less polished societies of the world. Every savage can dance." This is not just Darcy's su-
perciliousness, though his snobbish pride is certainly involved. It is Jane
Austen's way of reminding us of the very basic elements that are evinced in
a man and woman's moving rhythmically together, whether in a primitive
society or at the Court of St. James. (It is interesting that a little later in the
novel all Mr. Collins's pomposity and stupidity are summed up in a description of his dancing: "Mr. Collins, awkward and solemn, apologising instead
of attending, and often moving wrong without being aware of it, gave her

all the shame and misery which a disagreeable partner for a couple of dances can give. The moment of release from him was extasy."

Dancing as a courtship metaphor occurs for a third, though not a final time, in one of the drawing-room scenes at Netherfield. Anxious to attract Mr. Darcy to herself, Miss Bingley is playing a lively Scotch air on the piano. The result, however, is the opposite of what she intends. It leads Darcy to draw near to Elizabeth and ask if she does not "feel a great inclination . . . to seize such an opportunity of dancing a reel." Any kind of dancing would, of course, be inappropriate with Jane lying sick upstairs, but the lively reel seems totally unconventional and suggests Darcy's inner desires. Far more than his measured request for her hand under Sir William's tutelage, this approach to Elizabeth suggests strong attraction. Darcy is implying that they can cast off the measured forms of their society and unite in a lively dance. Elizabeth's pointed rejection of his request indicates her feelings perfectly. Although she smiles when she says it (as she invariably does when Darcy is by), she "does not want to dance a reel at all." Her resistance is inspired. That Miss Bingley reads the second volume to his first, wishes for a library like that at Pemberley, is enraptured by his sister's drawings, and is willing to sing to him, play for him, dance with him, walk with him, "mend his pen" for him, provokes only his driest wit. But Elizabeth's refusal to dance with him—like his earlier unwillingness to dance with her—heightens the tension between them.

Still another semimetaphoric measure of Darcy's attraction to Elizabeth can be found in the references to her eyes. For a man like Darcy, Elizabeth Bennet is both an attraction and a threat. She is free and lively, with the easy playfulness he lacks. His eye is satiric. It takes notice, but it does not react. Elizabeth's "pair of fine eyes," dark, sparkling, and expressive, are not only quick to perceive but to communicate. "The faculty of vision," Richard Chase reminds us in another context, "is often identified in the unconscious with the energy of sex." Darcy cannot quite say, because he does not really know, what attracts him to Elizabeth. But part of the attraction is surely a sense of her vitality, of a freedom and ultimately of a sexual energy unknown in his formal and insipid circles that entices him against his judgment. It is for this reason that Elizabeth's eyes become an issue between him and Miss Bingley, who realizes, though she too is unconscious of its real origins, the source of her rival's power.

But Darcy's ambiguous attitude toward Elizabeth, which Miss Bingley considerably exaggerates for him, is more frequently expressed through motion than eyesight. As the novel shows, a sedate stroll through cultivated parklands or gardens or an accompanied walk to town, is an appropriate

activity for a woman; but rapid, immoderate movement, especially when
unescorted, is both alluring and perturbing. Hence, when in her walk from
Longbourn to Netherfield to visit Jane, Elizabeth hikes over fields, jumps
over stiles, and springs over puddles, her very energy in doing so at once
heightens her value and renders her suspect in Darcy's eyes. He is "divided
between admiration of the brilliance which exercise had given to her complexion and doubt as to the occasion's meriting her coming so far alone."
It is only Miss Bingley's censoriousness about Eliza's muddy petticoats and
"blowsy" hair—a word the eighteenth century applied to beggars' trulls—
that provokes Darcy to defend her. And even here he is ambivalent, certain
he would not want his sister to "make such an exhibition of herself" and
sure, as he later acknowledges, that he does not wish to be allied to a family
that frequently makes a spectacle of itself.

But while Miss Bingley's unreasonable criticisms originate in jealousy
rather than good judgment, Darcy's hesitations seem to echo Jane Austen's
own ambivalences about the proper limits of female freedom. Without ever
denying or rejecting her characters' energies, Jane Austen, in all her novels,
tends to restrain the individual drives, particularly the sexual drives, within
the confines of reasoned behavior and punishes those who too far exceed its
limits. To do so, she uses movement symbolically. Thus, Mary Crawford's
unregulated delight in horseback riding, Marianne Dashwood's impetuous
running downhill, Louisa Hayter's leap from the Cobb, in two cases out of
three, lead to a literal misstep and fall, and, in all three cases, to the young
ladies' disappointment and defeat. As Sir John Middleton reminds us after
Marianne's stumble in *Sense and Sensibility,* such "tumbling about"—and
the word had the same sexual connotation in Jane Austen's time that it has
now—is no way to get a proper husband.

The conflict between Darcy and Elizabeth that propels the first half of
the novel is thus, as has often been seen, a very basic conflict in values. It is
an opposition of heart and head, of control and spontaneity, of elitism and
egalitarianism. As Samuel Kliger aptly sums it up, it is the contrast between
art and nature. Many of the differences between the hero and the heroine
represent attitudes originating in class—the landed proprietor's view versus
the outlook of a gentleman's daughter. But the more fundamental differences
are based on sex, with the hero and heroine embodying in dramatic form
what the eighteenth century thought to be intrinsic distinctions between male
and female temperaments. As Hannah More's antithetical portrait of the
sexes, written in the late eighteenth century, shows, Elizabeth and Darcy are
not just one man and one woman. They are representative sexual types:

Women have generally quicker perceptions; men have juster sentiments. Women consider how things may be prettily said; men, how they may be properly said. In women (young ones at least), speaking accompanies and sometimes precedes reflection; in men, reflection is the antecedent. Women speak to shine or to please; men, to convince or confute. Women admire what is brilliant; men, what is solid. Women prefer an extemporaneous sally of wit, or a sparkling effusion of fancy, before the most accurate reasoning, or the most laborious investigation of facts. In literary composition, women are pleased with point, turn, and antithesis; men, with observation and a just deduction of effects from their causes. Women are fond of incident; men, of argument. Women admire passionately; men approve cautiously. One sex will think it betrays a want of feeling to be moderate in their applause; the other will be afraid of exposing a want of judgment by being in raptures with anything. Men refuse to give way to the emotions they actually feel, while women sometimes affect to be transported beyond what the occasion will justify.

Darcy's containment, his distrust of "raptures," his self-proclaimed caution in forming his implacable judgments, all show how apt the description is for him. The feminine attributes of quickness, brilliance, spontaneity, and sprightliness seem equally applicable to Elizabeth. As Lionel Trilling states, the conflict in the novel and its ultimate resolution center upon "her female vivacity" and "his strict male syntax."

All the differences between Elizabeth and Darcy come to a focus in the proposal scene at Rosings, which is the pivotal episode of the book. Overtly, the dialogue focuses upon the social differences between them, with Darcy insisting on his social superiority, while Elizabeth argues that it is behavior, not rank, that makes the gentleman. But their overt discussions mirror an even more basic conflict. Also in conflict before them are the issues of superiority between male and female, with Darcy aggressively urging the claims of his male superiority, while Elizabeth acts out a traditionally defensive female role. The conventions of Jane Austen's fiction no longer allow the hero to assault the heroine physically, as Squire B. could do; but there is no doubt of his emotions toward this clever Pamela. The agitation of his manner and the charged energy of his speech—"In vain have I struggled. It will not do"— suggest a passion and a desire for possession that are almost palpable. Faced with an emotion that she does not yet desire, Elizabeth, like most fictional heroines, can only live by her wits. In a series of angry thrusts, brilliantly directed at his deep-held pretensions to fairness and honor, she wards off what can perhaps be seen as a verbal rape. Her final statement to Darcy that he has not behaved in a "gentlemanlike manner" is far less explicit than Jane Eyre's assertion to Rochester that she has full as "much soul as [he],—and full as much heart." But it voices the same feminine complaint against the man who will not recognize her selfhood.

On one level, then, the scene is all Elizabeth's—a triumph of feminist wish-fulfillment, in which the most desirable of males is meant to stand abased. But Jane Austen's mind is in all ways balanced. Her novels not only reconcile the claims of rival social classes and value systems, but reconcile the antitheses and hostilities of the sexes as well—perhaps because she knows that, in the case of the sexes at least, the very attraction and repulsion are often the signs and preludes of a deeper attraction. So it is that after the climactic oppositions of the proposal scene, the rest of the novel moves toward the redefinitions and readjustments of love. Darcy must move further because his faults have been greater; but Elizabeth, too, must change and must see Darcy, herself, and her family in a clearer, truer light. In describing the way in which Darcy and Elizabeth move toward one another both as individuals and as typically masculine and feminine protagonists, the novel uses the same techniques of language and gesture that it used in the earlier sections. However, walking rather than dancing becomes the chief metaphor of sexual relationship in this more sober second half, and Elizabeth is no longer smiling and teasing, but quiet and subdued.

As demonstrated through the walking metaphor, Elizabeth and Darcy literally cannot get together in the scenes before Pemberley. Coming upon Darcy and Miss Bingley in the paths at Netherfield, Elizabeth runs off gaily, saying she would spoil their picturesque grouping if she stayed with them. Discovering that Darcy takes the same rambles in the park at Rosings that she does, she tries to hint that she does not want to meet him. Even after the proposal scene, they walk at cross-purposes, like Shakespearean lovers in a wood, meeting only for a moment as he hands her his letter.

Only at Pemberley, when Elizabeth's attitudes are changing, do they finally walk together in what becomes a crucial scene. The whole Pemberley episode is a *tour de force* of perception and technique, in which the outward action is a metaphor of inward feeling. The brilliant ambiguity of Elizabeth's first response to Pemberley—"at that moment she felt that to be mistress of Pemberley might be something"—has frequently been pointed out. But the whole episode is described through a series of changing perspectives, each indicative of Elizabeth's growing insights. First there are the varying viewpoints of the approach to Pemberley—the ascent and descent with their broken views, and then the arrival at the house itself and a full retrospective panorama. Similarly, within the house there are fragmentary new glimpses into its master provided by his possessions, his portrait, and his housekeeper, and then the sudden view of the man himself as he unexpectedly materializes on the lawn. The deep blushes that spread over Darcy's and Elizabeth's cheeks when they meet are symptomatic of the awkwardness of their mutual attraction.

These points of view—his fixed, hers changing—are further symbolized by their walk through the park. Darcy has set out to meet her; she is his polestar and he steers by her. But for her the landscape is constantly shifting. Each turn in the walk, each rise or fall in the land, reveals to her new beauties and new insights until another twist of the path reveals Mr. Darcy himself, deliberately coming toward her. As they walk on together, their manner is sober—no smiles, no sparkle of wit, no repartee. Beatrice and Benedict are silent at last. But it is the silence of those who feel deeply.

The implications of silence and walking together are again explored in the second proposal scene at Longbourn. For a number of critics, this scene, like the proposal scenes in all her novels, is simply a frigid exercise in plot resolution, whose reticences are a sign she cannot handle sex. But this is far from true. As always, language and gesture tell an unspoken story, though here it is largely the language of speechlessness that she employs. We have only to look at Darcy's shift in pronouns from "I" to "you" (from "In vain have I struggled" to "You are too generous to trifle with me") to realize how far he has come in transcending his social and sexual egocentricity. And we have only to listen to Elizabeth, suddenly fumbling for words, to see how far she, too, has outgrown her old self. Jane Austen deliberately chooses to give Elizabeth's response in indirect discourse only, as if her confusion and intensity of feeling are beyond mere statement. Darcy's reaction, too, is given by indirection. He expresses himself, we are told, "as sensibly and warmly as a man violently in love can be supposed to do." But once again we can only guess at and supply from our own imaginations the potency and force of his feelings. They are too strong and too private for our hearing. Only his eyes, mentioned for almost the first time, tell all. They are suffused with "heartfelt delight." Fully alive at last, Darcy is no longer constrained within the rigidities of convention. He is free to ramble through the lanes with an Elizabeth only too glad to walk with him.

That there are ironies in this passage, that the chapter ends with Elizabeth's deciding that it is still too early to tease him, and that the next one begins with her claiming that it was his beautiful estate at Pemberley that made her love him, do not indicate that Jane Austen underestimated the force of sexual attraction—only that she understood the complexity of human relationships. Indeed, the last paragraphs of the book, which tell us little about Darcy and Elizabeth and a great deal about their various relatives, remind us that their love story can only fully be read in the context of the other couples around them: Mr. and Mrs. Bennet, Bingley and Jane, Lydia and Wickham, Mr. and Mrs. Gardiner, and the still-unmarried Georgiana.

If Mr. Bennet's marital disappointment in his silly wife shows us what happens when a person of lively talents fails to choose an equal mate, the marriage of Bingley and Jane illustrates the pleasures of wedlock between two people of no particular talents at all. Neither polar opposites nor exceptional people, they serve as foils to Elizabeth and Darcy. The obstacles to their marriage are purely external and the very ease with which this man and woman melt into one another points up the high degree of energy involved in the male-female fusion of Elizabeth and Darcy. The Bingleys' ductile metal strikes no sparks.

More interesting in their role as a normative couple are the Gardiners. The very last sentences of the book are dedicated to them: "With the Gardiners they were always on the most intimate terms. Darcy, as well as Elizabeth, really loved them; and they were both ever sensible of the warmest gratitude toward the persons who, by bringing her into Derbyshire, had been the means of uniting them." That Darcy's acceptance of the Gardiners stands for his recognition of a rising social class and for a broadened humanitarianism has often been noted. But the Gardiners are more than social indices; they represent sexual norms as well. Where Elizabeth's parents illustrate the possible future miseries of marriage, the Gardiners and their children suggest its promises. Can one doubt that they are comfortably wedded? Their constant conjectures about Elizabeth and Darcy suggest intimate bedtime conversation, and their slow arm-in-arm walk at Pemberley (arranged to allow Elizabeth time to be with Darcy) implies a tacit understanding of their common aims. They are actually surrogate parents to both Elizabeth and Darcy. Their highly practical and highly principled handling of Lydia's elopement sets a standard for warmth and firmness that Elizabeth and Darcy must learn to combine before they marry.

Georgiana Darcy, one of the few unwed characters at the end of the novel, serves as a foil to Lydia and as a further illustration of Jane Austen's attitude toward sex. Shy and restrained though she is, Georgiana is in many ways Lydia Bennet's double. Both girls are almost the same age at the period of their involvement with Wickham. Georgiana was fifteen when she planned to elope; Lydia had just turned sixteen when she married. Georgiana was nearly seduced from one seaside resort; Lydia ran away from another at Brighton. Each had an inadequate chaperone and both, significantly enough, were physically precocious. In an age when puberty arrived later than it does now, the fifteen-year-old Lydia is repeatedly described as "stout" and "well-grown," and Miss Darcy, too, has a well-formed figure. That both of them can fall prey to a man like Wickham is a sign not only that Jane Austen recognizes the temptations of the flesh but that she sees the equal dangers of a too repressive or too permissive upbringing, each of which equally may lead to sexual promiscuity. As in all things, it is the mean between feeling and reason that must be observed. The obstreperous Lydia is as unsuccessful an example of one kind of upbringing as the agonizingly shy Georgiana is of another. They represent the extremes to which Darcy's and Elizabeth's families are prone.

If Lydia's fate seems fixed by the end of the novel, there is the promise of a happier future for Georgiana. Immature enough to be considered Elizabeth's and Darcy's child, she must be retrained by the lessons their own love has taught them. The next-to-last paragraph of the novel, which emphasizes the freedom and spontaneity Elizabeth will teach Georgiana, is a corrective to her too-rigid upbringing. Ideally, she will be a child of Darcy's head and Elizabeth's heart, of his principles and her feelings, or—to oversimplify—of the union of rationality and emotion that their marriage represents.

To say that Jane Austen's novels are essentially sexless—intellectual exercises devoid of sex or defensive about it—seems to me wrong. Her use of allusions, puns, riddles, and sex symbols points to a specific knowledge about the manifestations of sexuality, if nothing else. Far from wondering, as one critic does, if she "knew anything of the part played by the flesh and the fleshly passions," we can only register surprise at her sophisticated devices for indicating them.

But more significant than her knowledge of physical sex is the fully human way in which she implies the broad range of feelings that man and woman have for each other. All of her books underscore both the social and sexual meaning of marriage. A good marriage for Jane Austen is always supportive of the organization of society. It involves an appropriate mixing of classes and value systems that sustains the traditional qualities of English life while allowing for change and renewal. But marriage is also a sexual act in her novels—usually a reconciliation between a man and a woman whose inner feelings and conscious knowledge have been at odds throughout the story. As I have tried to show in my analysis of *Pride and Prejudice,* the signs of such attraction may only be covert. But they ring true to the complexities of human emotion and to its intensities as well.

It may be argued that I have conjectured too much in interpreting these novels, that I have treated the characters as if they were living beings, whose words and gestures we can interpret and whose past and future we can guess. But this is surely what we are meant to do. Jane Austen herself went looking for Elizabeth's picture among the real portraits of an art exhibition—a symbol of the kind of involvement her fiction demands. Besides, the art of Jane Austen is an art of interstices—of lines finely drawn and space suggested. The unflagging delight of rereading her lies in our own increasing perception of those traits and motives that she merely suggests. One of the clearest suggestions is surely the subtleties of sexual relationship that lie behind the surface of convention and restraint.

RUTH apROBERTS

Sense and Sensibility, or *Growing up Dichotomous*

Sense and Sensibility has traditionally been considered, along with *North-anger Abbey*, a kind of early prentice work, and in spite of the delight it occasions and the light it spreads, "unsuccessful." I want to insist on its success, its importance within the Austen canon, and its importance in general. I want to suggest some connections with the poets, and show Austen, in this book particularly, performing some perennially important activities, such as testing abstractions against realities, laughing, and coping with the dissociation of sensibility. Even such a perceptive critic as A. Walton Litz has recently found the abstract tags of the title "obstacles to the maturing artist,"—"the author is caught in the web of a language which tends to describe 'types,' not individuals." I suggest, rather, that the novel has a sound base in that dichotomous abstraction of the title. *Sense and Sensibility, Pride and Prejudice, Persuasion*—"It is not for nothing," says Gilbert Ryle, "that these titles are composed of abstract nouns. *Sense and Sensibility* really is about the relations between Sense and Sensibility or, as we might put it, between Head and Heart, Thought and Feeling, Judgement and Emotion." This novel is, then, a part of what might be the oldest tradition of the verbal animal. Being in itself is altogether too hard to think about as the "blooming, buzzing confusion" which (in William James's phrase) it probably is, and in our linguistic fictions we posit aspects of it in order to deal with it: Anima and Corpus, Soul and Body, Mind and Body, Head and Heart. Most often

From *Nineteenth-Century Fiction* 30, no. 3 (December 1975). © 1975 by the Regents of the University of California.

there is something left over, the very self, which when it speaks poems we are in our linguistic desperation reduced to calling the *persona,* which is— of all things—a mask, the real self being so unthinkable.

Sometimes our linguistic fictions are abstractions, like thought and feeling. Sometimes they are clearly metaphor, Head and Heart, for instance, a physiological metaphor for things felt to be separable processes of being. Probably the physical head has no more proprietary claim to "thinking" than the heart has to "feeling." Sometimes they are obscurely metaphor, *anima* being at bottom the invisible but felt breath or wind, and *corpus* being the material, kickable substance. We know finally that these things are not absolute entities, but they are indispensable to thinking. As Bentham said of the fictions of language in general, they are "impossible but indispensable." For it is only by their means that we are able to say a great deal about the way things are; they open areas of discourse otherwise inaccessible.

The Emperor Hadrian could address his soul, his *anima,* in a five-line poem that has kept its force over the long space of time since the second century:

Animula vagula blandula
hospes comesque corporis
quae nunc abibis in loca
pallidula rigida nudula
nec ut soles dabis jocos.

The diminutives manage to objectify the tenderness felt for the soul, so vulnerable, fragile, tenuous, and errant we sense it to be. *Hospes,* yes: both host and guest of the body but more than either, as in the hospitality relationship that in the Near East is preeminent and sacred in its rights and obligations; *comes,* yes: that is the good working relationship, a comradeship. The soul threatened by the severed relationship must feel its future forlorn indeed, stark, bare, desolate. The emperor, however, marvels that his soul might lose what is apparently for him its most characteristic and essential function, the making of jokes! the most astoundingly mysterious aspect of consciousness, that recoil upon itself which is wit and laughter. One reason the poem is an enduring challenge to translators is the way it ends surprisingly, on the mystery of laughter in very humble terms. The Latin *dabis jocos* is just about as low as English "crack jokes." Among the translators of Jane Austen's time, the young Byron felt he had to reverse the order of the ending:

> Ah! gentle, fleeting, wav'ring sprite,
> Friend and associate of this clay!
> To what unknown regions borne,
> Wilt thou now wing thy distant flight?
> No more with wonted humour gay,
> But pallid, cheerless, and forlorn.

But let us note above all that the use of the body-soul dichotomy made this important and subtle statement of Hadrian's possible, and keeps it functional. Man must always have used such concepts as soon as he used language. This particular body-soul concept is the one that under the impulse of Christianity gives birth to a whole series of texts such as those many medieval debates of the Body and Soul, to keep to dichotomies; or, moving to pluralities, the dramas of the virtues and vices. Always the self is there, listening and observing and learning, both stage and audience for the debate or for the morality play. These old art forms worked well, we might surmise, because they are so obviously metaphorical. No one believes the soul can really talk to the body.

Personification of aspects of personality opens whole new worlds of theology too; and as Christianity exploited the body-soul dichotomy, the dichotomy tended to harden into doctrine, and ultimately the soul came to be considered literally the immortal part. The immortal soul, if we retain the sense of it as fictive, may be thought of as a useful fiction in the line of Hans Vaihinger's theory of fictions, and the *Als-Ob,* the As-If. Our actions may be the better or more successful if we act as if the soul was an immortal part which will take the consequences of our behavior. It can be argued that when the metaphor hardens into doctrine it becomes less useful. To "believe" that the soul is a literally immortal separable entity may make a closing off of the mind instead of an opening into new phases of discourse. We can become anxious about "belief," and malfunction can occur. Matthew Arnold deplored this literalism of belief, and called it the "prison of Puritanism"; in his diagnosis it lay at the root of the Victorian malaise. Something similar may be responsible for what T. S. Eliot deplored as the "dissociation of sensibility."

As literalism was developing in the late eighteenth century, along with the Evangelical movement, the most current philosophical dichotomy was the intellect-emotion one, preeminently the Sense and Sensibility of Jane Austen. The philosophical background has been well explored in Descartes, Locke, Hume, Berkeley, and Shaftesbury; the literary cult of sensibility—in Sterne, MacKenzie, and the poets—is a well-known chapter in the history of English literature; and the linguistic background reveals itself in an hour or so with the *Oxford English Dictionary,* or most conveniently and delightfully in C. S. Lewis's essay on "Sense (with Sentence, Sensibility and Sensible)." From the cluster of words growing out of the Latin *sentio* matrix, develops a set of words with widely divergent uses, from something like *logos* or "meaning," in *sentence,* to the Austen pair of sense-reason, and sensibility-responsiveness. Lewis quotes Dr. Johnson on the relevance of this last meaning to art: "the ambition of superior sensibility and superior eloquence dispose the lovers of arts to receive rapture at one time and communicate it at another"; and Cowper on its relevance to moral sympathy: "Grant, Kind heav'n, to me, Sweet Sensibility." And he takes the Dashwood girls of course as the *locus classicus* of the two uses. It is "a semantic situation," he says, which can hardly last, the two meanings being so divergent; and the "half-punning antithesis" of the Austen title preserves the unstable moment. Her terms are certainly used as mutually exclusive categories for experience, nicely caught in the title of the French translation of 1815: *Raison et sensibilité, où les deux manières d'aimer.*

Certainly the title sets the novel in the long and august line of fictive dichotomies from the old body-soul one, through such little allegories as Tennyson's "The Two Voices," and the Victorian commonplace of conscience as the "still small voice" of God within us (developed rather oddly out of the Elijah story), holding its adversary the beast-in-man in check; and the great nineteenth-century debate of Heart and Head, perhaps most nobly done by Dostoevsky; surviving in the twentieth century in the mind-body myth, which Ryle has been at pains to expose as fictive in his famous *Concept of Mind.* We are liable to error if we "believe" in the dualism. But meantime, all these dichotomies are, however "impossible," quite "indispensable." The danger is to forget the fictiveness, for once the terms become current, they reinforce themselves as concepts and are more and more liable to harden into things "believed in" as reality.

Jane Austen in *Sense and Sensibility* starts with a fictive dichotomy but warns us against it from the beginning. In the first description of the two girls, Elinor, though obviously representing sense, has feelings that are strong, and Marianne, though obviously representing sensibility, has a distinguished intellect. It is not a case where the author finds she must modify her theme in the course of the novel; she knows what she is about from the first. This is not going to be a morality play, nor a set of Jonsonian humors, nor a simplistic cautionary tale. But with the title in front of us, we are certainly at first invited to test the characters on its polarity. Austen is too often connected only with novelists, and we might have the courage to connect her with the poets, her contemporaries. Blake, characteristically forthright, asserts: "To generalize is to be an idiot." Austen, too, refuses us the generalization. Blake also asserts, forthright again: "Without contraries is no progression." I propose that Austen takes her contraries or antitheses not as ends, but as means, to a kind of progression or education. I think the antitheses characteristic of the Enlightenment are a kind of product or conclusion. But Austen's antitheses are not so much enlightened epigrammatic conclusions, but phases of process. Take from *Sense and Sensibility* a typical series of antitheses: Elinor and Marianne

> had too much sense to be desirable companions to the former [Lady Middleton]; and by the latter [the Steeles] they were considered with a jealous eye, as intruding on *their* ground, and sharing the kindness which they wanted to monopolize. Though nothing could be more polite than Lady Middleton's behaviour to Elinor and Marianne, she did not really like them at all. Because they neither flattered herself nor her children, she could not believe them good-natured; and because they were fond of reading, she fancied them satirical. . . . Their presence was a restraint both on her and on Lucy. It checked the idleness of one, and the business of the other. Lady Middleton was ashamed of doing nothing before them, and the flattery which Lucy was proud to think of and administer at other times, she feared they would despise her for offering.

This play of antitheses, diagrammed by "the former" and "the latter," "because" and "because," "the one" and "the other," "ashamed" and "feared," is a means toward discovery by contrasts. All these oppositions are temporarily useful structures, to be dropped in series and replaced by others.

One of Jane Austen's Victorian critics, Richard Simpson, had a keen perception of this antithesis as method. In general, he understood that in "growth through contradictions we see the highest exercise of the critical faculty." He notes that Austen rejects the simple black-and-white view, sees the good in the evil, and the evil even in the good, and all this is perceived in action.

> It is her thorough consciousness that man is a social being, and that apart from society there is not even the individual. . . . She contemplates virtues not as fixed quantities, or as definable qualities, but as continual struggles and conquests, as progressive states of mind, *advancing by repulsing their contraries* [my ital-

ics]. . . . A character . . . unfolded itself to her . . . as . . . a composite force, which could only exhibit what it was by exhibiting what it did.

Simpson goes on to relate this aspect of her art to Cowper, and we remember that of all her books it is this one where Cowper is most involved. According to Cowper, "By ceaseless action all that is subsists." "He that attends to his interior self, / That has a heart and keeps it; has a mind / That hungers, and supplies it; and who seeks / A social, not a dissipated life, / Has business." This novel is a Cowperian exercise, where it is initially proposed that we test all by the bipolar gauge of Sense-Sensibility or mind-heart, and yet we are warned from the first against taking this gauge as absolute. We find that not only must the heart be "kept"—protected, guided, disciplined—but also the mind must be "supplied"—fed, exercised, and developed. And the test is not the initial bipolar one finally, but something else that measures the adjustment or integration of mind-heart. The test is a social business, and social business is the determination of morality. Everyone is tested first on the Sense-Sensibility gauge, and events prove that gauge grossly inadequate. The John Dashwoods, early on in the splendid second chapter, where they cut down the inheritance of the girls all for their own good, make a fine demonstration of how sense or prudence can be the most egregious selfishness. Mrs. Jennings is wonderfully deficient in both sense and sensibility, and yet comes out very high on that other gauge. The evaluation of each character is adjusted and changed as the novel proceeds. The events are a series of multidimensional tests that demonstrate the fallacy of the premise. It even recalls Bertrand Russell's fable of the barber. In town A, you remember, you can divide all the men into two classes, those that shave themselves and those that are shaved by the barber. The categories seem perfectly unexceptionable. But events bring us in contact with Mr. Jones, the barber himself. And what do we do with *him*? Our categorization is revealed as inadequate.

This slight-seeming little novel bears the weight of much analysis, and is looking increasingly important in the Austen canon. Historically, it appears to use and to criticize the abstract intellection of the Enlightenment, and at the same time anticipates the novelistic realism of the nineteenth century. Austen would have us beat our dichotomies into pluralities, as more closely adapted to what will be felt to be the variety of reality, the relativistic view of life. When she departs from simple antithesis into the triplet, I think she moves significantly closer to relativism. When Marianne sings at the Middleton's party, there are three significant reactions:

Sir John was loud in his admiration at the end of every song, and as loud in his conversation with the others while every song lasted. Lady Middleton frequently called him to order, wondered how any one's attention could be diverted from music for a moment, and asked Marianne to sing a particular song which Marianne had just finished. Colonel Brandon alone, of all the party, heard her without being in raptures. He paid her only the compliment of attention.

There are two kinds of false rapture here, and one nonrapture. Elements one and two are clearly anti-Marianne; element three, or Brandon, is antirapture but pro-Marianne and so breaks out of the categories, thereby moving forward and anticipating how Marianne's simplicities will be modified.

Other events yield more complicated results. When the John Dashwoods, unaccustomed as they are to giving anything away, do give a dinner, there appeared "no poverty of any kind, except of conversation." "When the ladies withdrew to the drawing-room after dinner, this poverty was particularly evident," for the only topic was the comparative heights of two little boys.

> Had both the children been there, the affair might have been determined too easily by measuring them at once; but as Harry only was present, it was all conjectural assertion on both sides, and every body had a right to be equally positive in their opinion, and to repeat it over and over again as often as they liked.
>
> The parties stood thus:
>
> The two mothers, though each really convinced that her own son was the tallest, politely decided in favour of the other.
>
> The two grandmothers, with not less partiality, but more sincerity, were equally earnest in support of their own descendant.
>
> Lucy, who was hardly less anxious to please one parent than the other, thought the boys were both remarkably tall for their age, and could not conceive that there could be the smallest difference in the world between them; and Miss Steele, with yet greater address gave it, as fast as she could, in favour of each.
>
> Elinor, having once delivered her opinion on William's side, by which she offended Mrs. Ferrars and Fanny still more, did not see the necessity of enforcing it by any farther assertion; and Marianne, when called on for her's, offended them all, by declaring that she had no opinion to give, as she had never thought about it.

We have here four pairs of reactions, balanced against each other and within themselves in remarkable and hilarious symmetry. We all use contrasting pairs as a way of thinking, with parallelisms in our sentences or poems, in the analogies of metaphor, and in the doublings of allegory. Behind this activity we may see the outline of a mathematical structure. The Bourbaki school have described the mathematical method par excellence as the reduction of data to isomorphisms; and the structuralists take this to be the model of all human activity. An analogous principle has emerged out of Boolean algebra into a method for machines that is a binary—or isomorphological—system. All data may be programmed by this system, and one proceeds from data so obtained into new series of isomorphs and new results. The work of Kurt Gödel sustains the principle that no systems or results are final and complete—one moves on. I propose that Jane Austen's series of eight reactions to the conversational poverty situation are dealt with by isomorphs. First we have four relations balanced by four nonrelations. Then the first four are reduced to a pair of mothers, and a pair of grandmothers, in balance. Then the two mothers are discovered to balance each other precisely, indistinguishable in their partiality, their smug confidence and their hypocrisy. The two grandmothers are equally indistinguishable, both grown old in partiality and both even impatient with hypocrisy. The second set of four balances the first in some ways. Mothers:grandmothers = Steeles:Dashwoods in respect of closeness of interest and degrees of honesty. The two Steeles, however, differentiate themselves one from the other with the most ingenious and exquisite nicety, but the differences are pretense and we recognize the sisters as beautifully indistinguishable in corruption. Elinor and Marianne we know well enough to recognize their common ground in this exigency: both would be appalled at the intellectual desperation, and partly bored, partly "satirically" amused, since both are basically honest women. Similarities granted, the delicate distinctions can now appear in relief. Elinor, ever the more dutiful in social obligations, makes a compromise, satisfies her honesty by a single statement of opinion, being willing to offend one faction to a degree. Marianne, uncompromisingly honest, is willing to offend them all. In this testing event, we have discovered through the use of isomorphs a certain rich discrepancy which enables us to move on to a new level of discourse. Marianne's sensibility emerges as an unwillingness to sense the feelings of others and hence a reversal into lack of sensibility. Her feelings, initially authentic, through being fostered have taken on something histrionic which is inauthentic and which closes to her that empathy we owe to the people we encounter. Against the thoughtlessness of Marianne is set the extended social consciousness of Elinor.

On the same evening, when the gentlemen join the ladies, John Dashwood goes so far in generosity as to bring attention to Elinor's painting on a pair of screens. Again the members of the party are tested and the results recorded in sharp almost tabular form, revealing kinds and degrees of insolence and philistinism, till it is too much for Marianne. She cannot bear to have Elinor's art slighted, and she rudely snatches the screens from Fanny, "to admire them herself as they ought to be admired." It is an adorable action. Her love breaks the pattern of politeness, and we progress to a yet more advanced level of complication. The whole account of the evening is— I hope my analysis does not altogether disguise the fact—very funny. If the structuralists would find in mathematical isomorphisizing a model for distintively human activity, and if one feels with Hadrian that it is the essence of the distinctively human *anima* to make jokes, one might suspect there is a connection. It is true that by means of our isomorphs we discover and define discrepancies, which can make us laugh. To judge by the geometrical games Hadrian played in designing the Pantheon, he had thought a good deal about mathematics as well as his soul, and maybe he had an intimation of isomorphs. At any rate the funniness of the Austen novels is immeasurably important in the way it spreads back out over us in waves of benign awareness. Its working is absolutely unfathomable. Man, says Foucault, amounts to "a simple pleat in consciousness," and that might be a description of *homo sapiens, homo ludens,* or even, particularly, *homo jocans.*

Some of the scenes that open out new perspectives are grimmer in humor than the one of the Dashwoods' dinner party. The most difficult test for Elinor occurs when we know that Willoughby has betrayed Marianne, and we know that Elinor is in similar distress: Lucy Steele has told her under pledge of secrecy that she, Lucy, is engaged to Elinor's beloved Edward. Lucy calls on Mrs. Jennings, Marianne is suffering upstairs; Mrs. Jennings is called out, and Elinor is left alone with Lucy. This is bad enough, with Lucy's insufferable arrogance, but Elinor's torture is compounded when Edward himself is announced. "The very circumstance, in its unpleasantest form, which they would each have been most anxious to avoid, had fallen on them—They were not only all three together, but were together without the relief of any other person." Edward is virtually paralyzed, Lucy is sly and smirkingly quiet, and so Elinor must labor under the weight not only of her broken heart but of all the social duty. She is

> obliged to volunteer all the information about her mother's health, their coming to town, &c. which Edward ought to have inquired about, but never did.

Her exertions did not stop here; for she soon afterwards felt
herself so heroically disposed as to determine, under pretence of
fetching Marianne, to leave the others by themselves: and she
really did it, and *that* in the handsomest manner, for she loitered
away several minutes on the landing-place, with the most high-
minded fortitude.

It is some small comfort to us all that we may suspect her nobility to be a
little tempered with sadism: just let Edward face this charming fiancée of
his! But when Elinor returns with Marianne, Marianne in her naiveté says
everything that might increase the pain for Elinor. And Marianne thinks she
herself is the martyr! There is a mathematical kind of thoroughness in the
way Austen wrings each aspect of irony from the dialogue here.

The anguish of the testing is a learning process and it is not just Marianne who learns. We ourselves see that Mrs. Dashwood and Marianne have
adopted the fashionable new cult of sensibility out of motives which in themselves are hardly culpable: lively intelligence and sensitivity to life and art.
But the more they indulge themselves in the histrionics of sensibility, the
more Elinor, aware of the danger, is obliged to appear priggish in reaction.
The grave danger to personality becomes obvious in Marianne's case. She
has become vulnerable. Her severe physical illness symbolizes the moral danger; her physical resistance has been lowered by sensibility as has her psychic
resistance, and she is nearly lost in more ways than one. If the heroine of
Northanger Abbey suffers from "factual gullibility" in Ryle's terms, Marianne can be said to be a victim of "cultural gullibility." The dichotomy of
Sense and Sensibility is thus proved invalid, even dangerous, and we discard
it for other gauges that seem to sort better with behavioral actualities. Yet
because the dichotomy had seemed valid initially, we might be the more
prepared now to take our new gauges and standards as provisional. Learning
is a dialectical process and does not stop.

Learning is also a function of humanity. Innateness is not enough. We
remember that when Elinor reproves Marianne for visiting Willoughby's
house alone with him, Marianne retorts in Rousseauistic terms: "if there had
been any real impropriety in what I did, I should have been sensible of it at
the time, for we always know when we are acting wrong." But events contradict her, and it is part of the pattern of this book that the Rousseauistic
natural man is consistently put down. Children do not come off well in *Sense
and Sensibility*. It is foolish to classify Jane Austen as a child-hater, for we
know perfectly well that she was an excellent aunt and a great instigator of
laughter and joy. But there was no nonsense, one can be sure, about "Thou

best philosopher." The young John Dashwood runs no danger of being ide-
alized; he

> gained on the affections of his uncle, by such attractions as are
> by no means unusual in children of two or three years old; an
> imperfect articulation, an earnest desire of having his own way,
> many cunning tricks, and a great deal of noise.

The Middleton children are quite unable to assert any innate goodness
in the ambiance of stupidity and indulgence that their mother makes for
them. They are utter spoiled brats, of very limited usefulness.

> On every formal visit a child ought to be of the party, by way of
> provision for discourse. In the present case it took up ten minutes
> to determine whether the boy were most like his father or mother,
> and in what particular he resembled either, for of course every
> body differed, and every body was astonished at the opinion of
> the others.

And then, as we have seen, there is the John Dashwood party when the two
boys' heights afford the only straw of interest for desperate conversational-
ists. One imagines Elinor's and Marianne's distaste for those spoiled monsters; the Steeles, however, exploit the sentimental idealization of the young
for their own interests. They "doat," they say, on children, quite indiscriminately whenever the mother may be flattered thereby; they are in raptures
over behavior that should get a swift smack. This is a society that in reality
sacrifices children. Margaret, the younger sister of Elinor and Marianne,
would certainly never be so spoiled by her mother, but is at thirteen quite
naturally bound to be trying, and makes herself a party to the worst of Mrs.
Jennings's vulgar teasing. "As she had already imbibed a good deal of Marianne's romance, without having much of her sense," the prognosis is not
good. Since Austen also tells us she is "a good-humoured well-disposed girl"
we gather the material is good enough. The emphasis is on the telling value
of upbringing.

Ryle observes that Austen's "ethical vocabulary and idioms are quite
strongly laced with aesthetic terms"; and I think *Sense and Sensibility* is of
all her novels the one most concerned with art, language, and their relationship to morality. The superiority of Marianne and Elinor and their mother
consists in good part in their cultivation. Barton Cottage is full of books
and music, and the inhabitants habitually read poetry aloud, and paint, and
collect prints. The idle Philistines, the Middletons, Steeles, etc., are quite
astonished to find the Barton Dashwoods so frequently "employed." Ed-

ward's unfortunate entanglement with Lucy really came about from idleness. His mother denies him an active profession, he is not entered at Oxford till he is nineteen, and shy and self-deprecating as he is, he is vulnerable to Lucy. Man *is* language in a sense that Austen intimates here; this is a study of cliché in behavior as well as in language. Lucy Steele is retrograde on both counts. The values of cultivation and of virtue go for the most part hand in hand, though even here Austen refuses us the easy generalization: Mrs. Jennings is the walking exception, the vulgarian who is full of generosity. Whoever it was who said the exceptions to moral rules are about as frequent proportionately as the exceptions to grammatical rules, would find corroboration in the sort of life-grammar that Austen codifies for us. But to grant exceptions is not to insist any the less on the value of the rules. Grammar is simply hard.

Some time ago, Mark Schorer professed "our surest way of knowing the values out of which a novel comes lies in the examination of style, more particularly of metaphor," and he found in Austen a high proportion of terms of commerce, property, credit, interest, account, tax, insurance, and so on. Schorer did not apply this to mean that Austen's values were entirely material; he had far too fine a sense of them for that. But he accommodated his theory by asserting the "tension" between material and moral. Surely the moral interest is at the center. And the "surest way" of knowing her values is not to discover how she gives herself away by her metaphors but to observe what the novel is "about" in Ryle's plain sense. Metaphors are a means to an end. Our overriding business is to determine the virtuous life, and because that is difficult we turn to metaphor. And we find the terms of our metaphor in those interests that are all too familiar in our fallen state: commerce, property, credit, etc. So the moralist makes particular use of our frailty: "Lay up for yourselves treasures in heaven"; the figure is taken from banking. We must know where to put our "money." Similarly the parable of the talents is a figure taken from investment; and we had better be able to give a good accounting.

If the good artist is to be a good investment advisor, she will not allow us our easy generalities. From the first, Austen refused to let us take sense-sensibility as an absolute good-evil polarity, and, as her theme and variations act themselves out in the events, the odd thing is that sensibility rejoins virtue. The fashionable new lifestyle had its origin in the love of virtue: it was the eighteenth-century moralists who invented it. It becomes, however, excessively fashionable and its virtuous pretensions prove hollow, or even treacherous. We return to the principle, then, chastened and educated, to recognize that the fount of decency is the ability to feel, first for ourselves, and then, with good hope, for others. Austen's contemporary, Keats, asserts "the holiness of the heart's affections." "I have felt . . . ," says Wordsworth, and that is his authority. Mill discovers the prime importance of a "due balance among the faculties" and turns to Wordsworth for the necessary "culture of the feelings." There is a pattern of peripeteia in the movement of *Sense and Sensibility* that acts on various levels. In the main action, which is "the extraordinary fate" of Marianne Dashwood, "born to discover the falsehood of her own opinions, and to counteract, by her conduct, her most favourite maxims," the once despised Colonel Brandon becomes her beloved husband; she "could never love by halves; and her whole heart became, in time, as much devoted to her husband, as it had once been to Willoughby." Her capacity for passion is finally exercised, but in a way that was hardly to be expected. Austen is alert to a score of such peripeteias, major and minor: Mrs. Ferrars, Elinor observes after the reversals of the roles of Robert and Edward, "has actually been bribing one son with a thousand a-year, to do the very deed which she disinherited the other for intending to do." Little do we know, indeed, what reversals time will bring. There is a model for this in linguistic processes: out of the cluster of words from Latin *sentio* came the branching family of *sense* and *sensibility* to produce in time for Jane Austen a doublet that paradoxically represents something like opposites, and then moves back to converge into the *sentio-sensi* matrix: "I have felt. . . ." In a similarly peripatetic movement our heuristic fictions lead us back to the unity of being. Sensibility is, at least for a time, reassociated.

GENE W. RUOFF

Anne Elliot's Dowry: Reflections on the Ending of Persuasion

The endings of Jane Austen's novels present obstacles to anyone attempting to link her works to those of the other major writers of her age. The problems are not in those wholly fictive qualities which have preoccupied traditional Jane Austen criticism, such as the perfunctory cast of her endings or the parodistic tone which plays about them. In an era of unfinished masterworks, any ending at all may seem a technical accomplishment. Elemental issues are raised, though, by the way things turn out in Jane Austen's world—how the strength of human love is demonstrated and how, particularly, it is rewarded. Of Jane Austen's peers and contemporaries, Wordsworth would seem the most optimistic about the actual state of things in which man finds himself; yet when he celebrates the triumphs of the heart's affections, his most memorable victories tend to be wrenched from apparent defeats, as Michael, Margaret, Leonard Ewbank, and many others could bear witness. A pile of stones and an old dog are difficult to translate into Darcy, Pemberley, and ten thousand a year.

The simple fact that Jane Austen's heroines, heroes, and other characters of value invariably find their proper rewards suggests a belief that nothing is so radically wrong with the self or society that good sense, moderation, patience, and humor cannot finally make things work out. Few would claim that such a belief would be deeply Romantic. Jane Austen's apparent optimism that man's constituted society offers a possible and even proper home for his aspirations leads invariably to the charge, which is perhaps felt more

From *The Wordsworth Circle* 7, no. 4 (Autumn 1976). © 1976 by Marilyn Gaull.

often than voiced these days, that she is an unreflectively conservative defender of the status quo, ignorant of or choosing to ignore the ills which
grow from the social system into which she cheerfully integrates her heroines.
Why should the people be unhappy? Are there not landed gentry, country
parsons, and even wealthy naval commanders for them to marry?

That Jane Austen's novels do affirm the value of a social order is un-
deniable; but how a proper society comes into being within them, how its
values are grounded, and how its structure relates to commonplace hierar-
chies of wealth and rank are problematical. Of the five novels which come
before *Persuasion, Pride and Prejudice* can serve as an illustrative model.
The acute consciousness of social and economic status with which the novel
begins—the respective layers of the social pile represented by Bingley and
Darcy—prefigures a complex interplay of hierarchical motifs, quite similar
to those traced so convincingly by L. J. Swingle's essay on *Emma*. Darcy,
for example, is discovered to be "*above* being pleased"; Lady Catherine's
outstanding virtue is her *condescension*; and Elizabeth, on hearing Wickham's false revelations about Darcy, remarks that even she "did not suspect
him of *descending* to such malicious revenge" (all italics mine). The terms
above and *below,* in all their variants, dominate the narrative complications
of the work, assuming critical force in such lines as those in which Darcy
angrily responds to the curt rejection of his first proposal of marriage:
"Could you expect me to rejoice in the inferiority of your connections? To
congratulate myself on the hope of relations, whose condition in life is so
decidedly beneath my own?"

Given the prevalence of hierarchical patterning in the novel, one might
reasonably expect at its conclusion some emphasis on the levels which characters ultimately find. Instead, the ending of *Pride and Prejudice* is governed
by motifs of physical and psychological distance. In the reformed social order
which closes the book, Pemberley has become the center of societal values,
just as its inhabitants are at the center of human values. The worth of other
characters is mapped in terms of their proximity and access to Pemberley.
After Bingley buys an estate in a neighboring county, "Jane and Elizabeth,
in addition to every other source of happiness, were within thirty miles of
each other." The Gardiners are "always on the most intimate terms" with
Elizabeth and Darcy. Mr. Bennet "delighted in going to Pemberley, especially
when he was least expected," and Kitty improves greatly by spending "the
chief of her time with her two elder sisters." Among the characters who have
been obsessed with questions of degree and rank, Miss Bingley is forced to
drop her resentment of the marriage in order to "retain the right of visiting,"
while Lady Catherine is seen in only one visit to Derbyshire, still conde-

scending. Lydia and her Wickham are safely exiled in Newcastle, but while she is "occasionally a visitor" Darcy could, of course, "never receive *him* at Pemberley."

The concluding society of *Pride and Prejudice* is ordered schematically, but not in the way that had threatened to frustrate the most admirable of desires for happiness throughout the narrative. To a large extent, even the idea of society, in all its stratificational complexity, has been displaced by the idea of community. Consequently, the story of Elizabeth Bennet, an obvious enough rendering of the Cinderella myth, is less concerned with social mobility than social stability: she has not climbed a ladder; she has found and become a center. The novel indicates that a just and stable society cannot be formed by a shuffling and reshuffling of certificates of pedigree and statements of net worth, the respective fixations of Lady Catherine and Mrs. Bennet. A center is needed, a secure point from which civilized and humane values may emanate. For all their palpable differences, Pemberley has the same kind of meaning for Jane Austen that Grasmere has for Wordsworth: it is an organizing point for a society that has possessed only semblances of order. If it is a retreat, it is also a center for continuing moral regeneration.

Jane Austen's place endings move toward a point at which intimacy may be established and from which distance may be measured. That final location may, like Pemberley, have substantial value in and of itself; but its value is clearly subsidiary to its function as a place around which a community may form. "Elinor's marriage divided her as little from her family as could well be contrived, without rendering the cottage at Barton entirely useless"(*Sense and Sensibility*); she and Marianne finally live "almost within sight of each other." The fortuitous death of Dr. Grant allows Fanny and Edmund to move into the Mansfield parsonage "just after they had been married long enough to begin to want an increase of income, and feel their distance from the paternal abode an inconvenience" (*Mansfield Park*). Mr. Knightley gives up his residence at Donwell Abbey in order to move in with Emma and Mr. Woodhouse. The psychological and social benefits of a fixed and lasting home are treated eloquently in Wordsworth's well-known letter to Charles James Fox (14 January, 1801), where he proclaims the advantages of landed property. It provides, he says, "a kind of permanent rallying point for their domestic feelings, . . . a tablet upon which they are written which makes them objects of memory in a thousand instances when they would otherwise be forgotten." Good Burkean sentiments, we might nod, except that in both Wordsworth's and Jane Austen's presentations, disruption threatens the domestic feelings rather than the national security, and the home itself must be made safe before it can be confidently offered as an image of national order (in *The Improvement of the Estate,* [Alistair M.] Duckworth notes numerous parallels between Jane Austen and Burke). Given a rallying point, a sound community can form itself, and order can be established, at least on this small scale. Jane Austen's social views seem hardly optimistic from this perspective. As Professor Swingle has suggested, her strong sense of place aligns her with the Romantic fascination with enclosures—bowers, caves, islands, and other enclaves of the elect. Such a habit of mind is not characteristic of those who feel that things can be made right by a little tinkering and fiddling with the existing social machine.

But if Romanticism's affirmations often involve the successful discovery of a center, its darker musings are concerned with what happens when the center does not hold—when the bower is destroyed, the island invaded, the longed-for return to the childhood home crushed by the death of a beloved brother, or, to borrow Alistair Duckworth's phrase, the estate abandoned. Without a fixed point, can there be any secure foundation for the individual or social existence? Cain and Asmodeus, we remember, are nightmare figures of the age. Duckworth has commented tellingly on some of the ways in which the conclusion of *Persuasion* differs from those of the preceding novels: "the final marriage of the novel is not a 'social' marriage in the way that previous marriages are in Jane Austen; Anne's union with Wentworth fails to guarantee a broader union of themes and attitudes in *Persuasion* as say, Elizabeth's union with Darcy does in *Pride and Prejudice.* Nor, uniquely among Jane Austen's heroines, does Anne return to the stable and rooted existence of the land; she has 'no Uppercross-hall before her, no landed estate, no headship of a family'" (*The Improvement of the Estate*). With all this I would agree and add one further significant point of departure. The ending suggests no continuity of blood ties across generational lines: no visits from Mr. Bennet, no residence near Mrs. Dashwood or the Sir Thomas Bertrams, no living with Mr. Woodhouse. Here even the worthy Gardiners of *Pride and Prejudice,* the aunt and uncle who act as surrogate parents for Elizabeth, are replaced by the Musgroves, who are perhaps harmless enough but so lacking in stature as to be forgotten by the ending of the book. Anne feels her deprivation keenly: "The disproportion in their fortune was nothing; it did not give her a moment's regret; but to have no family to receive and estimate him properly; nothing of respectability, of harmony, of good-will to offer in return for all the worth and all the prompt welcome which met her in his brothers and sisters, was a source of as lively pain as her mind could well be sensible of, under circumstances of otherwise strong felicity.

She had but two friends in the world to add to his list, Lady Russell and Mrs. Smith. To these, however, he was very well disposed to attach himself."

Here are unmistakable signs that we are in at the founding of a new "community," one considerably different from those which have drawn together at the ends of the preceding novels. Lady Russell, with her deeply ingrained "prejudices on the side of ancestry" and the impoverished Mrs. Smith, who is, as Sir Walter Elliot puts it, "one of the five thousand Mrs. Smiths whose names are to be met with every where," seem an unlikely combination just in themselves. Their being added to the secure cluster of friends already surrounding Wentworth, principally Admiral and Mrs. Croft and Captain Harville and his family, leads one to wonder just what the common bond might be which holds this assemblage together. Certainly it is not the land. With the possible exception of Lady Russell, all are tenters, with temporary accommodations ranging in scale from the grandeur of Kellynch-hall to cramped lodgings in Bath, "a noisy parlor, and a dark bedroom behind." Anne and Wentworth are themselves given no geographical destination. Some sense of the mobility of habitation in *Persuasion* may be caught in Mrs. Croft's comments about living aboard ship: "Women may be as comfortable on board, as in the best house in England. I believe I have lived as much on board as most women, and I know nothing superior to the accommodations of a man of war."

Although the perspective into which Mrs. Croft places country houses—albeit with a "kind bow to Anne"—suggests the significance of those portions of the novel praising the naval life, it does not really justify the haste with which critics have commonly aligned its society into two alien camps, the inert landed gentry and the rising professional class, an aristocracy and a meritocracy. According to such a view, Anne Elliot's progress is marked by her steadily detaching herself from the gentry, her class by birthright, and attaching herself to Wentworth and his fellow naval officers. Anne cannot be said to leave her "feudal" past behind her as she rides the "revolutionary" currents, though, because she brings with her two of her oldest friends, neither of whom has shown the slightest predisposition toward the emerging professional class and one of whom is the most strenuous and—save Anne—the only genuine defender of the old order. That Anne should "bestow" Lady Russell and Mrs. Smith on Wentworth, and that he should accept them, creates an uncomfortable situation for readings which would pit professionalism against inheritance.

The ending of *Persuasion* is especially severe in its exclusions: it brushes aside all the Elliots except Anne, all the Musgroves, and even one naval officer, Captain Benwick, who has become engaged to Louisa Musgrove. We might, therefore, expect it to be equally exacting in its grounds for friendship, an issue which has commanded Jane Austen's attention since the juvenilia. Without a fixed geographical center, proximity can play no role in these newly formed relationships, nor to a large degree do a number of other familiar Austenian bonding agents—blood ties, cultural backgrounds, ages, and even dispositions. For all this, the figures who come together seem somehow solider than those who have closed the other novels. *Persuasion* embraces fewer charming eccentrics and tolerates fewer bores, and it proposes few startling reformations after the close of its dramatic action: no Kitty to be "improved," no Marianne to learn to love Colonel Brandon, no Sir Thomas Bertram to gain a rejuvenated sense of parental responsibility. At the end of both *Pride and Prejudice* and *Mansfield Park,* one is left with the feeling that the communities formed are stronger than either the individuals within them or the relationships among them would ordinarily allow. Problematical characters, weak and immature but not evil, are propped up by the related supports of generational continuity and landed property. In making do without these supports, *Persuasion* asks considerably more of its characters. The sort of parental incompetence tolerated in Mrs. Dashwood, the Bennets, and the Bertrams, for example, is not acceptable in the case of the elder Musgroves, even though they are generally pleasant and well meaning. Harmlessness is not on the novel's list of approved virtues.

In seeking the grounds of community in *Persuasion,* one might recall that a primary function of the estate in the earlier endings was to stimulate familial and cultural memory. The emotions engendered by the portrait gallery at Pemberley display this role at its most successful, just as the disarray into which Mansfield is thrown in Sir Thomas's absence shows its failure. Sir Thomas's response to the desecration of his billiard room dwells in a complicated way on the issue of family memory: "he felt it too much indeed for many words; and having shaken hands with Edmund, meant to try to lose the disagreeable impression, and forget how much he had been forgotten himself as soon as he could, after the house had been cleared of every object enforcing the remembrance, and restored to its proper state." This is the sort of word game through which Jane Austen often depicts the self-deluded. Upset by a failure of family memory, Sir Thomas tries to forget it by wiping out its visible signs. Obliterating this "disagreeable impression," of course, leads ultimately to others even more disagreeable, which will be less easily forgotten. An excessive reliance on houses or objects in general for recollection can be a tricky business, as prone to generate the self-indulgent and wallowing joys of nostalgia—one vice from which Fanny Price herself is not quite free—as vital and effective memories. *Persuasion* is even more centrally concerned with the vagaries of remembering and forgetting than *Mansfield Park,* but along with the estate it does without the various keepsakes and tokens which are Fanny's treasures in the old schoolroom. *Persuasion* places its highest value on the power of the individual memory, which, in the absence of such mnemonic aids as a stable home and family, must itself provide the continuity essential to the formation of a new community.

The importance of the theme of memory in *Persuasion* is implied ironically at the outset of the book, where we are allowed to read with Sir Walter Elliot his favorite page of the Baronetage: "there, if every other leaf were powerless, he could read his own history with an interest which never failed." Put off by a snobbery even more exalted than Lady Catherine's, we may fail to pay sufficient heed to the precise nature of that history which he reads with evident satisfaction: "Walter Elliot, born March 1, 1760, married July 15, 1784, Elizabeth, daughter of James Stevenson, Esq. of South Park, in the county of Gloucester; by which lady (who died 1800) he has issue Elizabeth, born June 1, 1785; Anne, born August 9, 1787; a still-born son, Nov. 5, 1789; Mary, born Nov. 20, 1791." Sir Walter has "improved" the account by adding the date and consequence of his youngest daughter's marriage and "by inserting most accurately the day of the month on which he lost his wife." The entry in the Baronetage has all the makings of family tragedy: the untimely loss of a wife, the still-born male heir, who would have secured the succession of the estate and guaranteed the future well-being of his unmarried sisters who, as matters stand, have no adequate provision. Whatever sorrow Sir Walter may ever have felt, though, is lost in his euphoric "vanity of person and of situation." Even the succeeding account of the exertions of his forebears in the service of the nation fails to call forth an inkling of personal inadequacy. He traces endlessly the skeletal account of a personal and hereditary past which seems scarcely to have touched him.

It has long been recognized that Anne Elliot differs from other Jane Austen heroines in having had a "past," in the sense of a romantic disappointment, and that, as the book's central consciousness, her view of its present actions is deeply interpenetrated by recollections of her past experience. At times, indeed, such as her first encounter with Wentworth at Uppercross, the present moment threatens to recede entirely, lost between her fearful anticipations of the event and her retrospective ponderings of its meaning. The key to Anne's character lies in a short reflection which follows the episode: "Alas! with all her reasonings, she found, that to retentive feelings eight years may be little more than nothing." On numerous occasions the retentive feelings of Anne are juxtaposed against the weak or faulty memories of those who surround her. Anne, for example, "could not hear that Captain Wentworth's sister was likely to live at Kellynch, without a revival of former pain." Whether her father, older sister, and Lady Russell make the same connection, though, is left to speculation: Anne is "assisted" in controlling her feelings "by that perfect indifference and apparent unconsciousness, among the only three of her friends in the secret of the past, which seemed to deny any recollection of it. She could do justice to the superiority of Lady Russell's motives in this, over those of her father and Elizabeth; she could honour all the better feelings of her calmness—but the general air of oblivion among them was highly important, from whatever it sprung." Anne must assume that Lady Russell remains silent in order to spare her feelings; her fidelity to the memory of Anne's mother and the hereditary responsibilities of the gentry would argue that she has not forgotten such an important crisis in Anne's life. Elizabeth and Sir Walter, however, may be either disdainful of or oblivious to the past: neither is ever to acknowledge a prior connection between Anne and Wentworth.

Sir Walter obliterates the past in his many looking glasses, anxious to think "himself and Elizabeth as blooming as ever amidst the wreck of good looks of every body else." Elizabeth, who seems at first to be haunted by a memorable grudge against William Walter Elliot, the heir presumptive of Kellynch Hall, forgets it as soon as the scapegrace seems to make himself available to her again. Mrs. Musgrove's maudlin outburst over her dead son is described as an improbable occurrence: "that Mrs. Musgrove should have been suddenly struck, this very day, with a recollection of the name of Wentworth, as connected with her son, seemed one of those extraordinary bursts of mind that do sometimes occur." Anne's sister Mary, so proud that her husband Charles will some day inherit Uppercross, shows no signs of recollecting that he first proposed to Anne. Henrietta Musgrove forgets Charles Hayter in her pursuit of Wentworth, and Louisa, in the absence of Wentworth, turns abruptly to Captain Benwick, who himself forgets his lost Fanny, for whom he has been pining Byronically, repeating "with such tremulous feeling, the various lines which imaged a broken heart, or a mind destroyed by wretchedness." A representative sample of the kinds of memories possessed by Anne's Uppercross associates is provided by Louisa's breathless account of a recent conversation: The Crofts "happened to say, that her brother, Captain Wentworth, is just returned to England, or paid off, or something, and is coming to see them almost directly; and most unluckily it came into mamma's head, when they were gone, that Wentworth, or something very like it, was the name of poor Richard's captain, at one time, I do not know when or where, but a great while before he died, poor fellow!" In the midst of such fuzziness, it is little wonder that Jane Austen inserts her notoriously succinct and brutal account of the "real circumstances of this pathetic piece of family history."

Faulty memories make personal relationships treacherously inconstant in *Persuasion,* and the relative strength of memory becomes a primary basis for ethical judgment. In the novel's climactic chapter, Captain Harville has been entrusted with delivering a miniature portrait of Captain Benwick, intended for Harville's dead sister Fanny, to Louisa Musgrove. After carefully recalling the circumstances of its being painted, he bursts out, "Poor Fanny! she would not have forgotten him so soon!" His statement sets off the famous debate with Anne on male and female constancy which, while itself remaining unresolved, underlines the moral distinction drawn throughout the novel between those who remember and those who do not, between those who are true to their pasts and those who are oblivious to, or evade, or disguise them. Consider the basis on which Anne judges William Walter Elliot: "she would have been afraid to answer for his conduct. She distrusted the past if not the present. . . . Though he might now think very differently, who could answer for the true sentiments of a clever, cautious man, grown old enough to appreciate a fair character? How could it ever be ascertained that his mind was truly cleansed?" In attempts to reconcile the past and present of the heir presumptive, Anne receives no assistance from his own accounts of himself. She distrusts the apparent discontinuity of his character, a discontinuity echoed, on a different level, by Benwick's rapid movement from obsessive grief over Fanny to love for Louisa. In *Persuasion* character is judged less in terms of behavior in a present situation than in terms of how individuals relate and relate to their own past experiences.

In a society pervaded by both clever and unwitting amnesiacs, how much people remember becomes an overriding concern. When Wentworth reappears, such questions multiply rapidly, as Anne must read his conversations for small signs, gestures, glances, any evidence that he might remember her in the way that she remembers him. That he does remember is clear from his initial unguarded comment upon seeing Anne: "Henrietta asked him what he thought of you, when they went away; and he said, 'You were so altered he should not have known you again.'" For change to be noted so vividly, the remembered image must be sharply etched. In general, though, it is Wentworth's conversations with his fellow officers which offer firm, if oblique, testimony to the strength of his memory. Much of the dialogue of *Persuasion* is anecdotal. Wentworth and Admiral and Mrs. Croft talk familiarly and lovingly of their various ships, encounters, and spoils while, in ironic counterpoint, the Misses Musgrove attempt to follow the conversation through their navy-list. The distinction between the summary knowledge provided by the list (another book of books, like the Baronetage) and the remembered personal history of the officers is made clear. The *Asp,* Wentworth's crucial first command, cannot be found in the list, because it has been taken from service. But above all, the stories of Wentworth and the admiral convey emotional knowledge, personal authenticity, a sense of having lived and experienced and remembered that is plainly lacking among the residents of both Kellynch Hall and Uppercross. One recalls that while Sir Walter is devoted to the Baronetage, Lady Russell and Anne remember the true meaning of the baronetcy; Mrs. Musgrove has to pillage her son's memorabilia, dragging forth his slender and illiterate correspondence, in order that her head, previously oblivious to his fate, should become "full of it, and of poor Richard!"

The anecdotal cast of the dialogue of *Persuasion* may, of course, be a sign of Jane Austen's deepening realism. Concerned as many novelists are with the dramatic analogue of scenic development, they sometimes overlook how much of our ordinary conversation—the best as well as the worst—consists of exchanged stories about ourselves. Sir Thomas Bertram, though, had serious motives for drawing Fanny's brother William out to talk about himself: "William was often called on by his uncle to be the talker. His recitals were amusing in themselves to Sir Thomas, but the chief object in seeking them, was to understand the recitor, to know the young man by his histories; and he listened to his clear, simple, spirited details with full satisfaction—seeing in them the proof of good principles, professional knowledge, energy, courage, and cheerfulness—every thing that could deserve or promise well" (*Mansfield Park*). Similar motives led Wordsworth to wander the public roads, and he made similar discoveries: "sounds in unison / With loftiest promises of good and fair" (*Prelude* [1850], XIII, 184–85). Equivalent roles are played in *Pride and Prejudice* and *Emma* by the letters in which Darcy and Frank Churchill, successfully and not so successfully, present their characters by giving an account of their actions, attempting to make themselves known by their histories. We may safely declare Jane Austen innocent of any knowledge of Wordsworth's unpublished masterpiece, but her tendency toward embedded narratives, so marked in *Persuasion,* would seem to proceed from similar considerations of the ways in which character should be presented.

Characters in *Persuasion* must render accounts of themselves. Some, like Sir Walter, Elizabeth, and the Musgroves, having experienced little and registered and retained even less, have precious little to tell. Others, like William Walter Elliot and Mrs. Clay, are thoroughly creatures of the present moment, vague or deceptive about their past lives. And still others, like Anne and Wentworth, the Crofts and Harvilles, and Lady Russell and Mrs. Smith, ultimately acquit themselves admirably, if not always painlessly. In their reconciliation scenes, Anne and Wentworth must retrace the past to come to terms with how things went wrong originally, how they might have been made right without the passage of eight lonely years, and how they very nearly misfired again. Mrs. Smith's account of the earlier life of Mr. Elliot does not spare her own youthful follies. When Lady Russell is faced with the truth about Mr. Elliot and with Anne's renewed attachment to Wentworth, "There was nothing less for [her] to do, than to admit that she had been pretty completely wrong, and to take up a new set of opinions and hopes." She is able to accomplish this confrontation with her past errors in judgment because "She loved Anne better than she loved her own abilities; and when the awkwardness of the beginning was over, found little hardship in attaching herself as a mother to the man who was securing the happiness of her other child." Anne's place in Lady Russell's life guarantees Wentworth's, just as Lady Russell's place in Anne's demands that he come to love her equally. The group which comes together at the end of the novel finds its bond in interlocking personal memories. Austen seems to suggest that a party of individuals with a firm sense of the integrity and continuity of the self will be able to overcome the fragmentation of society at large, which is so clearly imaged by the loss of the Kellynch estate and the near dissolution of the extended family as a social institution. In thinking of *Persuasion*'s principle for social unity, lines from *The Prelude* would again seem appropriate: "what we have loved, / Others will love, and we will teach them how" (1850; XIV, 446–47).

Jane Austen's earlier emphases on the discovery of a secure center and the maintenance of familial bonds, however inadequate the parents, are signs of her intense interest in cultural continuity. Her giving over these issues at the conclusion of *Persuasion,* accepting a world of fluidity of habitation, in which worthy older individuals must act, as Lady Russell explicitly does, in the place of parents, suggests a profound change in her attitudes on the possible foundations of a viable society. Controversy about the ending of the novel, most of which hinges in one way or other on the roles of Lady Russell and Mrs. Smith, may indicate that for many readers its vision of social continuity secured through the individual memory seems somehow inadequate. Old dreams die hard, and those of a secure place and generational continuity die harder than most. William A. Walling remarks of *Persuasion* that "Austen's art conveys to us a peculiarly modern terror: that our only recourse amid the accelerations of history is to commit our deepest energies to an intense personal relationship, but that an intense personal relationship is inevitably subject to its own kind of terrible precariousness." On the response of the modern reader, Professor Walling is undoubtedly correct; as far as Jane Austen herself is concerned, though, the terrors of her ending remain firmly circumstantial: "the dread of future war" and "the tax of quick alarm" paid by the sailor's wife are factors extrinsic to their personal relationship, which has already overcome obstacles equally threatening. An indication of Jane Austen's feelings about the adequacy of the grounds both of that relationship and of the small community which closes the novel may be found in the scene in which Anne and Wentworth find themselves alone and finally able to share their thoughts and feelings of the past moments and past years. "Soon words enough had passed between them," she writes, "to decide their direction towards the comparatively quiet and retired gravel walk, where the power of conversation would make the present hour a blessing indeed; and prepare it for all the immortality which the happiest recollections of their own future life could bestow." Such a belief in the power of memory—its ability to uphold and cherish and its power to make our noisy years seem moments in the being of the eternal silence—we have met with before, and in a writer whose central position in English Romanticism is uncontested.

SANDRA M. GILBERT and SUSAN GUBAR

Shut Up In Prose: Gender and Genre in Austen's Juvenilia

"Run mad as often as you chuse; but do not faint—"
—Sophia to Laura, *Love and Freindship*

They shut me up in Prose—
As when a little Girl
They put me in the Closet—
Because they liked me "still"—
—EMILY DICKINSON

Can you be more confusing by laughing. Do say yes.
We are extra. We have the reasonableness of a
woman and we say we do not like a room. We wish
we were married.
—GERTRUDE STEIN

She is twelve years old and already her story is written in the heavens.
She will discover it day after day without ever making it; she is curious
but frightened when she contemplates this life, every stage of which is
foreseen and toward which every day moves irresistibly.
—SIMONE DE BEAUVOIR

Not a few of Jane Austen's personal acquaintances might have echoed Sir Samuel Egerton Brydges, who noticed that "she was fair and handsome, slight and elegant, but with cheeks a little too full," while "never suspect[ing] she was an authoress." For this novelist whose personal obscurity was more complete than that of any other famous writer was always quick to insist

From *The Madwoman in the Attic: The Woman Writer and the Nineteenth-Century Literary Imagination.* © 1979 by Yale University. Yale University Press, 1979.

either on complete anonymity or on the propriety of her limited craft, her delight in delineating just "3 or 4 Families in a Country Village." With her self-deprecatory remarks about her inability to join "strong manly, spirited sketches, full of Variety and Glow" with her "little bit (two Inches wide) of Ivory," Jane Austen perpetuated the belief among her friends that her art was just an accomplishment "by a lady," if anything "rather too light and bright and sparkling." In this respect she resembled one of her favorite contemporaries, Mary Brunton, who would rather have "glid[ed] through the world unknown" than been "suspected of literary airs—to be shunned, as literary women are, by the more pretending of their own sex, and abhorred, as literary women are, by the more pretending of the other!—my dear, I would sooner exhibit as a ropedancer."

Yet, decorous though they might first seem, Austen's self-effacing anonymity and her modest description of her miniaturist art also imply a criticism, even a rejection, of the world at large. For, as Gaston Bachelard explains, the miniature "allows us to be world conscious at slight risk." While the creators of satirically conceived diminutive landscapes seem to see everything as small because they are themselves so grand, Austen's analogy for her art—her "little bit (two Inches wide) of Ivory"—suggests a fragility that reminds us of the risk and instability outside the fictional space. Besides seeing her art metaphorically, as her critics would too, in relation to female arts severely devalued until quite recently (for painting on ivory was traditionally a "ladylike" occupation), Austen attempted through self-imposed novelistic limitations to define a secure place, even as she seemed to admit the impossibility of actually inhabiting such a small space with any degree of comfort. And always, for Austen, it is women—because they are too vulnerable in the world at large—who must acquiesce in their own confinement, no matter how stifling it may be.

But it is precisely to the limits of her art that Austen's most vocal critics have always responded, with both praise and blame. The tone is set by the curiously backhanded compliments of Sir Walter Scott, who compares her novels to "cornfields and cottages and meadows," as opposed to "highly adorned grounds" or "the rugged sublimities of a mountain landscape." The pleasure of such fiction is, he explains, such that "the youthful wanderer may return from his promenade to the ordinary business of life, without any chance of having his head turned by the recollection of the scene through which he has been wandering." In other words, the novels are so unassuming that they can be easily forgotten. Mundane (like cornfields) and small (like cottages) and tame (like meadows), they wear the "commonplace face" Charlotte Brontë found in *Pride and Prejudice,* a novel Brontë scornfully describes

as "a carefully fenced, highly cultivated garden, with neat borders and delicate flowers; but no glance of a bright, vivid physiognomy, no open country, no fresh air, no blue hill, no bonny beck."

Spatial images of boundary and enclosure seem to proliferate whenever we find writers coming to terms with Jane Austen, as if they were displaying their own anxieties about what she represents. Edward Fitzgerald's comment—"She is capital as far as she goes: but she never goes out of the Parlour"—is a classic in this respect, as is Elizabeth Barrett Browning's breezy characterization of the novels as "perfect as far as they go—that's certain. Only they don't go far, I think." It is hardly surprising that Emerson is "at a loss to understand why people hold Miss Austen's novels at so high a rate," horrified as he is by what he considers the trivializing domesticity and diminution of her fiction:

> vulgar in tone, sterile in artistic invention, imprisoned in the wretched conventions of English society, without genius, wit, or knowledge of the world. Never was life so pinched and narrow. The one problem in the mind of the writer in both the stories I have read, *Persuasion,* and *Pride and Prejudice,* is marriageableness. All that interests in any character introduced is still this one, Has he or (she) the money to marry with, and conditions, conforming? 'Tis "the nympholepsy of a fond despair," say, rather, of an English boarding-house. Suicide is more respectable.

But the conventionally masculine judgment of Austen's triviality is probably best illustrated by Mark Twain, who cannot even bring himself to spell her name correctly in a letter to Howells, her staunchest American defender: Poe's "prose," he notes, "is unreadable—like Jane Austin's," adding that there is one difference: "I could read his prose on salary, but not Jane's. Jane is entirely impossible. It seems a great pity that they allowed her to die a natural death." Certainly D. H. Lawrence expresses similar hostility for the lady writer in his attack on Austen as "this old maid" who "typifies 'personality' instead of character, the sharp knowing in apartness instead of knowing in togetherness, and she is, to my feeling, thoroughly unpleasant, English in the bad, mean, snobbish sense of the word."

Repeatedly, in other words, Austen was placed in the double bind she would so convincingly dramatize in her novels, for when not rejected as artificial and convention-bound, she was condemned as natural and therefore a writer almost in spite of herself. Imagining her as "the brown thrush who tells his story from the garden bough," Henry James describes Austen's "light felicity," her "extraordinary grace," as a sign of "her unconsciousness":

> as if . . . she sometimes, over her work basket, her tapestry flow-
> ers, in the spare, cool drawing-room of other days, fell amusing,
> lapsed too metaphorically, as one may say, into wool gathering,
> and her dropped stitches, of these pardonable, of these precious
> moments, were afterwards picked up as little touches of human
> truth, little glimpses of steady vision, little master-strokes of imag-
> ination.

A stereotypical "lady" author, Austen is here diminished into a small per-
sonage whose domestic productions result in artistic creation not through
the exacting craft by which the male author weaves the intricate figures in
his own carpets, but through fortuitous forgetfulness on the part of the lady
(who drops her stitches unthinkingly) and through the presumably male critical establishment that picks them up afterwards to view them as charming
miniatures of imaginative activity. The entire passage radiates James's anxiety at his own indebtedness to this "little" female precursor who, to his
embarrassment, taught him so much of his presumably masterful art. Indeed,
in a story that examines Austen's curious effect on men and her usefulness
in male culture, Rudyard Kipling has one of his more pugnacious characters
insist that Jane Austen "did leave lawful issue in the shape o' one son; an'
'is name was 'Enery James."

In "The Janeites" Kipling presents several veterans from World War I
listening to a shell-shocked ex-Garrison Artillery man, Humberstall, recount
his experiences on the Somme Front, where he had unexpectedly discovered
a secret unit of Austen fans who call themselves the Society of the Janeites.
Despite the seeming discrepancy between Austen's decorously "feminine"
parlor and the violent, "masculine" war, the officers analyze the significance
of their restricting ranks and roles much as Austen analyzes the meaning of
her characters' limiting social positions. Not only does Humberstall discover
that Austen's characters are "only just like people you'd run across any day,"
he also knows that "They're all on the make, in a quiet way, in Jane." He
is not surprised, therefore, when the whole company is blown to pieces by
one man's addlepated adherence to a code: as his naming of the guns after
Austen's "heavies" demonstrates, the ego that creates all the problems for
her characters is the same ego that shoots Kipling's guns. Paradoxically,
moreover, the firings of "General Tilney" and "The Lady Catherine de Bugg"
also seem to point our attention to the explosive anger behind the decorous
surfaces of Austen's novels, although the men in the trenches find in the
Austen guns the symbol of what they think they are fighting for.

Using Austen the same way American servicemen might have exploited pin-up girls, the Society of Janeites transforms their heroine into a nostalgic symbol of order, culture, England, in an apocalyptic world where all the old gods have failed or disappeared. But Austen is adapted when adopted for use by masculine society, and she functions to perpetrate the male bonding and violence she would herself have deplored. Clearly Kipling is involved in ridiculing the formation of religious sects or cults, specifically the historical Janeites who sanctified Austen into the apotheosis of propriety and elegance, of what Ann Douglas has called in a somewhat different context the "feminization" of culture. But Kipling implies that so-called feminization is a male-dominated process inflicted upon women. And in this respect he illustrates how Austen has herself become a victim of the fictionalizing process we will see her acknowledging as women's basic problem in her own fiction.

Not only a parody of what male culture has made of the cult of Jane, however, "The Janeites" is also a tribute to Austen, who justifies her deification as the patron saint of the officers by furnishing Humberstall with what turns out to be a password that literally saves his life by getting him a place on a hospital train. By pronouncing the name "Miss Bates," Humberstall miraculously survives circumstances as inauspicious as those endured by Miss Bates herself, a spinster in *Emma* whose physical, economic, and social confinement is only mitigated by her good humor. Certainly Humberstall's special fondness for *Persuasion*—which celebrates Captain Harville's "ingenious contrivances and nice arrangements . . . to turn the actual space to the best possible account"—is not unrelated to his appreciation of Austen herself: "There's no one to touch Jane when you're in a tight place." From Austen, then, Humberstall and his companions have gained not only an analysis of social conventions that helps make sense of their own constricted lives, but also an example of how to inhabit a small space with grace and intelligence.

It is eminently appropriate that the Army Janeites try to survive by making the best of a bad situation, accepting their tight place and digging in behind the camouflage-screens they have constructed around their trenches. While their position is finally given away, their attitude is worthy of the writer who concerns herself almost exclusively with characters inhabiting the common sitting room. Critical disparagement of the triviality of this place is related to values that find war or business somehow qualitatively more "real" or "significant" than, for example, the politics of the family. But critics who patronize or castigate Austen for her acceptance of limits and boundaries are overlooking a subversive strain in even her earliest stories: Austen's courageous "grace under pressure" is not only a refuge from a dangerous reality, it is also a comment on it, as W. H. Auden implied:

You could not shock her more than she shocks me;
  Beside her Joyce seems innocent as grass.
It makes me most uncomfortable to see
  An English spinster of the middle class
  Describe the amorous effects of "brass,"
Reveal so frankly and with such sobriety
The economic basis of society.

Although she has become a symbol of culture, it *is* shocking how persistently Austen demonstrates her discomfort with her cultural inheritance, specifically her dissatisfaction with the tight place assigned women in patriarchy and her analysis of the economics of sexual exploitation. At the same time, however, she knows from the beginning of her career that there is no other place for her but a tight one, and her parodic strategy is itself a testimony to her struggle with inadequate but inescapable structures. If, like Scott and Brontë, Emerson and James, we continue to see her world as narrow or trivial, perhaps we can learn from Humberstall that "there's no one to touch Jane when you're in a tight place." Since this tight place is both literary and social, we will begin with the parodic juvenilia and then consider "the amorous effects of 'brass'" in *Northanger Abbey* to trace how and why Austen is centrally concerned with the impossibility of women escaping the conventions and categories that, in every sense, belittle them.

Jane Austen has always been famous for fireside scenes in which several characters comfortably and quietly discuss options so seemingly trivial that it is astonishing when they are transformed into important ethical dilemmas. There is always a feeling, too, that we owe to her narrator's art the significance with which such scenes are invested: she seemed to know about the burdens of banality and the resulting pressure to subject even the smallest gestures to close analysis. A family in *Love and Freindship* (1790) sit by the fireplace in their "cot" when they hear a knock on the door:

> My Father started—"What noise is that," (said he.) "It sounds like a loud rapping at the door"—(replied my Mother.) "it does indeed." (cried I.) "I am of your opinion; (said my Father) it certainly does appear to proceed from some uncommon violence exerted against our unoffending door." "Yes (exclaimed I) I cannot help thinking it must be somebody who knocks for admittance."
>
> "That is another point (replied he;) We must not pretend to determine on what motive the person may knock—tho' that someone *does* rap at the door, I am partly convinced."

Clearly this discursive speculation on the knocking at the door ridicules the propensity of sentimental novelists to record even the most exasperatingly trivial events, but it simultaneously demonstrates the common female ennui at having to maintain polite conversation while waiting for a prince to come. In other words, such juvenilia is important not only because in this early work Austen ridicules the false literary conventions that debase expression, thereby dangerously falsifying expectations, especially for female readers, but also because she reveals here her awareness that such conventions have inalterably shaped women's lives. For Jane Austen's parody of extravagant literary conventions turns on the culture that makes women continually vulnerable to such fantasies.

Laura of *Love and Freindship* is understandably frustrated by the banal confinement of the fireside scene: "Alas," she laments, "how am I to avoid those evils I shall never be exposed to?" Because she is allowed to pursue those evils with indecorous abandon, *Love and Freindship* is a good place to begin to understand attitudes more fully dramatized there than elsewhere in Austen's fiction. With a singular lack of the "infallible discretion" for which it would later become famous, Austen's adolescent fiction includes a larger "slice of life" than we might at first expect: thievery and drunkenness, matricide and patricide, adultery and madness are common subjects. Moreover, the parodic melodrama of this fiction unfolds through hectic geographical maneuverings, particularly through female escapes and escapades quite unlike those that appear in the mature novels.

Laura, for instance, elopes with a stranger upon whom, she immediately decides, the happiness or misery of her future life depends. From her humble cottage in the vale of Uske, she travels to visit Edward's aunt in Middlesex, but she must leave immediately after Edward boasts to his father of his pride in provoking that parent's displeasure by marrying without his consent. Running off in Edward's father's carriage, the happy couple meet up with Sophia and Augustus at "M," but they are forced to remove themselves quickly when Augustus is arrested for having "gracefully purloined" his father's money. Alone in the world, after taking turns fainting on the sofa, the two girls set out for London but end up in Scotland, where they successfully encourage a young female relative to elope to Gretna Green. Thrown out in punishment for this bad advice, Laura and Sophia meet up with their dying husbands, naturally in a phaeton crash. Sophia is fittingly taken off by a galloping consumption, while Laura proceeds by a stagecoach in which she is reunited with her husband's long-lost family who have been traveling back and forth from Sterling to Edinburgh for reasons that are far too complicated and ridiculous to relate here.

Of course her contrivance of such a zany picaresque does not contradict Austen's later insistence on the limits of her artistic province, since the point of her parody is precisely to illustrate the dangerous delusiveness of fiction which seriously presents heroines like Laura (and stories like *Love and Freindship*) as models of reality. While ridiculing ludicrous literary conventions, Austen also implies that romantic stories create absurd misconceptions. Such novelistic clichés as love at first sight, the primacy of passion over all other emotions and/or duties, the chivalric exploits of the hero, the vulnerable sensitivity of the heroine, the lovers' proclaimed indifference to financial considerations, and the cruel crudity of parents are all shown to be at best improbable; at worst they are shown to provide manipulative roles and hypocritical jargon which mask materialistic and libidinal egoism.

Living lives regulated by the rules provided by popular fiction, these characters prove only how very bankrupt that fiction is. For while Laura and Sophia proclaim their delicate feelings, tender sentiments, and refined sensibilities, they are in fact having a delightful time gratifying their desires at the expense of everyone else's. Austen's critique of the ethical effects of such literature is matched by her insistence on its basic falsity: adventure, intrigue, crime, passion, and death arrive with such intensity, in such abundance, and with such rapidity that they lose all reality. Surely they are just the hectic daydreams of an imagination infected by too many Emmelines and Emilias. The extensive itinerary of a heroine like Laura is the most dramatic clue that her story is mere wish-fulfillment, one especially attractive to women who live at home confined to the domestic sphere, as do such heroines of Austen's nonparodic juvenilia as Emma Watson of *The Watsons* and Catharine of the early fiction "Catharine."

Significantly, however, Emma Watson and Catharine are both avid readers of romance, just as Austen herself was clearly one of those young women whose imagination had, in fact, been inalterably affected by all the escapist literature provided them, then as now. Not the least of the curious effects of *Love and Freindship* results from the contradiction between the narrator's insistent ridicule of her heroines and their liveliness, their general willingness to get on with it and catch the next coach. Laura and Sophia are really quite attractive in their exuberant assertiveness, their exploration and exploitation of the world, their curiously honest expression of their needs, their rebellious rejection of their fathers' advice, their demands for autonomy, their sense of the significance and drama of their lives and adventures, their gullible delight in playing out the plots they have admired. The girls' rebellion against familial restraints seems to have so fascinated Austen that she reiterates it almost obsessively in *Love and Freindship*, and again in a hilarious letter when she takes on the persona of an anonymous female correspondent who cheerfully explains, "I murdered my Father at a very early period of my Life, I have since murdered my Mother, and I am now going to murder my Sister." The matricides and patricides make such characters seem much more exuberantly alive than their sensible, slow-witted, dying parents. It is this covert counterpoint that makes suspicious the overt "moral" of *Love and Freindship*, suggesting that though Austen appears to be operating in a repressive tradition, many of her generic moral signals are merely convenient camouflage.

At first glance, Sophia and Laura seem related to a common type in eighteenth-century literature. Like Biddy Tipkins of Steele's *The Tender Husband*, Coleman's *Polly Honeycombe*, and Lydia Languish of Sheridan's *The Rivals*, for instance, these girls are filled with outlandish fancies derived from their readings in the circulating library. Illustrating the dangers of feminine lawlessness and the necessity of female submission, female quixotes of eighteenth-century fiction typically exemplify the evils of romantic fiction and female assertion. The abundance of such heroines in her juvenilia would seem to place Austen in precisely the tradition Ellen Moers has recently explored, that of the educating heroine who preaches the necessity of dutiful restraint to female readers, cautioning them especially against the snares of romance. But Austen did not admire the prototypical Madame de Genlis; she was "disgusted" with her brand of didacticism and with the evangelic fervor of novelists who considered themselves primarily moralists.

Far from modeling herself on conservative conduct writers like Hannah Moore or Dr. Gregory or Mrs. Chapone, Austen repeatedly demonstrates her alienation from the aggressively patriarchal tradition that constitutes her Augustan inheritance, as well as her agreement with Mary Wollstonecraft that these authors helped "render women more artificial, weak characters, than they would otherwise have been." A writer who could parody *An Essay on Man* to read "*Ride where you may*, Be Candid where you can" [italics ours] is not about to vindicate the ways of God to man. Nor is she about to justify the ways of Pope to women. One suspects that Austen, like Marianne Dashwood, appreciates Pope no more than is proper. Even Dr. Johnson, whom she obviously does value, has his oracular rhetorical style parodied, first in the empty abstractions and antitheses that abound in the juvenilia, and later in the mouth of *Pride and Prejudice*'s Mary Bennet, a girl who prides herself on pompous platitudes. Finally, Austen attacks *The Spectator* repeatedly, at least in part for its condescension toward female readers. The Regency, as well as her own private perspective as a woman, inalterably separates Austen from the Augustan context in which she is so frequently

placed. Like her most mature heroine, Anne Elliot of *Persuasion*, she sometimes advised young readers to reflect on the wisdom of essayists who sought
to "rouse and fortify the mind by the highest precepts, and the strongest
examples of moral and religious endurance," but she too is "eloquent on a
point in which her own conduct would ill bear examination."

If Austen rejects the romantic traditions of her culture in a parody like
Love and Freindship, she does so not by way of the attack on feminine
flightiness so common in conduct literature, or, at least, she uses this motif
to mask a somewhat different point. *Love and Freindship* is the first hint of
the depth of her alienation from her culture, especially as that culture defined
and circumscribed women. Far from being the usual appeal for female sobriety and submission to domestic restraints so common in anti-romantic
eighteenth-century literature, *Love and Freindship* attacks a society that triv-
ializes female assertion by channeling it into the most ridiculous and unpro-
ductive forms of behavior. With nothing to do in the world, Sophia and
Laura become addicts of feeling. Like all the other heroines of Austen's
parodic juvenilia, they make an identity out of passivity, as if foreshadowing
the bored girls described by Simone de Beauvoir, who "give themselves up
to gloomy and romantic daydreams":

> Neglected, "misunderstood," they seek consolation in narcissistic
> fancies: they view themselves as romantic heroines of fiction, with
> self-admiration and self-pity. Quite naturally they become co-
> quettish and stagy, these defects becoming more conspicuous at
> puberty. Their malaise shows itself in impatience, tantrums, tears;
> they enjoy crying—a taste that many women retain in later
> years—largely because they like to play the part of victims. . . .
> Little girls sometimes watch themselves cry in a mirror, to double
> the pleasure.

Sophia and Laura do make a cult of passivity, fainting and languishing
dramatically on sofas, defining their virtues and beauty in terms of their
physical weakness and their susceptibility to overwhelming passions.

In this way, and more overtly by constantly scrutinizing their own physical perfections, they dramatize de Beauvoir's point that women, in typical
victim fashion, become narcissistic out of their fear of facing reality. And
because they pride themselves not only on their frailty but also on those very
"accomplishments" that insure it, their narcissism is inextricably linked to
masochism, for they have been successfully socialized into believing that their
subordinate status in society is precisely the fulfillment they crave. Austen is
very clear on the reasons for their obsessive fancies: Sophia and Laura are

the victims of what Karen Horney has recently identified as the "overvaluation of love" and in this respect, according to Austen, they typify their sex. Encouraged to know and care only about the love of men, Laura and Sophia are compulsive and indiscriminate in satisfying their insatiable need for being loved, while they are themselves incapable of authentic feeling. They would and do go to any lengths to "catch" men, but they must feign ignorance, modesty, and indifference to amatory passion. Austen shows how popular romantic fiction contributes to the traditional notion that women have no other legitimate aim but to love men and how this assumption is at the root of "female" narcissism, masochism, and deceit. She could hardly have set out to create a more heretical challenge to societal definitions of the feminine.

Furthermore, *Love and Freindship* displays Austen's concern with the rhetorical effect of fiction, not in terms of the moral issues raised by Dr. Johnson in his influential essay "On Fiction," but in terms of the psychological destruction such extravagant role models and illusory plots can wreak. De Beauvoir writes of "stagy" girls who "view themselves as romantic heroines of fiction"; and at least one of the reasons Laura and Sophia seem so grotesque is that they are living out predetermined plots: as readers who have accepted, even embraced, their status as characters, they epitomize the ways in which women have been tempted to forfeit interiority and the freedom of self-definition for literary roles. For if, as we might infer from Kipling, Austen herself was destined to become a sanctified symbol, her characters are no less circumscribed by fictional stereotypes and plots that seem to transform them into manic puppets. Like Anne Elliot, who explains that she will "not allow books to prove anything" because "men have had every advantage of us in telling their own story," Austen retains her suspicions about the effect of literary images of both sexes, and she repeatedly resorts to parodic strategies to discredit such images, deconstructing, for example, Richardson's influential ideas of heroism and heroinism.

Refusing to appreciate such angelic paragons as Clarissa or Pamela, Austen criticizes the morally pernicious equation of female virtue with passivity, or masculinity with aggression. From *Lady Susan* to *Sanditon*, she rejects stories in which women simply defend their virtue against male sexual advances. Most of her heroines resemble Charlotte Heywood, who picks up a copy of *Camilla* only to put it down again because "She had not *Camilla's* Youth, & had no intention of having her Distress." Similarly, Austen criticizes the Richardsonian rake by implying that sentimental fiction legitimizes the role of the seducer-rapist, thereby encouraging men to act out their most predatory impulses. Sir Edward of *Sanditon* is only the last of the false suitors who models himself on Lovelace, his life's primary objective being seduction. For Austen, the libertine is a relative of the Byronic hero, and she is quite sure that his dangerous attractions are best defused through ridicule: "I have read the *Corsair*, mended my petticoat, & have nothing else to do," she writes in a letter that probably best illustrates the technique. Because she realizes that writers like Richardson and Byron have truthfully represented the power struggle between the sexes, however, she does seek a way of telling their story without perpetuating it. In each of her novels, a seduced-and-abandoned plot is embedded in the form of an interpolated tale told to the heroine as a monitory image of her own more problematic story.

For all her ladylike discretion, then, Austen is rigorous in her revolt against the conventions she inherited. But she expresses her dissent under the cover of parodic strategies that had been legitimized by the most conservative writers of her time and that therefore were then (and remain now) radically ambiguous. Informing her recurrent use of parody is her belief that the inherited literary structures which are not directly degrading to her sex are patently irrelevant. Therefore, when she begins *Sense and Sensibility* with a retelling of *King Lear*, her reversals imply that male traditions need to be evaluated and reinterpreted from a female perspective: instead of the evil daughter castrating the old king by whittling away at his retinue of knights ("what need one?"), Austen represents the male heir and his wife persuading themselves to cheat their already unjustly deprived sisters of a rightful share of the patrimony ("Altogether, they will have five hundred a-year amongst them, and what on earth can four women want for more than that?"). When Maria Bertram echoes the caged bird of Sterne's *A Sentimental Journey*, complaining that the locked gates of her future husband's grounds are too confining—"I cannot get out, as the starling said"—she reflects on the dangers of the romantic celebration of personal liberty and self-expression for women who will be severely punished if they insist on getting out.

Whether here, or in her parodies of Fanny Burney and Sir Samuel Egerton Brydges in *Pride and Prejudice*, Austen dramatizes how damaging it has been for women to inhabit a culture created by and for men, confirming perhaps more than any of her sisterly successors the truth of Mary Ellmann's contention that

> for women writers, as for Negro, what others have said bears down on whatever they can say themselves. Both are like people looking for their own bodies under razed buildings, having to clear away debris. In their every effort to formulate a new point of view, one feels the refutation of previous points of view—a weight which must impede spontaneity.

Austen demystifies the literature she has read neither because she believes it misrepresents reality, as Mary Lascelles argues, nor out of obsessive fear of emotional contact, as Marvin Mudrick claims, nor because she is writing Tory propaganda against the Jacobins, as Marilyn Butler speculates, but because she seeks to illustrate how such fictions are the alien creations of writers who contribute to the enfeebling of women.

But though Ellmann's image is generally helpful for an understanding of the female artist, in Austen's case it is a simplification. Austen's culture is not a destroyed rubble around her corpse. On the contrary, it is a healthy and powerful architecture which she must learn to inhabit. Far from looking under razed buildings or (even more radically) razing buildings herself, Austen admits the limits and discomforts of the paternal roof, but learns to live beneath it. As we have seen, however, she begins by laughing at its construction, pointing out exactly how much of that construction actually depends on the subjugation of women. If she wishes to be an architect herself, however, she needs to make use of the only available building materials—the language and genres, conventions and stereotypes at her disposal. She does not reject these, she reinvents them. For one thing, she has herself admired and enjoyed the literature of such sister novelists as Maria Edgeworth, Mrs. Radcliffe, Charlotte Lennox, Mary Brunton, and Fanny Burney. For another, as we have seen, regardless of how damaging they have been, the conventions of romantic fiction have been internalized by the women of her culture and so they do describe the psychology of growing up female. Finally, these are the only available stories she has. Austen makes a virtue of her own confinement, as her heroines will do also. By exploiting the very conventions she exposes as inadequate, she demonstrates the power of patriarchy as well as the ambivalence and confinement of the female writer. She also discovers an effective subterfuge for a severe critique of her culture. For even as she dramatizes her own alienation from a society she cannot evade or transcend, she subverts the conventions of popular fiction to describe the lonely vulnerability of girls whose lives, if more mundane, are just as thwarted as those they read about so obsessively. For all their hilarious exaggeration, then, the incidents and characters of the juvenilia reappear in the later novels, where they portray the bewilderment of heroines whose guides are as inadequate as the author's in her search for a way of telling their story.

Just as Laura languishes in the Vale of Uske at the beginning of *Love and Freindship,* for example, the later heroines are confined to homes noteworthy for their suffocating atmosphere. The heroine of "Catharine" is limited to the company of an aunt who fears that all contact with society will engage the girl's heart imprudently. Living in her aunt's inexorably ordered house, Catharine has nothing to do but retreat to a romantically constructed bower, a place of adolescent illusions. Boredom is also a major affliction for Catherine Morland and Charlotte Heywood, who are involved in the drudgery of educating younger siblings in secluded areas offering few potential friends, as it is for the seemingly more privileged Emma, who suffers from intellectual loneliness, as well as the blazing fires, closed windows, and locked doors of her father's house. The Dashwood sisters move into a cottage with parlors too small for parties, and Fanny Price only manages to remove herself from her suffocatingly cramped home in Portsmouth to the little white attic which all the other occupants of Mansfield Park have outgrown. When the parental house is not downright uncomfortable because of its inadequate space, it is still a place with no privacy. Thus the only person able to retreat from the relentlessly trivial bustle at the Bennets is the father, who has his own library. Furthermore, as Nina Auerbach has shown, all the girls inhabit houses that are never endowed with the physical concreteness and comfort that specificity supplies. The absence of details suggests how empty and unreal such family life feels, and a character like Anne Elliot, for example, faces the sterile elegance of her father's estate confined and confused by one of the few details the reader is provided, the mirrors in her father's private dressing room.

One reason why the adventures of the later heroines seem to supply such small relief to girls "doomed to waste [their] Days of Youth and Beauty in a humble Cottage in the Vale" is that most, like Laura, can only wait for an unpredictable and unreliable knock on the door. What characterizes the excursions of all these heroines is their total dependency on the whim of wealthier family or friends. None has the power to produce her own itinerary and none knows until the very last moment whether or not she will be taken on a trip upon which her happiness often depends. All the heroines of Austen's fiction very much want to experience the wider world outside their parents' province; each, though, must wait until lucky enough to be asked to accompany a chaperone who frequently only mars the pleasure of the adventure. Although in her earliest writing Austen ridicules the rapidity and improbability of coincidence in second-rate fiction, not a few of her own plots save the heroines from stagnation by means of the overtly literary device of an introduction to an older person who is so pleased with the heroine that "at parting she declares her sole *ambition* was to have her accompany them the next morning to Bath, whither they were going for some weeks."

It is probably for this reason that, from the juvenilia to the posthumously published fragments, there is a recurrent interest in the horse and carriage. It is not surprising in the juvenilia to find a young woman marrying a man she loathes because he has promised her a new chaise, with a silver border and a saddle horse, in return for her not expecting to go to any public place for three years. Indeed, not a few of the heroines recall the plight of two characters in the juvenilia who go on a walking tour through Wales with only one pony, ridden by their mother: not only do their sketches suffer, being "not such exact resemblances as might be wished, from their being taken as [they] ran along," so do their feet as they find themselves hopping home from Hereford. Still, they are delighted with their excursion, and their passion for travel reminds us of the runaways who abound in Austen's novels, young women whose imaginations are tainted by romantic notions which fuel their excessive materialism or sexuality, and who would do anything with anyone in order to escape their families: Eliza Brandon, Julia and Maria Bertram, Lydia Bennet, Lucy Steele, and Georgianna Darcy are all "prepared for matrimony by an hatred of home, restraint, and tranquillity" (*Mansfield Park*). Provided with only the naive clichés of sentimental literature, they insist on acting out those very plots Austen would—but therefore cannot—exorcise from her own fiction.

But hopping home from Hereford also recalls Marianne Dashwood who, like Fanny Price, is vitally concerned with her want of a horse: this pleasure and exercise is not at these girls' disposal primarily because of its expense and impropriety. Emma Woodhouse is subjected to the unwelcome proposals of Mr. Elton because she cannot avoid a ride in his carriage, and Jane Bennet becomes seriously ill at a time when her parents' horses cannot be spared. Similarly, Catherine Morland and Mrs. Parker are both victimized by male escorts whose recklessness hazards their health, if not their lives. It is no small testimony of her regard for their reciprocal partnership that Anne Elliot sees the lively and mutually self-regulating style of the Crofts' driving of their one-horse chaise as a good representation of their marriage. Coaches, barouche-landaus, and curricles are the crucial factors that will determine who goes where with whom on the expeditions to places like Northanger, Pemberly, Donwell Abbey, Southerton, and Lyme.

Every trivial social occasion, each of the many visits and calls endured if not enjoyed by the heroines, reminds us that women are dependent on fathers or brothers for even this most limited form of movement, when they are not indebted to wealthy widows who censure and criticize officiously. Not possessing or controlling the means of transportation, each heroine is defined as different from the poorest men of her neighborhood, all of whom can convey themselves wherever they want or need to go. Indeed, what distinguishes the heroines from their brothers is invariably their lack of liberty: while Austen describes how younger brothers are as financially circumscribed as their sisters, for instance in their choosing of a mate, she always insists that the caste of gender takes precedence over the dictates of class; as poor a dependent as William Price is far more mobile than both his indigent sisters and his wealthy female cousins. For Austen, the domestic confinement of women is not a metaphor so much as a literal fact of life, enforced by all those elaborate rules of etiquette governing even the trivial morning calls that affect the females of each of the novels. The fact that "he is to purvey, and she to smile" is what must have enraged and repelled readers like Brontë and Barrett Browning. As Anne Elliot explains, "We live at home, quiet, confined and our feelings prey upon us."

According to popular moralists of Austen's day, what would be needed for a satisfied life in such uncongenial circumstances would be "inner resources." Yet these are what most of the young women in her novels lack, precisely because of the inadequate upbringing with which they have been provided by absent or ineffectual mothers. In fact, though Austen's juvenilia often ridicules fiction that portrays the heroine as an orphan or foundling or neglected stepdaughter, the mature novelist does not herself supply her female protagonists with very different family situations. In *A Vindication of the Rights of Woman* Mary Wollstonecraft explained that "woman . . . a slave in every situation to prejudice, seldom exerts enlightened maternal affection; for she either neglects her children, or spoils them by improper indulgences." Austen would agree, although she focuses specifically on mothers who fail in their nurturing of daughters. Emma Woodhouse, Emma Watson, Catharine, and Anne Elliot are literally motherless, as are such minor characters as Clara Brereton, Jane Fairfax, the Steele sisters, Miss Tilney, Georgianna Darcy, the Miss Bingleys, Mary Crawford, and Harriet Smith. But those girls who have living mothers are nonetheless neglected or overindulged by the absence of enlightened maternal affection.

Fanny Price "might scruple to make use of the words, but she must and did feel that her mother was a partial, ill-judging parent, a dawdle, a slattern, who neither taught nor restrained her children, whose house was the scene of mismanagement and discomfort . . . who had no talent, no conversation, no affection toward herself." Mrs. Price, however, is not much different from Mrs. Dashwood and Mrs. Bennet, who are as immature and silly as their youngest daughters, and who are therefore unable to guide young women into maturity. Women like Lady Bertram, Mrs. Musgrove, and Mrs. Bates are a burden on their children because their ignorance, indolence, and folly, resulting as they do in neglect, seem no better than the smothering love of those women whose officiousness spoils by improper indulgence. Fanny Dashwood and Lady Middleton of *Sense and Sensibility,* for example, are cruelly indifferent to the needs of all but their children, who are therefore transformed by such inauspicious attention into noisy, bothersome monsters. Lady Catherine de Bourgh proves conclusively that authoritative management of a daughter's life cannot be identified with nurturing love: coldly administering all aspects of her daughter's growth, overbearing Lady Catherine produces a girl who "was pale and sickly; her features, though not plain, were insignificant; and she spoke very little, except in a low voice."

Because they are literally or figuratively motherless, the daughters in Austen's fiction are easily persuaded that they must look to men for security. Although their mothers' example proves how debilitating marriage can be, they seek husbands in order to escape from home. What feminists have recently called matrophobia—fear of becoming one's mother—supplies one more motive to flee the parental house, as does the financial necessity of competing for male protection which their mothers really cannot supply. The parodic portrait in "Jack and Alice" of the competition between drunken Alice Johnson and the accomplished tailor's daughter, Lucy, for the incomparable Charles Adams (who was "so dazzling a Beauty that none but Eagles could look him in the Face") is thus not so different from the rivalry Emma Woodhouse feels toward Harriet Smith or Jane Fairfax over Mr. Knightley. And it is hardly surprising when in the juvenilia Austen pushes this fierce female rivalry to its fitting conclusion, describing how poor Lucy falls a victim to the envy of a female companion "who jealous of her superiour charms took her by poison from an admiring World at the age of seventeen."

Austen ridicules the easy violence that embellishes melodrama even as she explores hostility between young women who feel they have no alternative but to compete on the marriage market. Like Charlotte Lucas, many an Austen heroine, "without thinking highly either of men or of matrimony," considers marriage "the only honourable provision for well-educated young women of small fortune, their pleasantest preservation from want." And so, at the beginning of *The Watsons,* one sister has to warn another about a third that, "There is nothing she would not do to get married. . . . Do not trust her with any secrets of your own, take warning by me, do not trust her." Because such females would rather marry a man they dislike than teach school or enter the governess "slave-trade," they fight ferociously for the few eligible men who do seem attractive. The rivalries between Miss Bingley and Miss Bennet, between Miss Dashwood and Miss Steele, between Julia and Maria Bertram for Henry Crawford, between the Musgrove sisters for Captain Wentworth are only the most obvious examples of fierce female competition where female anger is deflected from powerful male to powerless female targets.

Throughout the juvenilia, most hilariously in "Frederic and Elfrida," Austen ridicules the idea, promulgated by romantic fiction, that the only events worth recording are marriage proposals, marriage ceremonies, engagements made or broken, preparations for dances where lovers are expected, amatory disappointments, and elopements. But her own fiction is essentially limited to just such topics. The implication is clear: marriage is crucial because it is the only accessible form of self-definition for girls in her society. Indeed, Austen's silence on all other subjects becomes itself a kind of statement, for the absences in her fiction prove how deficient are the lives of girls and women, even as they testify to her own deprivation as a woman writer. Yet Austen actually uses her self-proclaimed and celebrated acceptance of the limits of her art to mask a subversive critique of the forms of self-expression available to her both as an artist and as a woman, for her ridicule of inane literary structures helps her articulate her alienation from equally inadequate societal strictures.

JULIA PREWITT BROWN

Civilization and the
Contentment of Emma

There is a plaguing discrepancy, familiar to anyone who has written on
Emma, between reading the novel and writing about it. The novel's first
great strength lies in the ability to draw the reader in. We are made happy
in the traps that are laid for us; we roll in their nets and sleep. We read, in
the words of E. M. Forster, with mouth open and mind closed; and after we
have finished the spell is broken. Then we can begin to think about it, when
the remembered event and the inferred theme have lost their primary, exigent
brilliance. The pleasure of reading *Emma*, the very great pleasure, has little
to do with the kinds of linear meaning that may be found in most novels;
the pleasure comes from our willing immersion in the everyday concerns and
relationships of this world, and from a glow of suggestion in the narrative
that tells us: this is enough. The novel's very self-absorption makes it acceptable and wonderful. It is a world that believes in itself entirely, and
hypnotized, we too believe.

How is this irresistible self-absorption achieved and sustained? There
are many answers to this question. One concerns the structure of the novel.
Most novels written during the eighteenth and nineteenth centuries, and even
many later ones, are teleologically structured—either overtly, like *Pride and
Prejudice* and *Great Expectations,* or ironically, like *Tom Jones* and *Vanity
Fair.* To miss the outcome of these stories is to miss the meaning. This causal
structure is not realized in a few exceptions, notably *Tristram Shandy* and

From *Jane Austen's Novels: Social Change and Literary Form.* © 1979 by the President and Fellows of Harvard College. Harvard University Press, 1979.

Emma, whose conclusions are not, as it were, judiciously weighted. Although we may wonder, like Mr. Knightley, what will become of Emma, her destiny, either social or moral, has little to do with her actions. She is not punished for her misconduct; she does not earn the perfect happiness that is hers in the end. Nor are we disturbed by the non sequitur; although she is often in error, we never feel she is heading toward any retribution except enlightenment. Emma's fate does not identify her the way, say, Isabel Archer's fate makes her Isabel Archer. Emma is always Emma, an integrated, functioning whole; after all her surprises and self-criticism, we still enjoy her in the same way. When she says near the close of the novel, "Oh! I always deserve the best treatment, because I never put up with any other," we smile at her once again, or perhaps with her. Lionel Trilling calls this structure "forgiving," yet the idea of forgiveness still assumes a causal plot. That Emma is never properly humbled by fate has little to do with pride forgiven, but is a matter of personal being. Because she is Emma, acting out her extraordinary nature from beginning to end, we are satisfied. Our *not* thinking about matters of forgiveness is what makes our immersion in her concerns so effortless.

Just as the structure of *Emma* is not causal, it is also not hierarchical. Were we to draw a picture of the novel, it would not, I believe, bring before the reader the ladder of social and moral being that Graham Hough assigns. It would look more like a road map in which the cities and towns, joined together by countless highways and byroads, stood for people. Some of the roads are curved and smooth, like those between Emma and her father or Emma and Mrs. Weston; some are so full of obstacles that their destinations (Jane Fairfax, for example) are almost inaccessible. Mr. Weston and Miss Bates are like great indiscriminate towns from which radiate roads that join almost everyone.

As the image of a road map suggests, Highbury is a system of interdependence, a community of people all talking to one another, affecting, and changing one another: a collection of relationships. Miss Bates is emblematic of Highbury in this respect. In the words of E. M. Forster, "Miss Bates is bound by a hundred threads to Highbury. We cannot tear her away without bringing her mother too, and Jane Fairfax and Frank Churchill, and the whole of Box Hill." Emma herself is as firmly connected to her world as Miss Bates. Perceived in her many relationships with others, Emma is seen as daughter, sister, sister-in-law, aunt, companion, intimate friend, new acquaintance, patroness, and bride. And each connection lets us see something new in her.

The interaction of characters in the novel is extensive and dynamic. All characters intersect in some way. In addition to all the major combinations, we witness sufficiently realized contact between Jane Fairfax and Mr. John Knightley, Mr. Weston and Mrs. Elton, Mr. Elton and Mr. John Knightley; we learn what Mr. Woodhouse thinks of Frank Churchill, what Mr. John Knightley thinks of Mr. Weston, and what Isabella thinks of Harriet. These represent brief encounters and the almost spur-of-the-moment judgments that arise from them. For example, Mr. John Knightley has only to see Mr. Elton once during his holiday visit to know that Mr. Elton is interested in Emma. As always in Jane Austen, the smallest detail of behavior can justify the most definitive judgment.

Even the more sustained relationships seem to be composed of many individual encounters and the individual judgments that arise from them. For example, the relationships between Mrs. Elton and Jane Fairfax, Frank Churchill and his foster parents, Jane Fairfax and Emma, and Harriet and Robert Martin's sister are discussed several times by different persons, and on the basis of brief incidents. When compared to the pattern of dialogue in *Pride and Prejudice,* these dialogues and judgments seem random and self-absorbed—indeed, like "real" conversations—yet not the less reliable for being so. Mr. Woodhouse's judgment upon Frank Churchill—that the young man is "not quite the thing"—is unreasonably and uncharitably founded, yet correct; and it is acknowledged with dismay by those who hear it.

The novel is like Highbury itself; there is no limit to the combinations within it, or to the combinations speculated upon. Marriage, always the first and last relationship in Jane Austen, is confirmed in six couples in the novel and predicted in many more. (Harriet and Mr. Elton, Emma and Mr. Elton, Emma and Frank Churchill, Harriet and Frank Churchill, Jane Fairfax and Mr. Dixon, Mr. Knightley and Jane Fairfax, Harriet and Mr. Knightley.) Indeed, speculation about love relationships is the basis of the novel's plot, because the heroine is herself a relentless matchmaker. Yet to catalogue all of these real or imagined connections is misleading. In its unlikely and changing combinations, the catalogue gives an impression of social irrationality, overworked variety, and exhaustive socialization. Yet no other novel has more the opposite effect: of rich, unbroken continuity, of uncluttered awareness, routine contentment, cooperation, and harmony. This effect is achieved not only because of the interdependence of Highbury, its commune-like nature, but because events and characters are likened to one another in subtle ways, like so many hues of one color. This too helps to explain the magic and magnetic appeal of *Emma*; we are transfixed by the kaleidoscope patterning of its relationships.

The similarities between Emma and Mrs. Elton are often noted. Both are preoccupied with status; each adopts another young woman as protégé and satellite; both are self-centered and therefore blind. Jane Fairfax and Emma also are compared and contrasted; Miss Bates is Jane's Mr. Woodhouse. Miss Taylor is to Emma what Emma plans to be to Harriet. Mr. Perry has his counterpart in town, Mr. Wingfield. And so on.

The similarities always have psychological meaning. Characters have a tendency to repeat the relationships they have known; for example, Emma seeks a replacement for Mrs. Weston in Harriet. Isabella Knightley finds her Mr. Perry in town, another doctor who like his counterpart parodically embodies the atavistic, maternal relationship founded on one-sided knowledge and care. Both Jane Fairfax and Frank Churchill are orphaned; their original relationships disrupted, neither has a secure prototype to follow. It is difficult for Jane Fairfax to connect with others; she feels far more isolated in the presence of her aunt, for example, than Emma does in the presence of her father. Frank, on the other hand, has no notion at all of what a relationship is, of reciprocal endeavor and trust. Unlike Jane's unwavering attachment to him, his love does not include loyalty—he not only flirts with Emma but does so to torment his fiancée. Since neither has received the education of a steady and lasting parental relationship, as Emma has, they can only form an attachment that becomes "a source of repentance and misery to each." (Because of the unvalidated status of their relationship their marriage is left waiting at the end of the novel.)

Many of the transformations, actions, and events in *Emma* take place in the form of repetitions. Emma has three enlightenments; related respectively to Mr. Elton, Frank Churchill, and Mr. Knightley, they increase in intensity yet are essentially similar. Isolated events are also replayed in a changed key; Mr. Knightley rescues Harriet at the Crown Ball in a scene of great romantic delicacy involving Emma; the next day Frank Churchill rescues Harriet from the gypsies in a burlesque fashion. The crudeness of the second event drowns out the delicacy of the first and prepares the way for Emma's wanton blow at Miss Bates at Box Hill. The ball scene in which Mr. Knightley performs his wonderfully unobtrusive act of kindness reverberates with suggestion. It brings Emma and Mr. Knightley together for the first time; it joins them through an act of charity in the way Emma earlier planned to join Mr. Elton and Harriet the day they visited the cottage. And the look of approval Emma sends across the dance floor that night is later matched by his silent expression of approval for Emma when she visits Miss Bates the morning after Box Hill. The most resonant instance of transformation as repetition in Jane Austen, of course, is marriage. The three marriages that close the novel are different yet similar, repetitive of one another and of the marriages at the beginning of the novel. The rich overlay of experience, the almost Shakespearean imaginative continuity of the novel, is all but hypnotizing.

Because *Emma* is a novel about relationships and their natures, the "action" of the work is a dialectic. Every relationship in the novel has its unique dialectical rhythm; even the smoothest relationships encounter snags, such as the near-argument between Mr. Woodhouse and Emma about the treatment of brides. The novel's humor is almost always centered on the surprise creation of a dialectic through the sudden juxtaposition of unlikely personalities. The conversation between Mr. Knightley and Mrs. Elton about the picnic at Donwell Abbey, one of the most amusing exchanges in English fiction, does not perform at all; the humor lies in the contrast of character and is available to those who see it. Such moments border on farce because of the deadly seriousness of the characters themselves. And Mr. Knightley, the most serious of all, is not exempted from the farce of the situation; the contrast is not available to his subjective standpoint.

Three major dialectics in the novel involve Emma herself: the interior dialectic, of which only Emma is aware; the dialectic between Emma and Mr. Knightley; and the dialectic between Emma and Highbury. By the close of the novel they all seem to become the same dialectic. They are never resolved, only validated, in marriage; the only truth is the dialectic itself. Part of the novel's greatness is that it never moves to the death of total resolution.

Emma's personality opens like a fan before us. Seen in her innumerable relationships with others, she alters continually and gracefully, and the novel is deliberately paced to allow this. Mr. Woodhouse's daughter is not Harriet's patroness or Mr. John Knightley's sister-in-law. The Emma who condescends to Harriet, self-satisfied, smirking, and dictatorial, is not the Emma we see with Mr. Knightley, witty, open, and daring. And although she is tied by countless social relations, she is neither overshadowed nor borne down by them. We cannot think of her as we do some nineteenth-century heroines, changing under the circumstances like Darwinian organisms. Emma's inner nature, her stability as Emma, even as she is drawn this way and that— spoiled, criticized, disappointed, insulted, and loved—never alters; she is still Emma. Protean, elusive, capable of true goodness and deliberate cruelty, she is what she is—a reservoir of indeterminacy. She represents the genuine triumph of volition, for she is free to be better than she knows herself to be. She is faultless not in spite of her faults, but because of them.

Always doing "more than she wished and less than she ought" Emma is frequently divided between two impulses in her interior dialogue. There is a struggle, but never a war. In questioning her own treatment of the Martins, of Harriet, of Jane Fairfax, and of Miss Bates, she has some unsettling moments, yet her disposition is to like and accept herself wholeheartedly. Even after her most crucial, most soul-searching enlightenment, her final admission of her despicable treatment of Harriet, she swings back to a tolerably self-supporting state of mind. At length she begins to learn to treat others as generously as she treats herself, to accept the faultlessness of human interactions in spite of their faults. Emma's interior struggle is never laid to rest; the only resolution consists in trying to be better: "the only source whence anything like consolation or composure could be drawn, was in the resolution of her own better conduct." She never ceases to be one Emma and begins to be another.

Mr. Knightley, in his relation to Emma, takes the side of her that does or should do what she "ought." When she paints Harriet taller than she really is, only Mr. Knightley and this side of Emma acknowledge that she is doing it. Mr. Knightley seems to bring out the best in Emma; he makes her defend her right to be Emma, and in defending it, she becomes witty and challenging. "I shall not scold you. I leave you to your own reflections," says Mr. Knightley. "Can you trust me with such flatterers?" replies Emma. The tension between Emma and Mr. Knightley is as vital as that in a love affair in a novel by D. H. Lawrence. From their first words to each other, every encounter between them vibrates with their unique awareness of one another, their mutual knowledge disguised under apparent differences: "'You have made her too tall, Emma,' said Mr. Knightley. Emma knew that she had, but would not own it." And the secret knowledge of the other's character is not limited to Mr. Knightley. When he arrives at the Coles', Emma can tell he has come in his carriage and says:

> "There is always a look of consciousness or bustle when people come in a way which they know to be beneath them. You think you carry it off very well, I dare say, but with you it is a sort of bravado, an air of affected unconcern; I always observe it whenever I meet you under those circumstances. *Now* you have nothing to try for. You are not afraid of being supposed ashamed. You are not striving to look taller than any body else. *Now* I shall be very happy to walk in the same room with you."
>
> "Nonsensical girl!" was his reply, but not at all in anger.

Such encounters suggest an immediacy of awareness and intimacy that is undeniably sexual. There are no sexual "overtones" in *Emma*; the sexuality is there, in the minds and speech and emotional intensity of the characters, in the mental urgency of every encounter. The scene at the Crown Ball when

Mr. Knightley asks the defenseless and snubbed Harriet to dance is alive with the sense of a new understanding between Emma and Mr. Knightley. Until the end of the chapter, no words are spoken between them; like the love in *Persuasion,* their love is silent. Eye contact replaces speech: "her countenance said much, as soon as she could catch his eye again." And the wonderfully powerful: "her eyes invited him irresistibly to come to her and be thanked." One feels that this is what being in love is about, not all the talk, planning, and invention Emma imagines it is. It is the power to move, to know the other person.

The Crown Ball is a scene of extraordinary delicacy and love. Set off by the benevolent hum of Miss Bates's monologue, its strength lies in Emma's watching Mr. Knightley perform this act of kindness; her appreciation of it makes her a better Emma than the Emma who mistreats the Martins, the Emma who is above everyone. And Mr. Knightley, who would do what he does now for any woman in the novel, does it here for Emma, as they both know. The dialogue that follows registers the new intimacy with spirit, and without losing a sense of their individuality. The scene ends in dance:

> "Will you?" said he, offering his hand.
> "Indeed I will. You have shown that you can dance, and you
> know we are not really so much brother and sister as to make it
> at all improper."
> "Brother and sister! no, indeed."

Mr. Knightley knows he loves Emma at this point; characteristically, Emma does not yet know she loves him. But the reader is not ignorant and his knowledge gives the scene its exquisite emotion.

The scene is surrounded and intertwined with contrasts that set off its romantic delicacy. Preceded by Mr. Weston's indiscriminate hospitality, Frank Churchill's nervousness, and the Eltons' sneering self-importance, Mr. Knightley's act suddenly crystallizes the three concerned—himself, Harriet, and Emma—in a brilliant tableau. Miss Bates's interpolated monologue is a wonderful contrast to the delicate discriminations of the event. It is as though their love were founded in her jumbled benevolence.

The chapter itself is framed on one side by Emma's private admission of an entirely deflated interest in Frank Churchill, and on the other by Frank Churchill's mock-heroic rescue of Harriet, pointedly used to establish the real heroism of Mr. Knightley's action. The ball scene in *Emma* is flanked by events that, through contrasts, set off its intensity and validate its sincerity.

It seems to me that in this respect *Emma* is a great novel about "the association of man and woman"—to use T. S. Eliot's phrase. Emma and

Mr. Knightley actually make each other larger, more interesting. Without Mr. Knightley, Emma is a self-satisfied busybody; without Emma, Mr. Knightley is a dull and predictable English gentleman. Emma is responsible for Mr. Knightley's one unpredictable act in the entire novel, his standing up Mr. Elton one morning. Infuriated, Mr. Elton recalls: "I met William Larkins . . . as I got near the house, and he told me I should not find his master at home, but I did not believe him.—William seemed rather out of humour. He did not know what was come of his master lately, he said." Because each has always possessed a part of the other, the marriage between Emma and Mr. Knightley does not wrench either from an old identity into a new one. They do not seek to annihilate one another—the way, for example, part of Edmund Bertram is annihilated when he marries Fanny. Emma is still Emma and Mr. Knightley is still Mr. Knightley; Emma even wishes to continue to call him so. The only real difference is the knowledge of love between them, and the willingness to be influenced by the other that, as always, is central to Jane Austen's conception of love. After reading Mr. John Knightley's response to his brother's announcement of his engagement, Emma says:

> "He writes like a sensible man . . . I honour his sincerity. It is very plain that he considers the good fortune of the engagement as all on my side . . ."
> "My Emma, he means no such thing. He only means . . ."
> "He and I should differ very little in our estimation of the two,"—interrupted she, with a sort of serious smile—"much less, perhaps, than he is aware of . . ."
> "Emma, my dear Emma—"
> "Oh!" she cried with more thorough gaiety, "If you fancy your brother does not do me justice, only wait till my dear father is in the secret, and hear his opinion. Depend upon it, he will be much farther from doing *you* justice."

Here is the old Emma, asserting herself with the same archness and self-love, yet this time, with something new added—a kind of self-irony. "Oh! I always deserve the best treatment, because I never put up with any other."

Each wishes to make the other more like his or her self; yet each loves that part of the other that is not similar. This rapport between Emma and Mr. Knightley is, I believe, more central to the novel than Graham Hough's hierarchy of characters. Hough distinguishes five kinds of discourse in the novel and asserts that the "objective narrative" with its Johnsonian vocabulary and thoughtful, well-ordered, analytical generalizing sets "the standard by which all the rest is measured." Since Mr. Knightley's speech assimilates the objective narrative most completely, he is the highest on an unequivocal moral scale: "Mr. Knightley, who is never wrong, maintains this style of sober moral evaluation more consistently than anyone else . . . In his presence, conversation is always lifted from the familiar and the anecdotal to the level of general reflection; the characters become types; and the actual persons around him assume the air of personae in a moral apologue." Hough gives as an example Mr. Knightley's comments concerning Mrs. Elton and Jane Fairfax: "Another thing must be taken into consideration too—Mrs. Elton does not talk to Miss Fairfax as she speaks of her. We all know the differences between the pronouns he or she and thou, the plainest spoken amongst us; we all feel the influence of something beyond common civility in our personal intercourse with each other—a something more early implanted . . . And besides the operation of this as a general principle you may be sure that Miss Fairfax awes Mrs. Elton by her superiority both of mind and manner; and that face to face Mrs. Elton treats her with all the respect which she has a claim to." Yet Mr. Knightley's words simply are not true in the very example Hough gives. Mrs. Elton is irrepressible, so much so that she almost usurps the closing lines of the novel. Although we never see her alone with Jane Fairfax, we know from the liberties taken in finding Jane a position that Mrs. Elton's private behavior is as bold and intrusive as her public behavior. If Mrs. Elton is not awed by the "superiority both of mind and manner" of Mr. Knightley, who as Hough says is superior to all, she will not be awed by Jane Fairfax. Mr. Knightley is wrong in his evaluation here, as he is in his optimistic insistence that, were Frank Churchill to act more virtuously toward his father, his foster parents would bend and respect him for it. Mr. Knightley is a pastoral figure who insists on seeing the "actual persons" around him as "personae in a moral apologue." This is not the way Jane Austen views the world, nor can it be the vision she really supports. As Mary Ellmann has said, the endorsement of moral stolidity is reluctant, qualified by Mr. Knightley's pleasure in Emma's defects: "I am losing all my bitterness against spoilt children, my dearest Emma. I who am owing all my happiness to *you*, would it not be horrible ingratitude in me to be severe on them?" The weight of the novel is centered not in Mr. Knightley but in Emma, or in the contributing tension between them.

Mr. Knightley is the link between Emma's interior struggle and her struggle with Highbury. He seems to represent both her conscience and the community. Almost every time Emma sets herself against her conscience, she is also setting herself against Mr. Knightley and against the values of Highbury. (Her treatment of Robert Martin is the best example of this opposition.) Emma's interior coordination, her quest to know and approve of herself, is solidly linked to her exterior coordination, or her arrival at a juster relation to others and to the community.

Essays on *Emma* have a tendency to describe Highbury the way an ethnographer writes history, sorting through the picked bones of institutions and beliefs. The inner consistency, the living society, escapes attention. Class divisions and difficulties are stressed, and moral traits are eventually viewed as possessions of a particular class, or class attitude. I do not intend to decry this view, but pursued too far, it reduces the society of Highbury to a sack of struggling types in some manner creating order out of chaos. It is not the Highbury Emma sees standing on the doorstep of Ford's one morning:

> Mr. Perry walking hastily by, Mr. William Cox letting himself in at the office door, Mr. Cole's carriage horses returning from ex-ercise, or a stray letter-boy on an obstinate mule, were the liveliest objects she could presume to expect; and when her eyes fell only on the butcher with his tray, a tidy old woman travelling home-wards from shop with her full basket, two curs quarrelling over a dirty bone, and a string of dawdling children round the baker's little bow-window eyeing the gingerbread, she knew she had no reason to complain, and was amused enough; quite enough still to stand at the door.

Highbury, it is true, is made up of classes and their individual members. Yet however different the traits of personality and class, they are taken into a functioning society and reshaped by inner organizing forces. Miss Bates is perhaps the nearest symbol of Highbury; all classes join and cooperate in her, just as all gossip passes through her vacant mind. She is the repository of all that occurs and has occurred in Highbury. Her small apartment joins the older gentry (the Woodhouses and Knightleys), the new rich (the Coles), and the lower-middle to lower-class townspeople and clerks. She represents Highbury's fluidity and mobility, its tolerance of past and future classes, or part of the sensibility that helped England avoid a French Revolution.

Emma sets herself against this Highbury, as she does finally against Miss Bates at Box Hill. After every disagreement with Mr. Knightley she visits Miss Bates, as though humbly paying deference to Highbury itself. She does not like visiting Miss Bates for the very reason she should visit her: because it sanctions class fluidity. She does not wish to fall in with the "second and third rate of Highbury"; she wishes to have her own "set." Her greatest sin in the novel is cutting off Harriet's warm attachment to the Martins; as Lionel Trilling has said, she is a reactionary, out to stop social mobility. And Jane Austen gives her snobbery deliberately vindictive over-tones: "The regular and best families Emma could hardly suppose [the Coles] would presume to invite—neither Donwell, nor Hartfield, nor Randalls. Nothing should tempt her to go, if they did; and she regretted that her father's known habits would be giving her refusal less meaning than she could wish." If anything saves Emma after such deliberate unkindness, it is that she actually wants to, and does, go to the Coles' dinner. At bottom, Emma is the most social person in the novel: totally preoccupied with and loving all her relationships with people. This is the basis of the contrast between her and Jane Fairfax, who is a solitary, and who, in her marriage to a morally and intellectually inferior person, will continue to be a solitary.

One of the many ironies surrounding Emma's social preferences is that she will not admit the "true gentility" of Robert Martin, documented by the simple dignity of his written proposal to Harriet and his behavior to her after she refuses him, and yet will sit through an evening of "everyday re-marks, dull repetitions, old news, and heavy jokes" at the Coles' and decide them to be "worthy people, who deserved to be made happy." The reason for the contradiction lies in the conclusion to this quotation: "And left a name behind that would not soon die away." What Emma requires of her inferior acquaintances is that they aggrandize her. In her comment about Robert Martin she makes this clear: "The yeomanry are precisely the order of people with whom I feel I can have nothing to do. A degree or two lower, and a creditable appearance might interest me; I might hope to be useful to their families in some way or other. But a farmer can need none of my help, and is therefore in one sense as much above my notice as in every other he is below it." And we see the self-serving nature of her patronage of the lower class when she visits the sick cottager.

Emma's charity visit has undergone many interpretations, and almost always appears in any discussion of Jane Austen's class attitudes. In trying to answer the question of *Emma*'s relevance to us today, Arnold Kettle points out that it is not necessary for a novelist writing in Jane Austen's time to suggest a solution to the problem of class divisions and prejudice, but that it is morally necessary for the author to notice the existence of the problem. Jane Austen, he decides, fails to do so:

> The values and standards of the Hartfield world are based on the assumption that it is right and proper for a minority of the com-munity to live at the expense of the majority. No amount of sophistry can get away from this fact and to discuss the moral concern of Jane Austen without facing it would be hypocrisy. It

is perfectly true that, within the assumptions of aristocratic society, the values recommended in *Emma* are sensitive enough.
Snobbery, smugness, condescension, lack of consideration, unkindness of any description, are held up to our disdain. But the
fundamental condescension, the basic unkindness which permits
the sensitive values of *Emma* to be applicable only to one person
in ten or twenty, is this not left unscathed? Is there not here a
complacency which renders the hundred little incomplacencies
almost irrelevant?

This is highly persuasive criticism of *Emma,* and Kettle is right in saying
that "no amount of sophistry" can disguise the fundamental questions it
raises. Yet it persuades us mainly because the writer is so sure of his moral
stance—most literary criticism is far more slippery—and because that stance
happens to be a particularly appealing one. The moral judgment made
against *Emma* is disturbingly simple. First of all, there are no "aristocrats"
in the novel; even the Churchills are just inflated gentry. Nor does Jane
Austen view the landed class in the novel as parasitic; she sees it as a functioning part of a changing organism. Mr. Knightley manages his land, has
little cash, and has a younger brother who makes a living as a lawyer. Emma's
destiny as a woman—to be spoiled, overprotected, given a weak, trivial
education, and then left to her own devices—is hardly to be envied. And the
social world of the novel is peopled with upwardly and downwardly mobile
individuals. It is viewed not from the perspective of frozen class division but
from a perspective of living change. It is not France in the 1780s but England
at the beginning of the nineteenth century.

    Kettle's interpretation of the scene of Emma's visit to the sick cottager
forms the basis of his argument; it is in this particular scene that the moral
issue is "shelved," that the existence of the problem is unrecognized. Yet
while he notes the irony of Emma's remarks upon leaving the cottage, his
conclusions rest exclusively upon the visit and its aftermath. Emma's words
before she arrives at the cottage are equally significant. Having told Harriet
she will never marry, Emma explains why her own spinsterhood could never
make her ridiculous:

Never mind, Harriet, I shall not be a poor old maid; and it is
poverty only which makes celibacy contemptible to a generous
public! A single woman, with a very narrow income, must be a
ridiculous, disagreeable, old maid! the proper sport of boys and
girls; but a single woman, of good fortune, is always respectable,
and may be as sensible and pleasant as anybody else. And the

distinction is not quite so much against the candour and common sense of the world as appears at first; for a very narrow income has a tendency to contract the mind, and sour the temper. Those who can barely live, and who live perforce in a very small, and generally very inferior, society, may well be illiberal and cross.

The exaggerated expressions and conceited ironies of Emma's speech are characteristic of her conversation in Harriet's company. If Mr. Knightley's skepticism makes her witty, Harriet's servile awe makes her unreasonable. When asked, as they near the cottage, if she knows Jane Fairfax, Emma replies:

> Oh! yes; we are always forced to be acquainted whenever she comes to Highbury. By the bye, *that* is almost enough to put one out of conceit with a niece. Heaven forbid! at least, that I should ever bore people half so much about all the Knightleys together, as she does about Jane Fairfax. One is sick of the very name of Jane Fairfax. Every letter from her is read forty times over; her compliments to all friends go round and round again; and if she does but send her aunt the pattern of a stomacher, or knit a pair of garters for her grandmother, one hears of nothing else for a month. I wish Jane Fairfax very well; but she tires me to death.

The poverty that Emma speaks of in the first quotation and the sickness she feels in hearing about Jane Fairfax find their counterparts in the real "sickness and poverty . . . which she came to visit." The contempt Emma really feels for the poor is very clear in the first speech (poor and elderly spinsters are "the proper sport of boys and girls"); her willingness to allow them to be "illiberal and cross" is an extension of her contempt. In the cottage this attitude is elaborated: "She understood their ways, could allow for their ignorance and their temptations, had no romantic expectations of extraordinary virtue from those, for whom education had done so little." Emma's "allowance" for ignorance and temptation is no more than an assumption of them. Even after reading Robert Martin's letter, we recall, she still insists that he is ignorant. The snapping bitterness of her tirade against Jane Fairfax, who is less fortunate than herself and who will have to earn a living, is enough to prove that even the rich can be illiberal and cross: "One is sick of the very name of Jane Fairfax . . . I wish Jane Fairfax very well; but she tires me to death." When such an example of Emma's compassion is followed with "They were now approaching the cottage, and all idle topics were superseded. Emma was very compassionate," the irony is so obvious that I question Kettle's interpretation that the moral issue is being shelved. The self-satisfied feeling Emma derives from the visit culminates when, upon seeing Mr. Elton, she says, "Well, (smiling) I hope it may be allowed that if compassion has produced exertion and relief to the sufferers, it has done all that is truly important. If we feel for the wretched, enough to do all we can for them, the rest is empty sympathy, only distressing to ourselves." Once again, the reappearance of a single word, in this case "distressing," makes us aware of the gap between Emma's real and spoken intentions. Even the "distresses of the poor" finally disappear into "what is distressing to ourselves."

It is precisely the moral issue then that is being put forward, put forward on the most demanding level: the practical, individual level. What is being subordinated to it is the collective issue, or the theoretical view of conduct as an expression of class. Such a view would let Emma off the hook, would make her class more responsible for her attitude than her own being. For all Jane Austen's awareness of the effect of class on character, she is never naive enough to overlook the existence of individual volition. She would not have written off the "little incomplacencies" as readily as Kettle does. To Austen's view, the "hundred little incomplacencies" make life tolerable for everyone; are we not required to imagine the effects of Emma's complacency on Robert Martin and his family? Emma is wrong to snub the Martins, and to encourage Harriet to snub them, not because as a class the yeomanry deserve to rise, but because she aims to break a moral and emotional tie between Harriet and the Martins that has already formed. It is on this level, the level of individual practice, that social damage is incurred in Jane Austen. From this point of view Kettle's broad class complacency is an abstraction, an evasion. Changes in the quality of social life originate on the concrete, atomized level.

Emma herself learns this lesson in the course of the novel. Indeed, it is her first lesson, because until she recognizes her own immediate effect on others, on Harriet and the Martins and Miss Bates, until she actually experiences her tie to a community of others, all talk about social responsibility and class difference is lost on her. In *Emma,* Austen makes us see the primary obstacles to class consciousness.

Emma's feelings toward her social inferiors are governed not so much by an unwillingness to see, converse with, or help them as by an insistence on regulating their lives. She does not wish to participate in Highbury society unless she can lead, on the dance floor and elsewhere. In essence she wishes not to cooperate but to rule, as Frank Churchill's mock proclamations at Box Hill suggest. Miss Bates offends her because she is uncontrollable; Emma cannot stop or even regulate the flow of her boring remarks. The urge to control is the basis of her insult at Box Hill: Miss Bates's dull remarks must be "limited as to number—only three at once."

It is important to Emma to feel that Highbury needs her but that she does not need Highbury. She imagines herself the envy and idol of all her social inferiors: young Robert Martin "will connect himself well if he can"; and the Coles' main object in giving the dinner is to see Emma at their table. At every social event Emma sees herself as giving the honor rather than as possibly receiving it. E. M Forster's remark is appropriate to her: for some, it is perhaps better to receive than to give.

Emma's unwillingness to mix with Highbury has a personal analogue in her wish to remain single. Both reveal the same superior tendency to remain aloof, to oversee life without participating in it. Her first realization of love is appropriately attended by the first realization of her need for human society generally:

> The child to be born at Randall's must be a tie there even dearer than herself; and Mrs. Weston's heart and time would be occupied by it. They should lose her; and, probably, in great measure, her husband also.—Frank Churchill would return among them no more; and Miss Fairfax, it was reasonable to suppose, would soon cease to belong to Highbury. They would be married, and settled either at or near Enscombe. All that were good would be withdrawn; and if to these losses, the loss of Donwell were to be added, what would remain of cheerful or of rational society within their reach? Mr. Knightley to be no longer coming there for his evening comfort!—No longer walking in at all hours, as if ever willing to change his own home for their's!—How was it to be endured?

A great deal of the force of Emma's realization of love lies in the implicit recognition of dependence, of need, for another person. What astounds her is her own failure to see, year after year, the importance of Mr. Knightley's presence to her.

And once the love and need for another person is admitted, a sense of obligation naturally follows. It is significant that Emma achieves knowledge of her "heart" and knowledge of her "conduct" simultaneously: "It darted through her, with the speed of an arrow, that Mr. Knightley must marry no one but herself! . . . Her own conduct, as well as her own heart, was before her in the same few minutes. She saw it all with a clearness which had never blessed her before. How improperly had she been acting by Harriet! How inconsiderate, how indelicate, how irrational, how unfeeling had been her conduct! What blindness, what madness, had led her on!" Emma learns a "sense of justice" for the first time—in the words of *Mansfield Park*, a sense of "what is owed to everybody." Never in Jane Austen do we find a convenient separation between the personal and the social act. As Mr. Knightley tells Emma at Box Hill, her remark to Miss Bates—to Emma no more than a careless indulgence—is inevitably a public act: "You, whom she had known from an infant, whom she had seen grow up from a period when her notice was an honour, to have you now, in thoughtless spirits, and the pride of the moment, laugh at her, humble her—and before her niece, too—and before others, many of whom (certainly *some,*) would be entirely guided by *your* treatment of her."

The scene at Box Hill possesses great emotional intensity. Each time we read it—no matter how objective familiarity or reason may have made us—Emma's cruelty completely shocks us. There is something particularly moving and frightening about the rejection of the comic figure in art, such as the rejection of Falstaff or of a clown in a Charlie Chaplin film. Miss Bates's emotional vulnerability, her blind (indeed her comic) goodness in expecting others to be as simply affectionate as herself, gives the scene its special pathos. And however Mr. Knightley finally stresses Miss Bates's social vulnerability, his speech begins with the frankly appalled question, "How could you be so unfeeling to Miss Bates?"

Yet the lack of feeling is not what makes the scene so shocking. Emma's action violates the most basic human law found in any society whether barbarous or advanced: the protection of the weak. Miss Bates is defenseless, as the first description of her makes clear: "She had not intellectual superiority to make atonement to herself, or to frighten those who might hate her, into outward respect." What leads Emma to mistreat her? We cannot really answer this question any more than we can explain an act of violence in an absurdist work. It is hot; Emma is tired of herself and of Frank Churchill; she is bored; and her discontent flowers with terrifying naturalness into cruelty.

Emma delivers the insult because she "could not resist." And the remarkable impact of the scene comes from our understanding her action though we know it to be wrong. We understand it not through its overt causes—Emma's impatience and boredom, her exasperated attempt to entertain herself since no one else will entertain her—but through its covert reality: there is no reason for it; it is simply a case of unrestrained human hostility. In this moment, perhaps more than in any other moment in Jane Austen, it is impossible to entertain D. W. Harding's notion of the "social

detachment" that arises from having to restrain ourselves in society; indeed, only through restraint do the characters achieve a modicum of "social engagement." It is through resisting these irresistible impulses and hostilities that people in Austen's society can maintain a tolerably open atmosphere for the individual. Where, finally, do Emma's "honesty" and "sincerity" place Miss Bates but in a condition of social estrangement? Emma's famous cruelty takes place in the open air of Box Hill (itself a contradiction in terms), in a "natural" environment away from the home community. This choice of setting gives us a rather pointed indication of Jane Austen's opinion of human nature, of how human beings behave when the muzzle is off. To Jane Austen, nothing boxes the individual in more tightly than his own craving for freedom.

Unlike Emma, Mr. Knightley has, in his own words, the "English delicacy toward the feelings of other people," as his protection of the slow-witted and defenseless Harriet reveals. In his conversation with Mrs. Elton, Mr. Knightley states his understanding of human behavior, and we observe one of the most richly ambivalent problems in Jane Austen realizing itself.

> "It is to be a morning scheme, you know, Knightley; quite a simple thing. I shall wear a large bonnet, and bring one of my little baskets hanging on my arm. Here,—probably this basket with pink ribbon. And Jane will have such another. There is to be no form or parade—a sort of gipsy party.—We are to walk about your gardens, and gather the strawberries ourselves, and sit under trees;—and whatever else you may like to provide, it is to be all out of doors—a table spread in the shade, you know. Everything as natural and simple as possible. Is not that your idea?"
>
> "Not quite. My idea of the simple and the natural will be to have the table spread in the dining-room. The nature and the simplicity of gentlemen and ladies, with their servants and furniture, I think is best observed by meals within doors. When you are tired of eating strawberries in the garden, there shall be cold meat in the house."

Mrs. Elton's idea of a "gipsy party" is given added irony when we consider that the real gipsy party in the novel comes close to attacking Harriet for her money. Yet Mr. Knightley is not simply the spokesman for Jane Austen in his comment. As his name suggests, Mr. Knightley is a slightly anachronistic figure, and his equating "servants" with "furniture" reveals this. His world is a stable, pastoral world in which everything is in its place, people

have the predictable stability of furniture, and the virtuous person is always deferred to. This is not the world of Highbury, where gentlewomen sometimes slip to the near-servant status of governess or even, like Miss Bates, to a barely genteel poverty; where governesses become the mistresses of estates; where inhumane behavior surfaces in its members; and, above all, where an encounter of opposites like that between Mr. Knightley and Mrs. Elton can take place.

Highbury is kept on through an endless dialectic. Like a well-oiled machine, it runs on the cooperation and coordination of its parts. Lionel Trilling has come closest to recognizing the basis of cooperation of Highbury, but as I have already suggested, he is mistaken in calling it pastoral. His argument brilliantly articulates a modern bias, for many readers, particularly American readers, view Jane Austen in this way. Cooperation itself is viewed as an archaic phenomenon. But to Jane Austen cooperation was no more pastoral than the moral restrictions in the novels were mysterious taboos. As Trilling states, the pastoral idyll excludes the idea of activity and includes an idea of harmonic stasis. Yet Highbury is an imperfect, changing society. It functions smoothly because almost everyone makes a constant effort to maintain it: "Some change of countenance was necessary for each gentleman as they walked into Mrs. Weston's drawing-room;—Mr. Elton must compose his joyous looks, and Mr. John Knightley disperse his ill-humour. Mr. Elton must smile less, and Mr. John Knightley more, to fit them for the place." These accommodations are minor compared to the continual exertion required of almost all to abide the slowness of Mr. Woodhouse and the loquacity of Miss Bates. I cannot agree with Trilling that everyone except Emma, the "modern" personality, experiences only their charm and goodness. Mr. Knightley must strain to be heard by both, and Jane Fairfax's despair is haunting: "Oh! . . . the comfort of being sometimes alone!" Mr. Woodhouse and Miss Bates are both loved *and* tolerated. Similarly, Mr. Knightley's willingness to move to Hartfield does not assume a lack of will. He is the hero of *Emma* because his move *is* a sacrifice.

Highbury, like all the communities in Jane Austen, is conceived as possessing an almost personal identity and will. "Frank Churchill was looked on as sufficiently belonging to the place to make his merit and prospects a kind of common concern." "By birth [Jane Fairfax] belonged to Highbury." Like Meryton in *Pride and Prejudice,* Highbury ingests and rejects materials that come into it; be it John Knightley's sullenness or Emma's energy, that trait is reworked in such a manner that when it reappears as part of the social body it has been molded to fit a larger purpose. It has become part of the network of influences that, through checks and balances, ensure High-

bury's survival. In *Emma*, this process does not reduce the human spirit but expands it; the efforts required of all its members make them better people. The atmosphere of "intelligent love"—when it dominates—is well earned. Many of the dialogues seem to pull and stretch under the strain of accommodation; Emma's little disagreements with her father, Mr. Knightley's conversation with Miss Bates, even Mr. Weston's exchange with Mrs. Elton about his son. At moments the intelligent and sensitive person is forced into irony, and this irony is not a form of social detachment but a form of social adjustment. It is not like the superior sarcasm of Mr. Palmer in *Sense and Sensibility*, which is treated with astringent disapproval. When used sincerely, irony is a benevolent compromise: a way of maintaining social integrity without sacrificing personal integrity, as Emma's first conversation with Mrs. Elton reveals. Such irony is, on the simplest level, courtesy; it is also a method of comprehending reality. In a world where, for reasons beyond the control of the intelligence of the characters, "seldom . . . does complete truth belong to any human disclosure," irony is a more truthful and humble mode of comprehension than direct statement.

Many critics have pointed out that no one works in *Emma*. Yet everyone is working, morally and psychically, to sustain this cooperative enterprise of civilized living. As in *Mansfield Park*, a certain amount of sheer psychic energy is required to make the social order endure. This is difficult for us to fathom, for the modern reader inevitably looks upon inactivity as stagnation; Milton's Adam and Eve in the Garden of Eden before their fall seem to us like old-age pensioners. In *Emma*, those who contribute relatively little to the cooperative enterprise, John Knightley and Jane Fairfax, are either involved or preparing to be involved in the working world. John Knightley has always seemed to me a curiously modern type, a commuting professional man who divides his time entirely between work and family. He and Jane Fairfax lack the energy for Highbury, and through them Austen registers the effect that the breakup of a ruling, or leisure, class will have on refined and civilized values. Austen knew that a community like Highbury could be maintained only if its members took a constant, unflagging interest in one another's welfare. Emma herself instinctively acknowledges this when, upon noticing that Jane Fairfax is not very curious about the news of Mr. Elton's marriage, she remarks, "You are silent, Miss Fairfax—but I hope you mean to take an interest in this news." Like much of Austen's dialogue, even the most offhand comments join in the underlying continuity of the work.

Marriage in *Emma* signifies the validation, not the resolution, of the different dialectics. Frank Churchill's character, Mr. Knightley asserts, "will improve" after his marriage. And as Emma and Mr. Knightley continue to

retain their separate identities, we anticipate that cooperation and compromise will maintain the relationship. Emma has had three enlightenments, and we expect that she will experience more.

Mr. Knightley sets the pattern of compromise by moving to Hartfield, an action antithetical to modern ideas of marriage. Yet since the most serious sin in the novel is Emma's insistence that Harriet cut the Martins in order to preserve her own friendship, it follows that Mr. Knightley should not commit a similar unkindness in making Emma give up her father for him. Since he has no really important relationship to give up in leaving his estate, the sacrifice is proper. Perhaps more significantly, Mr. Knightley's move to Hartfield marks the first time in a Jane Austen novel in which the relationship begins to take precedence over the "place" or estate. Could we imagine Darcy moving to Longbourn? It is also a subtly feminist praise of Mr. Knightley, whose practical sensibility does not include the traditional masculine insistence that his future wife leave her family to become Mrs. Knightley, the mistress of Donwell.

Jane Austen was interested in the stability of form, in what kept the great basic plans of social organization, one of which is marriage, so steadfast throughout whole epochs. To say that this concern is outdated—as several of Austen's critics have reluctantly concluded—reveals a curious misconception. Most people marry, and almost everyone participates in some way in the larger institutions of our society. Yet it has been the preoccupation of a post-Darwinian age to see struggle as the natural state of things and therefore to judge a novelist who explores the implications of our cooperative history as somehow blind or narrow or even trivial.

Why, one may ask, in a novel about social cooperation, is an individual, and a willful individual at that, so undeniably the main subject? Why is the novel not called *Highbury*? The novel as written could not be called *Highbury*; it is clearly a tribute to this heroine whom the author mistakenly thought "no one but myself will much like." Emma even threatens to take control over the work and write her own novel about Harriet: to give her a family history, a personality, beauty and stature, a love affair, a husband, and a social position. This deference to Emma, to her creative impulse, registers the author's interest in the individual person, for whom, after all, society was organized to begin with. Those who forget this origin by placing an abstract social ambition above it—General Tilney, Mrs. Ferrars, Lady Catherine de Bourgh, Sir Walter Elliot—are never contemplated without disapproval. Emma reminds us of what Highbury is for; while she has not the right to remain aloof from it, she has the right to be dissatisfied with it.

Emma is based on a recognition of the life of the individual as a func-

tioning whole that must be coordinated internally before it can function externally. Those who do not coordinate internally—more simply, those, like Harriet, who never know themselves—become the willing victims of those exterior forces that, because they never see them, will always control them. When Arnold Kettle says that the sensitive values of *Emma* are available to one in twenty, he is being generous. They are available to even fewer than that, not even to Emma until the end of the novel. They are available mainly to the intelligent, and only partially to the less intelligent. One does not have to be intelligent to be good in Jane Austen, but one does have to be intelligent to be free, to see and evaluate one's choices. Partly for this reason, an Austen novel seems inexorable beside most Dickens novels. Often in Dickens, in order to be good—above all to be a good woman—one has to be simple-minded. Jane Austen makes us acknowledge the undemocratic truth that those who are born unintelligent are at a terrible disadvantage in the world. Her belief in the importance of education, one of her most constant and serious concerns, is an extension of this awareness.

This is all the more reason why in *Emma* Jane Austen insists on the necessity and finally the benevolence of social cooperation: because it alone protects the Harriets and the Miss Bateses of the world, cares for, tolerates, and loves them. "She must laugh at such a close! Such an end of the doleful disappointments of five weeks back! Such a heart!—such a Harriet!" *Emma* is a novel of human interdependence in every sense. It is Harriet who makes Emma accomplished, Mr. Knightley who makes her witty, Jane Fairfax who makes her average, and, in the closing lines, Mrs. Elton who makes her tasteful:

> The wedding was very much like other weddings, where the parties have no taste for finery or parade; and Mrs. Elton, from the particulars detailed by her husband, thought it all extremely shabby, and very inferior to her own.—"Very little white satin, very few lace veils; a most pitiful business!—Selina would stare when she heard of it."—But, in spite of these deficiencies, the wishes, the hopes, the confidence, the predictions of the small band of true friends who witnessed the ceremony, were fully answered in the perfect happiness of the union.

"In spite of these deficiencies" may be read "because of these deficiencies." In a world that indiscriminately blesses the marriages of Mr. and Mrs. Elton and Harriet and Robert Martin, the union between Emma and Mr. Knightley is surely one of "perfect happiness." We understand them through comparison.

SUSAN MORGAN

Guessing for Ourselves
in Northanger Abbey

Besides, my Muse by no means deals in fiction:
She gathers a repertory of facts,
Of course with some reserve and slight restriction,
But mostly sings of human things and acts—
                                              —BYRON

The urbane narrator of Byron's *Don Juan* found that "perfection is / Insipid in this naughty world of ours" (I, 18). To use Byron's phrase, Austen too, had a pedestrian muse. She wrote her niece, Fanny Knight, that "pictures of perfection as you know make me sick and wicked." We hear in that remark her response to Richardson's claim in his preface to *Clarissa Harlowe* that his heroine, insofar as she could be perfect and still be consistent with human frailty, is perfect. In *Northanger Abbey,* which I assume to be the first of the six completed novels (revised to an unknown extent long after it was written and published posthumously, it may be the only one of Austen's novels from her Steventon period), Austen declares her aesthetic principles, much as Wordsworth, in his Preface to the *Lyrical Ballads,* would declare his. She seeks, like Wordsworth, to present her own view of "human nature, at least in the midland counties of England."

Instead of the angelic Clarissa, Austen offers Catherine Morland, who has "by nature nothing heroic about her." Readers have always seen that Catherine, created with a simplicity which suggests both the inexperience and the aims of her author, is an antiheroine, much as Byron's Juan is an

---

From *In the Meantime: Character and Perception in Jane Austen's Fiction.* © 1980 by The University of Chicago. The University of Chicago Press, 1980.

antihero. Katrin Ristkok Burlin has remarked that in *Northanger Abbey* "Jane Austen came to terms with her art in a single, complex treatment of the theme of fiction." There have been many studies of Austen's relations to previous novelists, and her ideas about fictions are recognized to include not only her own and those of her predecessors, but those of her own characters as well. Henry Tilney properly delights in the work of Ann Radcliffe because it makes his hair stand on end and Catherine enjoys *Sir Charles Grandison,* that "amazing horrid book." But we must also see that Austen has a new idea of fiction, specifically a new idea of character, one closer to the ideas of Romantic poets than of previous novelists.

Attempts to describe Austen's innovations in *Northanger Abbey* have often focused on the ending of the book because it is there that her aesthetic principles and her characters' moral and perceptual problems come together. Having mocked gothic and sentimental conventions throughout the novel, Austen yet resolves the plot by dismissing the heroine unexpectedly and inexplicably from the abbey and having the hero oppose the angry commands of his father and gallop after her to offer his hand. What is this book about? In the famous closing sentence, Austen laughs once again at didactic novels and their readers as she leaves the moral of the story "to be settled by whomsoever it may concern."

Most readers have agreed that Catherine Morland's experiences cannot be adequately described as a progress from "visions of romance" to realities; that, as Andrew Wright put it, "good sense, ironically, is limited too." Indeed, neither Catherine's experience nor her author's new literary principles can be described as a move toward realism. Instead we need to recognize the question which the portrayal of an unheroic heroine invokes. If fiction does not offer models to emulate, what then can be taught—by Tilneys or by novelists? At the center of *Northanger Abbey,* at the center of Austen's new idea of fiction, is the problem of education. Austen's constant subject, the relations between ourselves and other people, appears here as teaching and learning, as a novel of education.

The *bildungsroman* form reflects the more serious question—serious aesthetically as well as morally—of how to balance possibilities for character change with the continuing integrity of self. Education, then, is Austen's metaphor for exploring the extent to which we can become better or worse, the extent to which we can be affected by our experiences, and still remain ourselves. It is the metaphor for the relation between character and plot. Trilling reminds us that Austen writes of "the idea of love based in pedagogy." This idea includes not only education but the limits of education. And it is taught to us by Catherine, that "occasionally stupid" character who "never could learn or understand any thing before she was taught; and sometimes not even then."

Northanger Abbey has its own lasting beauty. It has the added charm of being a beginning which tells us much about what will follow. We are helped in understanding *Northanger Abbey* by reading it, at least in part, through *Emma*. What the heroines of both novels need is not good sense but the imaginative perception to interpret their experiences creatively and continuously. The world proves richer than Catherine's preconceptions, and, after a period of blindness, she sees both the limitations of her own vision and the variety and range of other people. "Most grievously was she humbled. Most bitterly did she cry." But after this moment of crisis and enlightenment Catherine does not remain humbled. Once resolved on better judgment, "she had nothing to do but to forgive herself and be happier than ever." Austen examines how Catherine changes and how she does not, through the reflector of Catherine's relations to her teacher, Henry Tilney. How much does he teach her? And why does Henry, clever and charming Henry, come to love this ordinary girl? What he sees in Catherine may show us what we are to see in her as well.

In the first chapter of *Northanger Abbey* Austen assures us that Catherine Morland is "unpropitious for heroism." Catherine's qualities suggest what the young novelist thought of as constituting ordinary people rather than heroines. At ten, Catherine "had neither a bad heart nor a bad temper; was seldom stubborn, scarcely ever quarrelsome, . . . she was moreover noisy and wild, hated confinement and cleanliness, and loved nothing so well in the world as rolling down the green slope at the back of the house." The freedom, naturalness, and spontaneity of a child captured in this description are qualities which Catherine still has at seventeen. She tells Henry Tilney that she needs no refined taste for hyacinths to get her out of doors. She likes walks, in spite of that shocking ignorance of how to judge a view. She is full of enthusiasm, for Bath and for *The Mysteries of Udolpho,* in which, Austen tells us, appeared "what interested her at that time rather more than any thing else in the world, Laurintina's skeleton." When she is excited, Catherine violates the bounds of decorum, bursting unannounced into the Tilneys' lodgings to rectify John Thorpe's changing the day for her walk. Catherine also breaks the bounds of polite language. At the theater when Henry politely demurs that he could have no right to be angry with her for not having kept their appointment, she replies with unconventional directness, "Well, nobody would have thought you had no right who saw your face." The reply to Henry is disarming and the theater scene is one of the moments we most feel the power of this unheroic heroine's charm. Her

natural and eager frankness is irresistible in its naiveté. During their conversation at the play she assures Henry that "'if Mr. Thorpe would only
have stopped I would have jumped out and run after you.' Is there a Henry
in the world who could be insensible to such a declaration? Henry Tilney at
least was not." And neither is the reader.

Catherine's liveliness and her ability to be "all happiness," "all eager
delight," give her an appreciation of mundane pleasures which contrasts with
jaded taste, particularly with Isabella Thorpe's artificiality and "boasted absence of mind." But Catherine's vitality is only part of her charm. Just before
launching her into "all the difficulties and dangers of a six weeks' residence
in Bath," Austen, in what will prove to be her regular method of introducing
characters, guides us by providing this "certain information" of what Catherine's "character is meant to be": "her heart was affectionate, her disposition cheerful and open, without conceit or affectation of any kind—her
manners just removed from the awkwardness and shyness of a girl; her
person pleasing, and, when in good looks, pretty—and her mind about as
ignorant and uninformed as the female mind at seventeen usually is." Catherine has that most essential quality of an Austen heroine, an affectionate
heart. She also has, in that openness of disposition which her author will
continue to appreciate and will later have Mr. Knightley and Anne Elliot
value so highly, the possibility for change. Catherine at eighteen will be less
"ignorant and uninformed."

When her story opens, Catherine lacks experience. She fails twice in her
judgments of people, first in thinking Isabella good and then in thinking
General Tilney evil. Both result from one flaw: she jumps to conclusions.
Catherine allows herself to be ruled by other people's fictions, a passivity
that makes everyone look silly. Thus she responds so wholeheartedly to Henry's lecture on the picturesque that she "voluntarily rejected the whole city
of Bath, as unworthy to make part of a landscape." More seriously, such
responses negate the self, a problem which appears with more rigidity and
self-destructiveness in Marianne Dashwood. One reason Austen creates
Catherine with natural vitality is to heighten our sense of what she loses
when she accepts other people's views. Absorbing sentimental conventions,
Catherine betrays her own energy and perceptions.

Northanger Abbey offers fallen versions of the heroine, as fictions rather
than as images of life. Catherine is a novice "in training for a heroine." Her
teacher in sentimental conventions is another false heroine, Isabella Thorpe.
There are interesting parallels between Isabella and Emma, who tries to make
a heroine out of Harriet Smith. Both are beautiful and twenty-one; for selfish
reasons both adopt and try to improve girls who are naive, sweet, and sev-

enteen. By the time of writing *Emma* Austen's interest has moved from the pupil or victim to the teacher, clearly the more culpable of the two. In *Northanger Abbey* the false teacher, unlike Emma, is presented rather simply as a hypocrite. But whereas Emma deludes herself, Isabella, with a coldness of heart Emma could never have, considers herself the heroine, and is mainly interested in deceiving others. Emma makes things up for the best of all possible reasons, to make life interesting, while Isabella's motives are mercenary. Actually, Isabella reverses her role. She plays at possessing an acute sensibility but in reality she has only sense. And to possess sense without feeling is to be shrewd, calculating, practical, and cold. It is also to fail in perceptiveness. Isabella cannot understand other people because she doesn't sympathize with their points of view. In spite of Catherine's explicit confessions of affection for Henry, Isabella still thinks Catherine might accept John Thorpe's proposal. She is incapable of believing that the proposal came without Catherine's encouragement, because she can only judge Catherine in her own terms. Isabella is appropriately vanquished. She loses both James Morland and Captain Tilney because she misjudges them as well. But that propriety is seldom repeated in Isabella's literary descendents. After *Northanger Abbey* Austen's idea of appropriate deserts is not so innocently moral, and her calculating people—Lucy Steele, Charlotte Lucas, Mrs. Elton, Mrs. Clay—more or less get what they want.

Like Isabella, Catherine sees others in terms of herself. Henry, laughing at her explanation that Captain Tilney wished to dance with Isabella out of good nature, tells her, "How very little trouble it can give you to understand the motive of other people's actions. . . . With you it is not, How is such a one likely to be influenced? What is the inducement most likely to act upon such a person's feelings, age, situation, and probable habits of life considered?—but, how should *I* be influenced, what would be *my* inducement in acting so and so?" Neither direct knowledge of one's own motives nor the acceptance of other people's versions can substitute for the moral activity of perception. Trying to see from another's point of view as a means of overleaping the limits of self does not have nearly the weight in *Northanger Abbey* it will have in *Emma*. But the idea is there, and Austen will develop it into a major narrative technique.

Catherine believes Isabella's self-presentation as a sentimental heroine. Her credulity is an early and more obvious form of Elizabeth Bennet's acceptance of Mr. Wickham's sad tale. Most surprising is how Catherine continues to accept Isabella's version when Isabella violates it in every scene. Claiming she wants to get away from two staring young men, Isabella rushes after them, while muttering that one was really quite handsome. After insisting that no power on earth could get her to leave her seat, she dances all evening with Captain Tilney. The examples are endless. Yet Catherine accepts the world as Isabella describes it, not just because she is inexperienced but because she thinks perception is a matter of straightforward description. People are what they say and say what they mean. And since people tell the truth one need not be at pains to understand them, or to try to make one's own sense of the world. Catherine has yet to realize that truth is multiple and particular and incomplete, and that judgment is an active process of exploration and understanding. This naiveté, unlike that of other seventeen-year-olds like Fanny Burney's Evelina, is not the sweet innocence which thinks too well of others to notice that they lie. Far from being a virtue, such simplicity is a fault.

The moral of the story (it seems most to concern literary critics) is not that people should speak with simple openness. To say what you mean, to tell the truth, is far too simple a dictum to be an adequate expression of, or response to, the complexities of personality and experience. Nor is *Northanger Abbey* a plea for the spontaneous and the natural. As Kenneth Moler has said, "Jane Austen insists . . . that her central character add a degree of 'art' to her natural goodness." The villains are not the only ones who manipulate words. Henry Tilney can play the wit, the jaded dandy, the gothic storyteller. Henry parries Catherine's close questions on why his brother flirts with Isabella, knowing her to be engaged, by the telling evasiveness of his own questions. The truth, unacceptable to Catherine, is that Henry's brother and her dear Isabella are both unprincipled and self-indulgent. Henry is not alone in the complexities of his language. Austen is also the creator of Elinor Dashwood, who tells polite lies, and of Emma, who is as appealingly devious as Catherine is appealingly frank.

When Henry leaves for Woodston two days early in order to prepare for his father's visit, Catherine is baffled. She blindly trusts to Henry's judgment. Still, "the inexplicability of the General's conduct dwelt much on her thoughts. That he was very particular in his eating, she had, by her own unassisted observation, already discovered; but why he should say one thing so positively, and mean another all the while, was most unaccountable! How were people, at that rate, to be understood?" If "at that rate," if words don't directly reflect thoughts and feelings, if people are not immediately known, if, in short, we live in a world where things are not as they appear, how are people to be understood? At that moment Catherine Morland defines what will be the essential dilemma of the characters in Austen's fiction.

The problem of understanding others, of accounting for the unaccountable, is what Catherine is in the novel to learn. She needs to for the very reason that life is unaccountable, people are not logical, words not literal, and meanings seldom accessible and clear. Catherine is beginning to recognize (to borrow Virginia Woolf's phrase) that the world is larger and more mysterious than she had supposed. Expressing this idea as moral education is a convention through which Austen explores the more essential question of how one is to see and act when the truth does not lie before us as we move. This problem connects *Northanger Abbey* with *Emma* and with all her other novels. And her study of this problem, as Austen declares in *Northanger Abbey,* separates her from her predecessors in fiction.

Northanger Abbey, both in its aesthetic principles and moral concerns, explores human experience in its everyday sense. How do people see themselves and each other? And how can they learn and grow? Catherine's problems in understanding her experience are the same ones Austen must consider in creating it. Despite awkward handling, the relation between the burlesque of other kinds of fiction and Catherine's education is intrinsic to Austen's vision. The connection between *Northanger Abbey* and *Emma* is that in *Emma* Austen has clarified her purpose to the point where moral and aesthetic concerns are virtually identical.

Austen mocks sentimental and gothic conventions because they are unnatural and therefore incredible. Fantastic claims of eternal friendship and murder most foul are beautifully contrasted with the mundane concerns of choosing "between her spotted and her tamboured muslin" and hoping that Henry Tilney will appear ahead of John Thorpe to ask for a dance. One difficulty of the technique is how to maintain interest in Catherine during those moments when she behaves like a gothic heroine in what we know is not a gothic context. In spite of her hopes, there have been no dark deeds. And without an objective correlative, Catherine's fears will seem dull unless the specific nature of those fears reveals something about her.

The low point of the novel for me comes at the abbey, when Catherine becomes increasingly suspicious of the general and concludes by imagining that he has murdered his wife. Since no reader can credit such a suspicion, the episode demonstrates how Catherine has allowed gothic literary conventions to distort her vision of actual events. However, the weakness of the episode is that it does not matter which convention Catherine adopts. Catherine could easily have decided that Mrs. Tilney had wasted away, or committed suicide, or, indeed, was still alive and hiding with a dark-eyed rescuer in Spain, sighing often at the memory of those unwillingly abandoned children. Any one of these phantasms fulfills the requirement that General Tilney be a domestic tyrant who has driven his wife to ruin. That Catherine has her gothic fancies is important, but their content is not. As Tave comments,

"Romance is really rather dull." Thus the novel lags during those sections in which Austen does not demand that the reader care about the content of Catherine's thoughts, only that we know she is astray.

Northanger Abbey does not come alive again until Catherine runs into Henry in the hall. The tension of their surprise, their veiled mutual affection, her mortification and his disapproval, combine to give the scene vitality. The reader, absolved from the boredom of condemning Catherine's silliness, is once again required to be discerning, to attend to the particular content of the characters' thoughts and feelings, because, once again, what they feel and say matters. All of Catherine's agitation about the chest, all of her tremulous fears about the contents of the closet and the fate of Mrs. Tilney, reveal little about her. Any heroine would respond similarly. Those delicate sentiments are worthless compared to what has been learned of Catherine in that single moment when she tells her brother, James, how grateful she is that he has come to Bath on purpose to visit her. We see her ignorance, her ingenuousness, and her affectionate heart.

Austen's continued interest in and mastery of how to keep false versions of reality compelling can be brought out by comparing Catherine's fancies of murder with Emma's more telling suspicion that Jane Fairfax might be having a liaison with the husband of her dearest friend. Both are literary fantasies, certainly beyond familiar experience. But the latter is more particular, more sharply focused, in that the object of Austen's attack is not the source of the fantasy but rather the character's state of mind. Indeed, we are told that although Emma draws up long lists of books, she seldom reads them. Her fantasies are more personally revealing than Catherine's and less clichéd. Their content matters. Emma's suspicion of a liaison combines her just sense that the twin mysteries of Jane's return to Highbury and her extraordinary reserve have something of romance in them with her most unjust sense of devaluing Jane by attributing an illicit affair to her. We see both Emma's insightfulness and its misuse. By reducing the effects of reading, Austen makes Emma more willful and thus more culpable for what she imagines than Catherine is.

Catherine sees herself literally and rather crudely as a created character enacting someone else's fiction. She applies literary conventions to her new experiences, and fails to understand them so long as she lacks that flexible vision which comes through releasing herself from superimposed meanings. With Emma, more vain and more powerful than Catherine, the case is more complex. Emma is quite beyond seeing herself in someone else's frame. Like her author, she creates fictions. More precisely than Catherine, she depicts in her role Austen's premise that the central moral question is how we see.

Emma begins with a wrong vision. Yet her creations are almost as sophisticated as her author's. Harriet Smith, as the fair, blue-eyed beauty of unknown yet noble birth, is a sentimental commonplace. But Emma's version of Jane Fairfax is subtle and realistic. She provides this dark-haired and sophisticated girl with an illicit love but spares her the role of villainy by invoking no moral absolutes with which to condemn her. Jane, in Emma's story, is one of those mixed characters that Catherine learns of in *Northanger Abbey*.

In *Emma* Austen has developed the themes of *Northanger Abbey* so that the difference between fantasy and reality is not that reality is more realistic, that is to say, more probable and mundane. It is as likely that Jane Fairfax should have fallen in love with her companion's suitor as that she should have met Frank Churchill at the seaside and become secretly engaged. As early as the conclusion of *Northanger Abbey* Austen's work has shown readers that, as Tave has said, "the art of the novel of common life holds its own surprises, some subsuming and some exceeding the excitements of romance." Facts can be at least as exciting as fictions. Emma's faults are better presented than Catherine's, because the moral failure which leads to Catherine's misconceptions is tied to the extreme and improbable content of those misconceptions.

The distance between Emma's ideas about Jane and the truth is small compared to that between Catherine's fears that the general is a murderer and the fact that he is not an amiable man. Yet Austen's point about both suspicions is finally much the same. To acknowledge a necessary relation between principles of art and principles of perception suggests that at the center of *Northanger Abbey* is a theory of imagination. Langbaum's claim that "the whole conscious concern with objectivity as a *problem,* as something to be achieved," is specifically romantic, is as relevant to *Northanger Abbey* as to *Emma*. Catherine's immaturity lies in her not being conscious of the problem. She thinks perceiving means a passive gathering of accepted forms of truth. She thinks girls who become engaged do so for certain reasons and will act in certain ways. She believes that the meaning of an engagement is established.

Catherine learns that truth is not a settled or a general thing, and that there is a relation between creativity and perception, between what she makes up and what she sees. When she tells Henry and Eleanor on the walk around Beechen Cliff that "invention is what delights me," Catherine has yet to recognize that invention can be a power which provides access to reality. That is why she only likes novels, why she doesn't like invention in history. Yet it is on these same grounds that Eleanor defends history. For history blends information "which may be as much depended on, I conclude, as any thing that does not actually pass under one's own observation" with all those "little embellishments." Historians, in short, "display imagination." *Northanger Abbey* is not a lesson in relinquishing the false world of the imagination for the true world of clear vision. It is a lesson in the imaginative nature of vision.

That her gothic speculations are actually a failure of imagination is shown by Catherine's fancies failing to come alive for her. When she sets off to investigate Mrs. Tilney's room, Catherine hopes to find proof of the poor victim's suffering, "in the shape of some fragmented journal, continued to the last gasp." This callous hope is not a grotesque proof of coldness of heart precisely because Catherine is not really imagining Mrs. Tilney's pain. We laugh and forgive. And even Catherine can't take her fancies completely seriously. In the midst of her worst suspicions, she is always polite to the general. Imagination is an awareness of one's own limits, an awareness which frees vision. It also includes the realization that there is something about others which is inaccessible. General Tilney as the murderous tyrant is entirely defined. But as the man whom Catherine "did believe, upon serious consideration, to be not perfectly amiable" he has possibilities for development, even for becoming a father-in-law.

Catherine does come to have some thoughts not befitting a heroine:

> Charming as were all Mrs. Radcliffe's works, . . . it was not in them perhaps that human nature, at least in the midland counties of England, was to be looked for. . . . Among the Alps and Pyrenees, perhaps, there were no mixed characters. There, such as were not as spotless as an angel might have the dispositions of a fiend. But in England it was not so; among the English, she believed, in their hearts and habits, there was a general though unequal mixture of good and bad. Upon this conviction, she would not be surprised if even in Henry and Eleanor Tilney, some slight imperfection might hereafter appear.

The idea that people are fallible, neither angels nor devils but somewhere in between, is the central premise of *Northanger Abbey*. It is Catherine's major lesson, the assumption on which human relations must be based and from which Austen constructs her theories about imagination and fiction. It means that there are no fixed formulas or conventions which Catherine can apply to her experience in order to understand it.

Catherine's attempt to understand is limited. She often makes mistakes. But Austen isn't interested in teaching her characters how to be right. Instead, she insists that they recognize and value the possibility of being wrong. The problem with heroines is that they are never wrong. And since by definition they are good, they are also complete and predictable. The only change possible for them is to decline and fall. That is why their most essential experience is to be threatened by seduction. It is also why some variation of attempted rape is such a common event in the plots of eighteenth-century novels. For a "true quality heroine," character change is character violation.

Austen transforms the notion of character, and thereby the notion of plot, by creating Catherine Morland. Experience is no longer a landscape heroines pass through, arriving at the finish either fallen or unscathed. Limits free characters for experiences undreamt of by either perfect or fallen heroines. In presenting Catherine, Austen connects moral imperfection to openness, to the possibility for change. For limits are also capacities. Because Catherine has "the common feelings of common life," she can be special, in the sense of being a particular person rather than a paradigm. And in her common and limited life Catherine needs imagination, which overleaps the borders of self.

Henry's lecture in the abbey hall is directed toward bringing Catherine back to a relationship of openness to the life she knows, because her education must come from experience: "Remember that we are English, that we are Christians. Consult your own understanding, your own sense of the probable, your own observation of what is passing around you." Catherine does learn to know herself and her situation. When she is about to leave Northanger Abbey, at the very moment she most feels the insult and humiliation of such a departure, Catherine looks beyond her own pride and promises to write Eleanor that she is safely home. To sympathize with Eleanor's feelings presages Emma's moral imagination in the proposal scene when she encourages Mr. Knightley to confide in her. Catherine can surmise Eleanor's emotions and respond appropriately because she believes in Eleanor's goodness of heart. Austen here creates what will recur in her fiction as a classic scene of generosity and self-control.

Right seeing, far from being a conclusion, is to be continually achieved. The proper use of imagination is continuous, a creative process of perception and judgment. This idea has affinities with what may be "the single morality of romanticism," the belief that "formulation itself must never be allowed to settle into dogma, but must emerge anew every day out of experience. It must be lived, which is to say that it must carry within it its subjective origin, its origin in experience and self-realization." Imagining goes on as long as a person can see and think and feel, because truth in *Northanger Abbey* is never complete.

"Little as Catherine was in the habit of judging for herself," she does come to see its necessity. Her involved imagination is charmingly demonstrated in those conjectures about Henry's reaction to her being turned out of his father's house. Her speculations do not require that Henry behave like the outraged hero in a novel: "To the General, of course, he would not dare to speak: but to Eleanor—what might he not say to Eleanor about her?" Austen gives Catherine the means to see beyond herself: "An imagination resolved on alarm" is supplanted by an imagination whose object is "the anxieties of common life." Catherine's sweetly mistaken guesses about Henry are an early version of Elizabeth Bennet's conjectures about Mr. Darcy's reaction to Lydia's elopement or to the persuasions of Lady Catherine de Bourgh. For Elizabeth, even more fully than for Catherine, the moment of self-revelation is followed not by accurate vision but by an actively engaged attempt to see accurately.

Catherine's recognition that there is more to other people than her experience of them means that she can no longer jump to conclusions. When General Tilney so rudely evicts her, Catherine searches in vain for a motive. It will turn out that the general's strange behavior is based on false information given by John Thorpe, a fact Catherine cannot know. Nor could we expect her to understand the general's behavior "by her own unassisted observation." The narrator herself stresses the inaccessibility of "all this" information by telling us that it was she who united the portions from various sources and that Henry was himself assisted by "his own conjectures." This plot device of the secret becomes a regular method for Austen, most centrally in *Sense and Sensibility*. It ensures that her characters must make judgments about others while faced with a necessarily elusive truth. After all, even Eleanor and Henry "had seen with astonishment" their father's approval of Catherine and had not "the smallest idea of the false calculations which had hurried him on." Early in the novel Austen had assured us that "strange things may be generally accounted for if their cause be fairly searched out." The search itself holds her interest and ours.

Near the end of the novel Mrs. Morland sums up the value of Catherine's forced journey home:

> It is always good for young people to be put upon exerting them-
> selves; and you know, my dear Catherine, you always were a sad
> little shatter-brained creature; but now you must have been forced
> to have your wits about you, with so much changing of chaises
> and so forth; and I hope it will appear that you have not left any
> thing behind you in any of the pockets.

Readers of romances will recognize that what Catherine has left behind her is her heart. Her plain-looking, plain-speaking mother of twelve speaks for good sense, and good sense is limited. Yet, in that charmingly literal way which looks forward to Mrs. Jennings, Mrs. Morland is right. Catherine has learned to exert herself. She has learned to have her wits about her. "Embedded in all Jane Austen's novels is a pedagogic story." And, like all Austen's novels, *Northanger Abbey* is a love story. To think about what Catherine has learned is also to think about Henry Tilney, the teacher of "a moral art."

Catherine had perceived her world according to simple conventions, described it in simple language. Henry helps her to free her vision from the strictures of preconceptions. When Catherine questions him about Captain Tilney's behavior with Isabella, Henry insists that she draw her own conclusions, think for herself. Against her plea that "I only ask what I want to be told," Henry offers indirection and evasiveness. He will not tell. As he says, "Nay, if it is to be guess-work, let us all guess for ourselves. To be guided by second-hand conjecture is pitiful. The premises are before you." If Henry draws Catherine's attention to the problems of understanding other people, he also offers her a means of resolution. Henry teaches Catherine to trust her own observations and sense of the probable. He teaches her to guess for herself.

But that isn't all. When we think about what Henry is doing in this novel and what he has to offer Catherine, we must look beyond those scenes in which he lectures her. Catherine is delighted by his cleverness, though she often finds him incomprehensible, and though she sometimes fears that "he indulged himself a little too much with the foibles of others." Henry's methods are too odd for a representative of reason. His conversation had "fluency and spirit—and there was an archness and pleasantry in his manner which interested, though it was hardly understood by her." Eleanor too remarks to Catherine that Henry has odd ways. He enraptures Mrs. Allen by knowing the bargain price of a true Indian muslin. He shocks Catherine by comparing dancing and marriage, and surprises her by liking to read gothic novels. And he initiates Catherine into the pleasures of not saying what one means. Henry's delight in words and their precise use and misuse is the most important way he communicates his sense of the variety and subtlety of the familiar world.

Henry attracts Catherine and the reader not because he is a mentor of good sense but because he is so interesting. Henry has an active imagination, freed from conventional structures, free to perceive and judge the world around him. He is not perfect, but he has learned how to use the powers of his mind and heart, and Catherine is understandably impressed. Thus when

Catherine drops her fancies for a clear vision of the world she finds it an exciting place. Her real feelings for her new friends have a depth and interest which her imaginings never approached. That, of course, is what Henry has known and offered all along. And appropriately, it is Henry who, in the finest spirit of romance, defies his father for the sake of true love. Good sense, for Austen, is always limited, because she insists on the charm as well as the right of facts to dominate fictions. Good sense without imagination means a plain speaking which may rise to the level of a pun. Good sense, in short, cannot account for Henry Tilney.

Trilling, in his famous brief reference to *Northanger Abbey,* suggests:

> We are quick, too quick, to understand that *Northanger Abbey* invites us into a snug conspiracy to disabuse the little heroine of the errors of her corrupted fancy—Catherine Morland, having become addicted to novels of terror, has accepted their inadmissible premise, she believes that life is violent and unpredictable. And that is exactly what life is shown to be by the events of the story: it is we who must be disabused of our belief that life is sane and orderly.

This remark, in its alluring vividness, rightly reminds us that the pattern of the plot is not a move from disorder to order but to an enlarged vision which can acknowledge the disorder of life. But, of course, there is a certain legerdemain here, in the identification of the "inadmissible premise" of novels of terror with the premise of Austen's novel. Her point is precisely that life is not like novels of terror, not because life is orderly but because novels of terror are. They are conventional and formulaic even (and particularly) in their horrors. And it is because life is not, because it cannot be understood or lived according to a set of conventional emotions or, on the other hand, according to the plain good sense of Mrs. Morland, that Catherine needs her imagination. Life is various and strange. And Henry, with his wit, elegance, nonsense, sympathy, and passion, is the most strange of all.

How much does Henry speak for his author? Is he a reliable or an unreliable authority? These questions, traditionally asked of Henry, mistake his function. Henry must be understood not just according to his lectures, not by simply measuring the rightness or wrongness of his remarks, but by his very presence in the novel. We gain nothing by deciding at what point Henry and his author part company. They were always separate. Differences between author and characters do not mean that we are to be continually judging—approving or condemning. Austen has a more concrete moral sense than that. And she offers better relations between author and character or reader and character than that. Henry is not to be abstracted from his context, any more than Mrs. Jennings or Admiral and Mrs. Croft or any of Austen's beautifully particular creations are to be abstracted from theirs. That is not the kind of lesson she teaches. This young man, introduced quite properly by the master of the ceremonies and proved upon Mr. Allen's inquiry to be "not objectionable as a common acquaintance for his young charge," is, like Jane Fairfax in *Emma,* a promise of the delights to be discovered in common life. It is through Henry's many-faceted charms more than through his father's violence that Austen makes her claim to Catherine and the reader for the value of life over fiction. Henry is more than a guide or a reward. He is proof that real people are more interesting than characters in books, and that people, when they are in books, may have something of the complexity and elusiveness that shapes them in reality.

The story of Henry and Catherine ends, like that of Emma and Mr. Knightley, in "perfect happiness." And, like Emma and Mr. Knightley, Henry and Catherine are far from the ideally matched lovers of conventional romance. We easily see why Catherine would fall in love with Henry. He is witty and charming, intelligent and kind, and "then his hat sat so well, and the innumerable capes of his great coat looked so becomingly important!" But it may be less easy to see why Henry would fall in love with Catherine. The author herself accents the imperfectness of the match near the end of the story when she confesses that Henry's "affection originated in nothing better than gratitude, or, in other words, that a persuasion of her partiality for him had been the only cause of giving her a serious thought." Gratitude as the beginning of love is a continual theme in Austen's fiction, perhaps most appealingly portrayed in Elizabeth's growing affection for Mr. Darcy. Obviously connected to self-love, it is also an emotion which by its very nature acknowledges obligation and commitment. Gratitude is why Henry gives Catherine "a serious thought." But why would he go on thinking about her? What does he love about her? Henry, like his author, "admires goodness more than cleverness," but Henry does more than convey Austen's approval of goodness. Austen tells us that Catherine, by finding Henry irresistible, became so herself and that he "felt and delighted in all the excellencies of her character and truly loved her society." Henry's affection for Catherine connects teaching that seventeen-year-old and learning to love her. Austen will go on to explore the vanity of such a relation, in Emma's taking up Harriet Smith. But in *Northanger Abbey,* responding to sentimental and gothic conventions, she is concerned with pedagogy primarily in terms of its possibilities in relation to her idea of character.

At the end of *Pride and Prejudice* Elizabeth remarks to herself about

Mr. Darcy that he had not yet learned to be laughed at. The wonder is not that Mr. Darcy could learn to be laughed at but that such an education would not already have occurred. How could Mr. Darcy have spent time with Elizabeth and delighted in her company and grown to love her and have avoided such a lesson? The answer, I think, is the resiliency of character. It is less surprising in Fitzwilliam Darcy than it is in someone with so teachable a disposition as Catherine Morland. But the proud and reserved Mr. Darcy is similar to that ignorant and uninformed seventeen-year-old in ways which help us to understand Catherine and *Northanger Abbey*. Both fall in love with characters of wit, of impertinence, of playfulness of mind, which both find alien to their own styles. The Morlands are plain speaking, the Darcys formal and serious. And both characters learn, Catherine pliantly and Darcy reluctantly, to admire and to love that wit, for it teaches them that the world is stranger and more interesting than they had seen on their own. But to admire and to love, to learn and to see the world differently, is not to become witty themselves. And it is surely part of our assurance of their happy futures together that Darcy will often find Elizabeth's laughter a surprise and Catherine will find Henry's verbal games a mystery.

The teachableness which Austen finds so amusing in her young heroine is amusing in part because it is also of limited value. It is, in fact, a significant virtue that Catherine cannot learn before she is taught, "and sometimes not even then." Catherine has had more than one teacher who tried to shape her opinions, to give a little art to her naturalness. The Thorpes tried manipulation, Henry and Eleanor encouraged her to attend to herself. When Henry offers Catherine explicit rules for understanding what she sees, the result can only be the comic moment on top of Beechen Cliff. Neither good art nor good understanding come from prescribed structures. We laugh when Catherine rejects all of Bath as unworthy to form a landscape because she has absorbed her lesson so well as actually to have learned nothing at all. In this instance her teachableness is comically superficial and thus a guarantee of her not losing herself.

The walk Henry and Eleanor and Catherine take around Beechen Cliff is the scene in which Austen discusses explicitly the subject of pedagogy—specifically as a relation between lovers but more generally as a common pattern of human relations. What is at issue are the differences between learning as growth or as loss of self, and between teaching as generosity or as manipulation. In this scene Austen defines the limits of pedagogy by reminding us that human relations must be more than forms of education. The scene focuses on false forms of education between Henry and Catherine but, most importantly, between their real feelings and the sentimental pattern of a love relation in which the female is educated in "the norms of the mature, rational" male world.

The subject of the walk is instruction. Henry, in his niceness about language, questions Catherine on what he believes is her misuse of words and she replies that, in fact, she meant exactly what she said, to instruct can mean to torment. Catherine's engaging directness as she describes what she was "in the habit of seeing almost every day of my life at home," how her siblings learn to spell and "how stupid they can be for a whole morning together," is delightfully persuasive. Learning may never have been a torment to Henry, but no reader can doubt that Catherine speaks from the truth of her experience. And the narrator, introducing the subject of taste in drawing, and Catherine's ignorance once again, turns specifically to the literary convention of female ignorance. Observing that "the advantages of natural folly in a beautiful girl have been already set forth by the capital pen of a sister author," the author adds about men "that though to the larger and more trifling part of the sex, imbecility in females is a great enhancement of their personal charms, there is a portion of them too reasonable and too well informed themselves to desire anything more in a woman than ignorance." Austen's focus here is not on her characters but on a convention too simple to represent either character or relations between characters. As Catherine has just demonstrated to Henry, the ignorant have their truths that the clever need to learn.

When Henry later in the conversation explains to Eleanor and Catherine that what Catherine meant by the shocking thing coming out of London was a new novel, he also invokes the conventional belief in women's lesser abilities and, by implication, their need to be taught. Continuing the ironic tone established by the author, Henry laughs at the notions of male clarity and rationality, assuring Catherine that "no one can think more highly of the understanding of women than I do. In my opinion, nature has given them so much, that they never find it necessary to use more than half." Catherine, the literalist, fears Henry has been speaking seriously. If the reader has any doubt, we need only recall that Austen has Henry's wit include Eleanor, who is neither ignorant nor uninformed. And it is Eleanor who stresses the true object of Henry's satire, those literary clichés, by assuring us as well as Catherine that "he must be entirely misunderstood, if he can ever appear to say an unjust thing of any woman at all, or an unkind one to me."

By the end of the walk around Beechen Cliff Austen has made clear that if Catherine is eminently teachable and Henry a good teacher, if she is ignorant and he is clever, it does not follow that Catherine's education will consist of learning to see from Henry's point of view or, indeed, that there is anything inevitably superior in his point of view. When, as in the case of her sibling's education being a torment, Catherine consults her own observation and understanding, she does quite well. When she blindly adopts a set of conventions on what is picturesque, she is absurd. Catherine, learning from Henry, does not reflect his opinions. She learns to develop her own. Nor is what he teaches her rational and male and what she grows out of irrational and female. One cannot distribute values by gender. Eleanor Tilney too is wise in ways that Catherine is not. But her friendship, unlike Isabella's, does not require imitation or identity of opinion. Neither Henry nor Eleanor are to be understood as models. We would not want Catherine to lose those particular qualities for which we like her in this business of being educated, any more than we would want Emma to forswear her self-love.

What pedagogic and romantic conventions typically share is the assumption that education is a discovery of identity. And to assume an identity of taste and opinion, either innate or taught, is to limit the idea of character, to reduce the possibilities of life. Isabella Thorpe, reporting to Catherine a conversation with Catherine's brother James, tells her that "really, our opinions were so exactly the same, it was quite ridiculous! There was not a single point in which we differed; I would not have had you by for the world; you are such a sly thing, I am sure you would have made some droll remark or other about it." When Catherine, always a disappointment in these conversations, does not respond to this hint as she ought, Isabella must play Catherine's part as well and insists that "I know you better than you know yourself. You would have told us that we seemed born for each other." Isabella is a hypocrite, but Austen is also attacking the convention itself.

The subject of ideal lovers is of continuing interest to her. It reappears in *Sense and Sensibility,* with Marianne Dashwood as a sincere version of Isabella. Marianne, who accepts as truth the fiction that lovers are born for each other and can never disagree, imposes her fixed opinions on Willoughby. And Marianne is deceived—as much by her commitment to the conventions as by Willoughby. In *Pride and Prejudice* Mr. Collins assures Elizabeth Bennet that "My dear Charlotte and I have but one mind and one way of thinking. There is in every thing a most remarkable resemblance of character and ideas between us. We seem to have been designed for each other." Here hypocrisy has become indistinguishable from sincerity and we shudder for the ways in which Mr. Collins's claim is becoming true. In *Emma* Austen offers a grotesque and compressed comment on lovers' accord, in Mr. Elton's incessant "Exactly so!" And of course Lady Russell tempts Anne Elliot with the symmetry of a marriage to Mr. Elliot.

Austen's lovers usually don't seem made for one another. Emma will tell Frank Churchill that "there is a likeness in our destiny; the destiny which bids fair to connect us with two characters so much superior to our own." And when Frank gallantly responds he speaks not of Jane's character but of her looks: "Is not she an angel in every gesture? Observe the turn of her throat. Observe her eyes, as she is looking up at my father.—You will be glad to hear (inclining his head, and whispering seriously) that my uncle means to give her all my aunt's jewels. They are to be new set. I am resolved to have some in an ornament for the head. Will it not be beautiful in her dark hair?" This is appreciation, but is it the kind we would have wished for Jane Fairfax? Does it do justice to her real superiority to speak of her dark hair and the turn of her throat? Yet it seems that their union is happy. And if the reader feels that Jane Fairfax is too good for Frank, we must remember that our knowledge of these two is notably brief and that in life people constantly fall in love and marry for reasons that are incomprehensible to those around them. That is what makes love interesting and matchmaking dull. If Jane and Frank's appropriateness for each other is obscure, their prospect of happiness is not.

Lovers in the midland counties are not required to be perfectly matched, in their characters or their opinions. It would be unjust to Henry Tilney and to his joy in Catherine's eager affection to base the progress of his affection for her on her ability to be improved by him. Austen does not offer a full reason for Henry's loving Catherine. In this book feelings are "rather natural than heroic," and we may simply conclude, with the Morlands, that "nothing, after all, could be more natural than Catherine's being beloved." Her charms, however much Henry taught her, are all her own. Education is not mimetic. It is an expression of self. If *Emma* helps us to see that what Catherine needs is imagination, Catherine's education helps prepare us for the powerful view of self-love Austen creates in *Emma*.

What can be taught, by Tilneys and by novelists, is a new integrity of character. In *Northanger Abbey* necessary change is not diminution, and being actively responsive to the power of others is not imitation. "Perfect happiness" does not require that kind of union. How people influence each other is of continuing interest to Austen. It reappears in Mr. Bingley's relation to Mr. Darcy as well as Harriet Smith's relation to Emma. We see it in the pressure exerted upon Fanny Price by the people who surround her. And it becomes the major subject of Austen's last, and perhaps most beautiful, completed novel, *Persuasion*.

The relations between Henry and Catherine are imaged early in their story, on that Thursday evening in Bath at the cotillion ball. Austen remarks in *Emma* that "It may be possible to do without dancing entirely," and the delightful implication is that the people in her novels cannot. Fanny Price must open her ball, Anne Elliot plays while others dance. "There is good dancing everywhere that men and women have mastered the arts of time and space, to move with meaning." One of the most memorable of Austen's scenes is that conversation at the cotillion ball when Henry compares marriage to a country dance. His analogic imagination in this scene is counterpointed by Catherine's inability to see the comparison. If he seems clever and she seems dull we must remember Eleanor's advice not to take Henry too seriously. Henry, after all, is flirting with Catherine, and the point of his far-fetched analogy is to lure her to a declaration that it is he she wants to be dancing with. And Henry at last succeeds, to their mutual delight. The conversation is wonderful as much for Catherine's resisting literalness as for Henry's metaphor. We misunderstand the scene unless we recognize that neither position is less valued, that both are necessary expressions of character. Insofar as a country dance can ever be an emblem of marriage these two will continue to dance together, each separate, and each pleasing the other with the difference.

GARY KELLY

Reading Aloud in Mansfield Park

It is remarkable how much discussion of reading and books there is in Jane Austen's novels. A character's interest in reading books and ability to discriminate among them are used by Austen as an index of that character's general powers of discrimination, from *Northanger Abbey* through to *Sanditon*. Reading, then, is used by Austen as a paradigm for the process of perception and judgment; it may also be instrumental in the plot of the novel. In *Northanger Abbey* and *Sense and Sensibility,* novels still closely bound to literary parody, Catherine Morland and Marianne Dashwood make embarrassing mistakes in judgment and action because they have read the wrong books, or read them too uncritically. In *Pride and Prejudice,* however, the kind of reading emphasized is not so much reading of books as reading of letters, especially in the first half of the novel. In fact, the turning point of the novel is the point when Elizabeth, after reading Darcy's letter, realizes how wrong she has been in "reading" him, herself, Wickham, and her family. As she says. "Till this moment, I never knew myself." It is in this sense— reading as a general process of perception and judgment—that *Pride and Prejudice* is a novel of education, education in the art of reading; for as Austen shows over and over in her novels, education is not the acquisition of information nor a matter of native talent but the cultivation of the mind, and reading books, like reading people and situations, like conversation and manners, is something one must cultivate and improve, in oneself and others,

From *Nineteenth-Century Fiction* 37, no. 1 (June 1982). © 1982 by the Regents of the University of California.

whatever one's natural "temper" may be. But in all her novels Austen also tests the novel-reader, in various ways, in order to recognize the way she herself is renovating the conventions of the novel; and thus the reader of the novel too is cultivated, is improved as a reader by the act of reading and re-reading one of Austen's novels.

Austen tests the reader, too, in order to recognize the diversity and the discriminations through her oeuvre as a whole. Characteristically, for example, she reversed the grounds of her central character and went from an improvable reader as her heroine in *Pride and Prejudice* to a character already thoroughly cultivated as a reader for her central character in *Mansfield Park*. Thus there is no dramatic moment of self-recognition for Fanny Price as there is for Elizabeth Bennet. Fanny is a good reader because, unlike her cousins Julia and Maria Bertram, her education is not neglected, nor made a matter of merely social attainments, but is in the special care of her cousin Edmund, a younger son of a landed gentleman and thereby destined for a career as a public reader, that is, a preacher. Their relationship begins, interestingly enough, with Edmund helping her write a letter to her beloved brother William. Such a beginning bids fair to the reader aware of how significant the writing and reading of letters is in all Austen's novels; yet Fanny is considered "stupid" by the rest of the family, especially since she shows no desire to learn the more showy, public "accomplishments" of either music or drawing but prefers to stick to the silent and private act of reading. Edmund, however, "reads" her right:

> He knew her to be clever, to have a quick apprehension as well as good sense, and a fondness for reading, which, properly directed, must be an education in itself. . . . he recommended the books which charmed her leisure hours, he encouraged her taste, and corrected her judgment; he made reading useful by talking to her of what she read, and heightened its attraction by judicious praise. In return for such services she loved him better than any body in the world except William.

Love begins with reading, with reading together, with literature ("the books which charmed her leisure hours, . . . encouraged her taste, . . . corrected her judgment"). And so, having taught her to read, "having formed her mind and [thus] gained her affections, he had a good chance of her thinking like him." This kind of relationship is of course a commonplace in late eighteenth-century sentimental novels. Unfortunately, and ironically, the rest of the novels shows us that Fanny does not always think like Edmund in that more important extension of reading books, namely "reading" people: he "misreads" Mary Crawford, and almost thinks he loves her; he "misreads" Fanny, and does not realize that she loves him as a lover, not a brother or cousin, until finally Mary Crawford's very charm, her easy wit and facile conversability give her away, and Edmund exclaims near the end of the novel, somewhat as Elizabeth Bennet had exclaimed in the middle of *Pride and Prejudice*, "the charm is broken. My eyes are opened." Able to see at last what Fanny had seen all along, Edmund in time learns to see more, to see what was in front of his eyes all along. Time performs its healing once again.

Mansfield Park is a novel of education, then, one might say of the romance of education, a sub*genre* in the literature of Sensibility. But having allowed her heroine true judgment almost from the outset, Austen strips her of power, almost of physical power to act. Thus Fanny is in yet another way the conventional Sentimental heroine, always acted upon, never acting for herself. Yet the convention is inverted, because in this novel Fanny's true judgment and the simplicity (another Sentimental value) of her principles confer on her a power Sentimental heroines lack, and to make this clear Austen deprives her heroine of any power or significance in her own social world. Unlike Elizabeth Bennet (*quite* unlike—for that is how Austen likes to move from one novel to the next), Fanny is sickly, and silent; and so she is surrounded by those who have too much to say, or who say it far too well. Fanny's particular anguish is to have true judgment (the appropriate analogue in Austen's novels to a cultivated competence as a reader) but to be unable to act on or even utter it. Furthermore, when she does speak, Fanny seems strangely restrained and "stilted," or "unnaturally" exclamatory in her utterance. Fanny's stilted or exclamatory speech, however, stands in the novel as the appropriate stylistic counter to the facile and witty conversational style of Mary Crawford. In all this, then, as shown by the critical controversy over whether Mary or Fanny is more "likeable," the reader of the novel is challenged to read Fanny, and thus the novel, properly (i.e., with a sense of the appropriate relativities); but Austen guides the reader, if the reader is alert enough to be guided, by her management of a set of related themes in the novel, namely eloquence, reading aloud, and the profession (in at least two senses) of the clergy.

The issue of choice of profession is the first major issue to be raised in the novel, as a crucial element in the secondary plot of the courtship of Edmund and Mary Crawford. In a characteristic effect of technical "placing," Austen enriches the dramatic quality of the debate by having it take place during the first major social "occasion" of the novel, namely the visit to Sotherton, and in the "wilderness" outside of the abandoned and neglected chapel at Sotherton house. The visit to Sotherton is of course important, as

several critics have pointed out, because of the many cross-currents of coquetry, flirtation, and courtship to be observed (and in particular observed
by Fanny) there. It is also the first of those several occasions in the novel
when Fanny is silently present at a dialogue between Edmund and another,
the other in this case being Fanny's "worldly" rival Mary Crawford. Mary
here, like her brother much later in the novel, seems to find the clergy on
the whole to be an uninteresting profession. She raises the subject first,
revealing her conventional notions as to the choice of profession:

> "So you are to be a clergyman, Mr. Bertram. This is rather a
> surprise to me."
> "Why should it surprise you? You must suppose me designed
> for some profession, and might perceive that I am neither a law-
> yer, nor a soldier, nor a sailor."
> "Very true; but, in short, it had not occurred to me. And you
> know there is generally an uncle or a grandfather to leave a for-
> tune to the second son."
> "A very praiseworthy practice," said Edmund, "but not quite
> universal. I am one of the exceptions, and *being* one, must do
> something for myself."
> "But why are you to be a clergyman? I thought *that* was always
> the lot of the youngest, where there were many to choose before
> him."

Mary's ideas as to what becomes of the younger sons of a landed gentleman
are utterly conventional, and so she is repeatedly surprised in this short
passage of dialogue. She had always considered choice of profession only as
a matter of sheer economic necessity and personal convenience, that is, of
sheer personal interest. Edmund, however, does not regard the matter from
the point of view of mere individualism (for the Crawfords are indeed extreme individualists, as their words and actions throughout the novel show).
Rather, Edmund has a sense of what a profession is as a social institution
and what is owing from the individual to that institution. And so he asks
Mary Crawford, naming the institution rather than, as she has been doing,
the profession which serves it, "Do you think the church itself never chosen
then?" Her reply shows that for her, yet again, the only consideration is self-
interest: "what is to be done in the church? Men love to distinguish themselves, and in either of the other lines [law or the military], distinction may
be gained, but not in the church. A clergyman is nothing." Edmund's response indicates his social rather than individualistic concept of the profession:

"A clergyman cannot be high in state or fashion. He must not head mobs, or set the ton in dress. But I cannot call that situation nothing, which has the charge of all that is of the first importance to mankind, individually or collectively considered, temporally and eternally—which has the guardianship of religion and morals, and consequently of the manners which result from their influence. No one here can call the *office* nothing. If the man who holds it is so, it is by the neglect of his duty, by foregoing its just importance, and stepping out of his place to appear what he ought not to appear."

As so often in Austen's novels, a great deal of eighteenth-century intellectual and ideological debate is concentrated here. Mary Crawford's emphasis on love of distinction was a commonplace of that kind of worldly wise rationalism considered, by more cautious late eighteenth-century British commentators, to be characteristic of French materialists and free thinkers and their British imitators. Where that kind of thing might lead, any well-informed reader of *Mansfield Park* in 1814, looking back over the previous quarter century, would be all too aware. Similarly, any well-informed reader of Edmund Bertram's defense of the church as an important moral and therefore an important social institution could be forgiven for sensing an echo of the greatest British attacker of individualism and defender of traditional social institutions, that other Edmund, one of the greatest public speakers of the age, Edmund Burke. The association of the two Edmunds is brought very close to the reader's notice midway through the novel when Mary and Fanny discuss young Bertram's Christian name. Mary dislikes it, finding it "so younger-brother like"; Fanny disagrees:

"How differently we feel!" cried Fanny [in one of the many exclamations she allows herself]. "To me, the sound of *Mr.* Bertram [the usual address for the older brother, the one to inherit the estate] is so cold and nothing-meaning—so entirely without warmth or character!—It just stands for a gentleman, and that's all. But there is nobleness in the name of Edmund. It is a name of heroism and renown—of kings, princes, and knights; and seems to breathe the spirit of chivalry and warm affections."

The best-known breather of "the spirit of chivalry and warm affections" in Austen's day was of course Edmund Burke. Even Edmund Bertram's recognition that the office is important and to be reverenced, if the officeholder is not (a point he makes forcibly in the next chapter when Mary points to

her own brother-in-law, Dr. Grant, as an example of the unclerical clergyman), is quite of a piece with the social thought and institutional concern of
Edmund Burke. So too is Bertram's placing of the clergyman between the
world of "state" and "fashion" on one hand and "the mob" on the other,
for these social polarities were just those posited by Burke, just those between
which the true "gentleman" should situate himself; they were also those
unnaturally associated together, according to Burke, in the unnatural project
of the French Revolution and in the activities of that Revolution's aristocratic
and vulgar British sympathizers. Burke's sociology is plausible content then,
to be read into Edmund Bertram's earnest defense of the church against the
polished and witty, fashionable cynicism of Mary Crawford; and can it be
insignificant that Mary, like her brother Henry later in the novel, sees the
profession of clergyman as that of mere sermonizer, of mere public speaker
of a special kind? How important the profession of public speaking could
be in the moral, social ("manners"), and institutional life of the nation
Burke's own career had exhibited.

Thus Mary Crawford's reply to this little sermon of Edmund's is quite
to the point, while missing its significance altogether.

> "*You* assign greater consequence to the clergyman than one has
> been used to hear given, or than I can quite comprehend. . . .
> How can two sermons a week, even supposing them worth hear-
> ing, supposing the preacher to have the sense to prefer Blair's to
> his own, do all that you speak of? govern the conduct and fashion
> the manners of a large congregation for the rest of the week?
> One scarcely sees a clergyman out of his pulpit."

For Mary Crawford the clergyman is of little "importance" or "consequence"; she thus unwittingly links Edmund with Fanny, that other person
of no "importance" or "consequence" to vulgar opinions. Furthermore, for
Mary Crawford a clergyman is a mere public reader who may at least have
enough "sense" to read aloud someone else's texts besides his own of a
Sunday. She cannot conceive of a clergyman outside of his pulpit, as a member, a leading member of society, a social individual giving social leadership.
Her conception of the clergyman is limited, as Edmund is quick to realize,
and to suggest, as he tells her, "*You* are speaking of London" (precisely
where Henry Crawford would have to shine if he were to become a clergyman, as he tells Edmund later), "*I* am speaking of the nation at large." It is
the clergyman as national leader that Edmund has in mind, then, a larger
conception altogether than Mary's, as her next remark indicates: "The me-

tropolis, I imagine, is a pretty fair sample of the rest." Edmund's reply indicates clearly that in fact he excludes the "metropolis" from the "nation":

> "We do not look in great cities for our best morality. . . . A fine preacher is followed and admired; but it is not in fine preaching only that a good clergyman will be useful in his parish and his neighbourhood, where the parish and neighbourhood are of a size capable of knowing his private character, and observing his general conduct, which in London can rarely be the case. The clergy are lost there in the crowds of their parishioners. They are known to the largest part only as preachers."

Here Edmund gently agrees with Mary Crawford and anticipates her brother's protest that *he* could only ever be a preacher in London, thus indicating the limited, merely metropolitan knowledge the Crawfords have of the nature and social function of the clergy.

> "And with regard to their influencing public manners [Edmund continues], Miss Crawford must not misunderstand me, or suppose I mean to call them the arbiters of good breeding, the regulators of refinement and courtesy, the masters of the ceremonies of life. The *manners* I speak of, might rather be called *conduct,* perhaps, the result of good principles; the effect, in short, of those doctrines which it is their duty to teach and recommend; and it will, I believe, be every where found, that as the clergy are, or are not what they ought to be, so are the rest of the nation."
>
> "Certainly," said Fanny with gentle earnestness.

There is no clearer statement in Austen's fiction, I think, of the relationship of "principles" and "conduct," of the *ideal* social function of the professions along with a recognition of the frequent actual failure of mortals to live up to those ideals, and of the inseparability of the moral and social institutions of the community. Mary Crawford, like her brother later in the novel, can only see the Church as a field of play for the individual and the individualist; she cannot see it as the two Edmunds see it, as an institution inherited by the individual and to be inhabited and brought to life by him, like Edmund Bertram's rectory at the "family" living of Thornton Lacey, the rectory Sir Thomas Bertram refuses to see unoccupied by an absentee vicar, the rectory Mary romances over, the rectory Henry Crawford imagines himself "improving" (volume II, chapter 7, during the game of "Speculation," the very center point of the novel). More particularly, we should note here the way that Edmund's "sermon" (as Mary will call a similar utterance of his later

in the novel) places her witty metropolitan worldly wisdom as in fact a kind
of provincialism, thus undermining her values for the reader for the rest of
the novel, while anticipating perfectly Henry Crawford's discourse on fashionable metropolitan preaching (volume III, chapter 3, discussed below). Of
course it is perfectly appropriate too that the silent listener, Fanny, should
be the one to speak first in agreement with Edmund (just as in the next
chapter it is Fanny who defends the ideal and the practice of the profession,
in her longest utterance up to this point in the novel); and could the reader
do anything but agree with Edmund too, after reading this perfect demonstration not only of his fitness to be the kind of preacher he images in his
"sermon" here, but of his ability to write and deliver his own sermons and
not those plagiarized, as Mary suggests, from a volume of sermons by someone such as Blair?

In fact, even Mary Crawford's reference to Blair would reveal, to the
informed reader, the depth of ignorance that lies beneath her shallow wit-
tiness here and her brother's too easy eloquence later, for Blair was much
better known in the late eighteenth century as the popularizer of the ethical
school of rhetoric of Cicero, Quintilian, and Adam Smith than as the author
of sermons. Two quotations from Blair's *Lectures on Rhetoric and Belles
Lettres* will make clear how close Edmund's idea of the public speaker is to
the ethical tradition and how far the idea of the Crawfords' is from it, how
close Edmund's own practice to and how far Henry Crawford's from the
ideal public speaker described by Blair—how close, in fact, Crawford is to
Blair's, Quintilian's, and Tacitus's description of the "mere declaimer." "It
is the business of the philosopher," Blair writes, "to convince me of truth;
it is the business of the orator to persuade me to act agreeably to it, by
engaging my affections on its side." That is, public speaking is superior to
philosophy because it is concerned with action, with the relationship between
moral truth and moral conduct. So much the more for preaching, especially
since, according to Blair, one must oneself believe what one would convince
others of. Nowhere is the connection between belief and persuasion, reason
and feeling, more crucial than in preaching:

> The end of all preaching is, to persuade men to become good.
> Every Sermon therefore should be a persuasive Oration. Not but
> that the Preacher is to instruct and to teach, to reason and argue.
> All persuasion . . . is to be founded on conviction. The under-
> standing must always be applied to in the first place, in order to
> make a lasting impression on the heart: and he who would work
> on men's passions, or influence their practice, without first giving

them just principles, and enlightening their minds, is no better than a mere declaimer.

This last is precisely what the Crawfords would do; and so they are mere declaimers, as Mary's words here and Henry's actions later in the novel show. That the Crawfords should so disastrously lack a real understanding of the nature of sermons and preaching is the revelation, then, to both Fanny and Edmund, of their mental and moral deficiencies, their dangerous ability to perform a text without understanding it, or holding it as a matter of conviction. They are good readers both, but in a very limited sense, for by the standards of rhetoric of the day, standards Austen could count on the properly educated reader knowing about, they are bad readers, because they are not concerned with belief, only with applause or admiration. That is why the novel makes so much, in its crucial scenes, of public speaking. That is why the Crawfords are consistently witty, and socially attractive, and why Edmund and Fanny are consistently silent, or earnestly candid when they do speak. That is why the reader of the novel is challenged to see the proper relation between them.

That Henry and Mary are declaimers of skill is shown clearly enough in the episode of the theatricals, the other major social occasion of volume I. The episode has been treated in detail by many critics, and it is only necessary to point out here that the issue involved in the acting of Elizabeth Inchbald's *Lovers' Vows* is a moral and ethical one, a matter of serious social consequence: by reading aloud something written and published by someone else, people may say to one another, and in public, what social convention would not permit them to say in ordinary circumstances unless they were willing to abide by the consequences of their speaking. To make speeches of love to another person in private, let alone in public, was a marrying matter. To speak one's love was to undertake to accept the ethical consequences of such verbal action; to do otherwise, to speak love while not intending to accept the consequences, or to speak love that was not felt, was coquetry or mere seduction and did lead, often, to social banishment. There are among the young people at the Park those who wish to speak love without consequence and those who wish to speak love not felt; but all except Edmund and Fanny are united in wishing for the precedent text, the pretext which will enable them to do so, and this desire is seen very clearly in the maneuvers and disputes in casting the parts (volume I, chapters 14 and 15). Of course the subject matter of the play, sexual seduction and "liberal" social views, is relevant too, but it is the enacting of the play's love texts without any consequence, or without responsibility for any consequence, that is improper, and inappropriate. Acting, as distinct from reading aloud the love texts, is in fact far less important to the actors (except perhaps Mr. Yates); it is what is in the lines of the play as subject matter that agitates the young people at the Park, including Edmund and Fanny. Furthermore, a deliberate blurring of the line between life and text is not only being allowed but actually sought after, to the extent that several of the actors confess difficulty or embarrassment in delivering certain lines of dialogue to certain other persons in the play.

With such embarrassment, of course, the nature of the social action being undertaken here is clearly revealed: conventionally, embarrassment is the breakdown of the social surface of personality under the pressure of emotion from within, a surging of the self through the surface of social convention—that is why embarrassment was so prized by writers of the culture of Sensibility. Thus Mary Crawford approaches Fanny to play Edmund's part in private rehearsal so that Mary can "harden" herself against the public trial (just before Edmund approaches Fanny for the same service), and Mary exclaims, "I did not think much of it [the embarrassing speech] at first—but, upon my word—. There, look at *that* speech, and *that*, and *that*. How am I ever to look him in the face and say such things?" That Mary should have thought so little of "it" at her first reading of the play contrasts nicely of course with Fanny's immediate fullness of understanding of the play's appropriateness for the players and therefore its inappropriateness to be performed by them, on her first reading. The important point, however, is that Mary does recognize the text as a pretext for her to say what she means to Edmund; her fear of embarrassment is also a recognition that she will be understood; but she will go ahead in spite of these recognitions, and she should not, if she is to be taken seriously as a woman to be taken "upon her word" (the utter conventionalities of conversation often have special meaning in Austen). Fanny sees that; the reader should see it too, even though Austen does make it easy to side with Mary, Mrs. Norris, and all the rest who see, or pretend to see, the theatricals as mere amusement and diversion. For after Mary's confession that she knows she is doing what should (even for her) cause embarrassment, that she must "harden" herself, how can any careful reader think she is right to go ahead? Yet there has been such acceptance by critics, or the protest that for Fanny and Edmund such things are made too great a matter. This may be so; but the novel itself shows how great matters can grow from small ones and how living an honorable and moral life is a question of attention to small matters, not just carrying off the great ones.

Fanny of course is a person who, often to her distress, cannot feign, and here she protests, when pressed as the last holdout to join the play, "I could not act any thing if you were to give me the world. No, indeed, I cannot act." There is of course a wealth of ambiguity in her protest, because Fanny's statement may be taken literally in reference to dramatic acting, or as a confession of physical incapacity resulting from moral disapproval (a consistency of principle and action), or yet again as a reference to Fanny's peculiar passivity and retiredness throughout the novel; that is, the literal level of her statement refers to those hearers too shallow and too obsessed with their immediate selfish gratification in getting her assistance in the theatricals, the secondary level of meaning is clearly addressed (at least for the novel-reader) to Edmund, who has allowed principle to be vitiated by circumstance and desire into the inconsistent action of acting, and the third level of significance can properly be considered by the novel-reader (and the narrator) as a kind of dramatic irony arising out of our recognition that Fanny's passivity and backwardness can indeed be preservatives against un-principled acting. Furthermore, Fanny's refusal to act here gains added res-onance for the reader as the novel's plot progresses, for when Fanny does take action in the novel, it is again refusal to act; most important, in volume III, it is a refusal to marry Henry Crawford, and marriage, as we know from J. L. Austin, is a very important form or ceremony of public utterance, one which, performed in the proper circumstances, changes one's condition in life. The fact that Fanny has so little to say, and the fact that, thanks to the narrator, we know she does feel much, means that for us it is always clear that Fanny means what she says; thus by contrast we become aware of how little meaning there is in what is said by others. Fanny's refusal to act, then, is usually dramatized in the novel as a refusal or reluctance to speak.

Henry Crawford is of course the finest talker in the novel, the finest actor, and the finest reader, that is, the one best at reading aloud from a text; and it is precisely this last ability which fascinates Fanny in spite of herself. So it is the more dramatic and demonstrative a reversal when Craw-ford, in running off with Maria Bertram Rushworth, shows how little his fine talk means, just as, on a lesser scale, it is Mary Crawford's fine talk which engages Edmund, and which gives her (the "real" her, the morally shallow her) away to him in the end. Crawford's abilities as fine talker and fine reader are seen in the episode of the theatricals in volume I, but even more so in volume III, after he has become Fanny's suitor. Knowing his power, and reading well aloud is a power, as Edmund's defense of the clergy has made clear, Crawford is quick to seize an opportunity when he and Edmund come upon Fanny and Lady Bertram in the drawing room. Fanny had been reading to her aunt from Shakespeare, but fell silent on hearing someone approach:

> Crawford took the volume. "Let me have the pleasure of finishing that speech to your ladyship," said he. "I shall find it immediately." And by carefully giving way to the inclination of the leaves, he did find it, or within a page or two, quite near enough to satisfy Lady Bertram, who assured him, as soon as he mentioned the name of Cardinal Wolsey, that he had got the very speech.— Not a look, or an offer of help had Fanny given; not a syllable for or against. All her attention was for her work. She seemed determined to be interested by nothing else. But taste was too strong in her. She could not abstract her mind five minutes; she was forced to listen; his reading was capital, and her pleasure in good reading extreme. To *good* reading, however, she had been long used; her uncle read well—her cousins all—Edmund very well; but in Mr. Crawford's reading there was a variety of excellence beyond what she had ever met with. . . . It was truly dramatic.—His acting had first taught Fanny what pleasure a play might give, and his reading brought all his acting before her again; nay, perhaps with greater enjoyment, for it came unexpectedly, and with no such drawback as she had been used to suffer in seeing him on the stage with Miss Bertram.

Crawford's reading from a dramatic text again recalls the theatricals of volume I; indeed, Crawford makes a joke about the connection, directed at Fanny, when he assures Lady Bertram that he will have no theater in his future country residence in Norfolk. It is also important to recognize that it is Crawford's "variety of excellence" in reading, his versatility, which draws Fanny, and versatility is the skill at "turning," something one can be too good at, as Crawford's defection to Maria later in the novel shows. However, the irony in the situation for the reader of the novel is that Fanny's response to Crawford's reading is not given by the narrator alone: as Fanny attends to Crawford's reading of Shakespeare, Edmund also silently "reads" Fanny, for *us*:

> Edmund watched the progress of her attention, and was amused and gratified by seeing how she gradually slackened in the needlework, which, at the beginning, seemed to occupy her totally; how it fell from her hand while she sat motionless over it—and at last, how the eyes which had appeared so studiously to avoid him

throughout the day, were turned and fixed on Crawford, fixed on him for minutes, fixed on him in short till the attraction drew Crawford's upon her, and the book was closed, and the charm was broken. Then, she was shrinking again into herself, and blushing and working as hard as ever; but it had been enough to give Edmund encouragement for his friend, and as he cordially thanked him, he hoped to be expressing Fanny's secret feelings too.

In other words, Edmund speaks for Fanny, though the reader of the novel, privileged by the narrator with knowledge of Fanny's full range of feelings, can read even more, can read a kind of dramatic irony through Edmund's only partially informed reading of Fanny.

The discussion then turns to Shakespeare, and Crawford claims, in his gentleman's dilettantish way, that one knows Shakespeare without having to read him: "Shakespeare one gets acquainted with without knowing how. It is part of an Englishman's constitution. His thoughts and beauties are so spread abroad that one touches them every where, one is intimate with him by instinct." In other words, one need not actually study or "know" this one unquestioned "classic" of vernacular literature, that most important social and cultural institution, in order to be "acquainted" with it; the reader of the novel, conscious of Austen's own attitude to literature by the very character of the text he or she holds in his or her hands, as well as by the many critical discussions of literature throughout Austen's fiction, must feel the superficiality of Crawford's gentlemanly nonchalance about an important aspect of the national cultural tradition. Edmund, educated at Eton and Oxford, and soon to become a professional reader (a clergyman) and one of the most common of his day (for university lecturers then were few), demurs, while still managing to praise Crawford for Fanny's benefit, and the subject of reading aloud is pursued further and related to education in general:

> The two young men were the only talkers, but they, standing by the fire, talked over the too common neglect of the qualification, the total inattention to it, in the ordinary school-system for boys, the consequently natural—yet in some instances almost unnatural degree of ignorance and uncouthness of men, of sensible and well-informed men, when suddenly called to the necessity of reading aloud, which had fallen within their notice, giving instances of blunders, and failures with their secondary causes, the want of management of the voice, of proper modulation and emphasis, of foresight and judgment, all proceeding from the first cause, want

of early attention and habit; and Fanny was listening again with great entertainment.

Edmund then turns the subject in another direction, that of his own future profession, and the subject of reading aloud is really sharpened up and turned in to the issue, also started in volume I, in the dialogue between Edmund and Mary Crawford, of the true nature of the clergy as a social institution.

> "Even in my profession"—said Edmund with a smile—"how lit-
> tle the art of reading has been studied! how little a clear manner,
> and good delivery, have been attended to! I speak rather of the
> past, however, than the present.—There is now a spirit of im-
> provement abroad; but among those who were ordained twenty,
> thirty, forty years ago, the larger number, to judge by their per-
> formance, must have thought reading was reading, and preaching
> was preaching. It is different now. The subject is more justly
> considered. It is felt that distinctness and energy may have weight
> in recommending the most solid truths; and, besides, there is
> more general observation and taste, a more critical knowledge
> diffused, than formerly; in every congregation, there is a larger
> proportion who know a little of the matter, and who can judge
> and criticize."

Crawford takes the subject up with enthusiasm, asking how particular parts of the service should be delivered, and then turns to that form of discourse, besides drama, written deliberately to be read aloud:

> "A sermon, well delivered, is more uncommon even than prayers
> well read. A sermon, good in itself, is no rare thing. It is more
> difficult to speak well than to compose well; that is, the rules and
> trick of composition are oftener an object of study. A thoroughly
> good sermon, thoroughly well delivered, is a capital gratification.
> I can never hear such a one without the greatest admiration and
> respect, and more than half a mind to take orders and preach
> myself. There is something in the eloquence of the pulpit, when
> it is really eloquence, which is entitled to the highest praise and
> honour. The preacher who can touch and affect such an hetero-
> geneous mass of hearers, on subjects limited, and long worn
> thread-bare in all common hands; who can say any thing new or
> striking, any thing that rouses the attention, without offending
> the taste, or wearing out the feelings of his hearers, is a man

whom one could not (in his public capacity) honour enough. I should like to be such a man."

This passage clearly and finally indicates how superficial is Crawford's understanding of the priest's calling and how much like his sister's shallow understanding, revealed earlier in the novel. And how self-condemning is that phrase "in his public capacity," tucked away in parentheses; obviously for Crawford it is all the same: plays or preaching, the important thing is not the text but the performance, and the applause. So, as too-ready talkers do, he proceeds to damn himself utterly in the space left by Fanny's silence and Edmund's amusement:

> "I never listened to a distinguished preacher in my life, without a sort of envy. But then, I must have a London audience. I could not preach, but to the educated; to those who were capable of estimating my composition. And, I do not know that I should be fond of preaching often; now and then, perhaps, once or twice in the spring, after being anxiously expected for half a dozen Sundays together; but not for a constancy; it would not do for a constancy."

By this point in the novel the reader should be able to recognize that it is precisely "a constancy" that Crawford is incapable of in anything, even his love for Fanny; the thing about the fine and excessive talker, however, is that he is unaware of the full meaning of what he says. So Fanny, silent Fanny, speaks at last, in a manner of speaking, as she had spoken to Edmund at the novel's and their relationship's beginning; she "involuntarily shook her head." Crawford rushes to interrogate her, to surmise what she might mean, to interpret her gestures; but in doing so he must, like Edmund, speak for her, and so condemn himself out of his own mouth. (Meanwhile Edmund, to clear a space for Crawford to work, turns his back, sits down, and proceeds to read a text, the newspaper, half aloud.) Fanny's actions speak louder than words, louder than the words of anyone in the novel, as Sir Thomas and Lady Bertram, and eventually Edmund, discover. The richer irony, then, is that Fanny Price, unlike Elizabeth Bennet and even more unlike Emma Woodhouse, is, as Tony Tanner says, "a true heroine because in a turbulent world it is harder to refrain from action than to let energy and impulse run riot."

We are not done, however, with the subject of reading aloud, of sermons and sermonizing. For in the novel's penultimate chapter, after Edmund has

had his eyes "opened" by Mary Crawford's superficial reaction to the elopement of her brother with his sister, he tells her so, and she mocks him:

> "A pretty good lecture upon my word. Was it part of your last
> sermon? At this rate, you will soon reform every body at Mans-
> field and Thornton Lacey [Edmund's first cure]; and when I hear
> of you next, it may be as a celebrated preacher in some great
> society of Methodists, or as a missionary into foreign parts."

Such is Mary's moral superficiality that she merely doubles her crime with
this attempt at witty deflection, for the subject has by this point in the novel
been deeply mined from the novel's thematic core and repeatedly connected
with the novel's secondary plot of the courtship of Mary and Edmund.

It is a case of the great talkers, then, against the eloquent mute and the
unfledged preacher, for Edmund too has difficulty bringing himself to speak,
and he only speaks earnestly, because always in earnest. It is accurate silent
reading against deceptive or too easy public reading, silent persuasion against
dissuasive because excessive and excessively easy, that is facile volubility.
However, the mute and the earnest persuade on principle too, the principles
of rhetoric laid down by Blair.

> The signification of our sentiments, made by tones and gestures
> [he writes], has this advantage above that made by words, that it
> is the Language of nature. It is that method of interpreting our
> mind, which nature has dictated to all, and which is understood
> by all; whereas, words are only arbitrary, conventional symbols
> of our ideas; and, by consequence, must make a more feeble
> impression.

We know from the work of sociologists such as Erving Goffman that this is
wrong, that gestures and tones are as conventional as words. Nevertheless,
the Sentimental convention that gestures are natural and authentic, language
artful and artificial, is made use of by Austen, but only to make another
criticism of convention: Mary and Henry Crawford have all the repertoire
of gestures of seductive elegance but lack a moral center. Gestures, as well
as words, can be used to deceive. Only the attentive reader, such as Fanny
Price, can tell the difference, and even she, like the reader of the novel, can
be temporarily fascinated; but then, that is what memory, which Fanny
praises in one of her "rhapsodies," is for—to save us from the fascination
of the moment. Time, which memory represents, rather than the immediacy
of the Sentimentalist, is the true value in *Mansfield Park,* and is represented
simply as the chief moral and ethical virtue which Fanny has, the virtue also

essential to the Christian life, and to the social role of the clergyman, namely perseverance. Austen, too often seen only as a satirist of Sensibility, does appropriate the Sentimental suspicion of language here, then, as in all her novels, but less drastically elsewhere, to a vigorous argument for the appropriate (Fanny would say "proper") use of appropriate language, whether the language be gestures, tone, words, or "manners" in general. And here in *Mansfield Park* she has deepened the criticism of language and reading precisely by depriving her heroine of the kind of "playfulness and epigrammatism" of speech relished by Elizabeth Bennet, and Elizabeth's creator. And so Austen deliberately challenges the reader to find Edmund, and especially Fanny, significant, to read them right, and therefore to read Austen herself right, for it is by reversing so much of the material and treatment in *Pride and Prejudice* that Austen does so. If Fanny is a better reader than Elizabeth, we are challenged to love perfection; if Fanny (as a fictional character) atones for her intellectual superiority by being deprived of Elizabeth's outspokenness, we are challenged to avoid feeling sorry for her. But in essentials Elizabeth and Fanny are only as different as the difference between Elizabeth's "obstinacy" and Fanny's "perseverance," between Elizabeth's "courage" in love and Fanny's "heroism."

Thus Jane Austen examines the nature of true eloquence in *Mansfield Park* and shows the relationship between moral character and public utterance through the theme of reading aloud. But she also places that theme in the context of vital social institutions. When she wrote that the subject of *Mansfield Park* was to be something very different from that of *Pride and Prejudice,* was to be "ordination," she wrote true. The subject of *Mansfield Park* is ordination, in all the richness of significance of the word and the social and religious institution. For ordination signifies order, and orders; it signifies above all the initiation (echoes of Austen's debt to Fanny Burney and others) of an individual into a moral and social institution, in this case the particular institution of the Church. In ordination one reads aloud a text, and one thereby performs an act by which one's condition in life is transformed by being made part of (not extinguished by) a social institution. It is, as such, an act beyond the comprehension of mere individualists like Mary and Henry Crawford; it is also an act that stands for, is paradigmatic of, the initiation of the individual into his or her inheritance of a whole array of social institutions, including language, conduct (or "manners"), literature, religion, property, social class, and so on. These institutions are not questioned *as institutions* by Jane Austen, though individual instances of the institution may be questioned, just as Edmund does not question the convention or custom (for it was that, and *not* an institution in Austen's day,

in England) of primogeniture. That refusal is seen very clearly when Fanny
(who thinks like Edmund) is so shocked at Mary Crawford's thought that
Tom Bertram's death would "free" Edmund from the younger son's necessity
of seeking a profession. Edmund, like Fanny, knows that the crucial question
is how the individual chooses to take on the institution and the convention,
to inhabit it meaningfully, to marry self with society *through* the institution.
Ordination is thus truly a marriage, one that is made to stand in the way of
Edmund's marriage to Mary Crawford; one for which Fanny Price is so
perfectly suited from the beginning of the novel—how could she be otherwise
when her mind was "formed" by Edmund? For marriage too is a reading
aloud which transforms one's condition in life.

   Mansfield Park is about reading, then, about the nature of eloquence,
silent and vocal, about the moral and ethical content of eloquence, about the
institutional context of eloquence, and about its social effects. *Mansfield Park*
is about reading as an act of the profoundest significance for the individual
and for his and her society, and thus *Mansfield Park* uses reading aloud both
as a paradigm for and dramatization of this significant acting. And yet that
is not all; for in its drama of reading between Fanny and Edmund, Henry
and Mary Crawford, *Mansfield Park,* as the critical controversy on the characters shows, presents us too with a challenge in reading, a challenge to read
mute eloquence and formal utterance correctly, to read volubility and witty
facility for what they are, above all to read the play of fictional conventions
and thus participate in Austen's own critical renewal of a social institution
which her work was, for us, instrumental in founding—the institution of
literature. In this novel, as far as true love goes, was that not where it all
began?

ANN MOLAN

Persuasion in Persuasion

Persuasion is generally regarded as a rather different novel from what we might have expected from Jane Austen's earlier achievements, and the obvious question is whether it is a new departure or a petering out. As many critics have noticed, there are technical imperfections that Jane Austen might well have removed had she lived—rather like the change she did make to the resolution so that it no longer looked like a favour to her heroine from the hand of fate. But if there are some grounds for some critics' reservations about the novel, there are none for supposing it a lesser achievement than Jane Austen's earlier work. Clearly, it is different; but it is also, I think, a real development.

It is important to notice how different it is in style and attitude from the earlier work, for the more or less familiar social setting and encounters tend to obscure this. Unlike other heroines', Anne Elliot's circumstances demand that she *release* her imagination, her fancy, from a reality which is fully recognized as only too intractable. Where earlier novels had portrayed many kinds of vanity, this explores the possible vanity of human wishes. In *Persuasion* there is a kind of seriousness and searchingness that can contemplate, far more steadily than in any of the earlier novels, the impotence of human yearnings to fashion or find their fulfilment, for this is a real possibility with Anne. The scope and terms of the novel are indicated in an early remark about Anne: "How eloquent could Anne Elliot have been,—how eloquent, at least, were her wishes." We are to discover that the eloquence

From *The Critical Review* (Australia), no. 24 (1982). © 1982 by Ann Molan.

of wishes, of fancy, and the insistence of them, is not a matter of the rhetoric of will, or of daydreaming or of romantic self-delusion, but of persuasion.

The title of the novel actually focuses most of its central interests. In any human situation, what one confronts and what one brings to the encounter, the possibilities within and without the self, what one is persuaded *of* and what one is persuaded *by,* weave an intricate knot of compulsions and restraints. This, I would argue, is at the centre of *Persuasion*; and much of the novel's energy comes from the way the various strands of the knot join, resist, and determine each other. Anne's case does not represent the rival claims of feeling and of prudential caution, or even of autonomous decision and persuadability. Such oppositions collapse upon examination, for persuadability is as much a factor in Anne's eventual happiness as it was in her earlier loss of Wentworth. In other words, Jane Austen penetrates the intrinsic doubleness of persuasion, its ability to destroy and fashion, its ineradicable presence in all human dealings, and the riskiness of deciding one's lot by something uncertifiable. Where there is some margin for doubt or personally attributed meaning, persuasion becomes important and correspondingly risky—as we see in Anne's earlier "persuasion" that marrying Wentworth would have disastrous consequences, and (later in the book) in her "persuasion" that she could reawaken his love. All "persuasions" and all persuading are seen to issue from the need to sustain something as well as the need to venture something; and this applies to the pleas of feelings as well as the pleas of reason, or of cold, hard facts. And if there is a self-preserving necessity in Anne's persuading herself of a real value in the places where she is obliged to spend her time, yet the exertion this requires from a spirit not limply pliable indicates a hope, a demand on life, that will later persuade her rather differently.

The tone of *Persuasion* has a seriousness born of the steady contemplation of the way things can go awry or go nowhere at all. Anne Elliot is very much alone in her world, more than most of the other Austen heroines; but there are ways of being alone, and ways of coping with it, which are set against hers quite early in the novel and ensure that our sympathies are neither sentimental nor undiscriminating. Elizabeth uses her long-nursed resentment about William Elliot to "fill the vacancies" of her life, for instance; Mary's response to having "not seen a creature the whole morning" is one of manipulative hypochondria. By contrast, Anne has more substantial inner resources, which helps make us see that the seriousness of her predicament is correspondingly deeper.

Unlike Jane Austen's other heroines', Anne's life is closing down, its horizons becoming narrow and unexpandable. She has done with the world, the world has done with her, and if only she can reconcile her heart to it, her task seems to be to acquit herself well as a useful second-rank member of the community. This is far from the case with the other heroines. We enter upon their lives at the point where their scope is broadest because so much is potential, when the constrictions of belonging to one family are being shed before the constrictions of entering another one have been adopted. Nor is this simply a matter of Anne being older than they. Age is important but not in some automatic way, for it matters more what Anne's life has meant for her to that age, and the fact that her opportunities for happiness seem to have been used up and come to nothing. Yet what matters even more are the feelings and capacities for feeling that age has brought with it. Emma is in a position to be "vexed" (and her age is part of that); Anne, on first seeing Wentworth, to have "a revival of former pain." The difference between "pain" and "vexation" signals a lot here. On Wentworth's appearance in Bath, Anne is overcome by "agitation, pain, pleasure, a something between delight and misery." Even such mixed feelings as these are a welcome relief from incidents of unalloyed suffering, as when Anne finds herself uncontrollably but quietly weeping in the midst of a joyous gathering, because Wentworth is engaged with someone else. Words of a different tone and cadence from "vexation" are necessary to render the disturbances that come to Anne's heart and mind.

As Jane Austen presents her, Anne is not the victim of a rigidly limiting social world. Anne has cast away her own happiness, allowing herself to be persuaded to choose a course that actually limits her to her own family—a family that hardly amounts to a home. She has not been hard done by or duped. It is important that Anne's father did not forbid the marriage to Wentworth, and that she was not absolutely obliged to obey Lady Russell's advice. To import the Cinderella theme (as D. W. Harding does, with some qualifications, in his introduction to the Penguin edition) obscures Anne's agency in her life, which we need to appreciate if we are to take her story seriously. Jane Austen gives due weight to all the tangled factors restraining and enticing Anne, so that we are by no means persuaded to any simple verdict about her early decision, such as that of Frederick Wentworth or Lady Russell. The very ordinariness of her case is part of its complexity: it was no whirlwind, fairy-tale romance of star-crossed lovers, but rather, "he had nothing to do, and she had hardly any body to love." The lovers exist in a world which they didn't create, but in which they must live. What should Anne have done, then? As we are made to see it, there is no minimizing the extreme difficulty and hazard of her deciding to marry Wentworth. She is very young, and her feelings are untested. We remember Anne's own mother (and Fanny Price's mother plunged into penury), and the unhappiness that a mistake of this kind inflicted on them. And we need not doubt that Sir Walter would be as good as his word in cutting her off. The cost of accepting and complying with the demands of her social world, and the cost of repudiating them, are both given their full weight. For Anne, the latter course would mean breaking every connection she has, and rejecting the advice of the one sensible person around, Lady Russell. If Jane Austen had made her heroine just a year or two older, it might have made our judgment easier, not because of the legal age of independence, but because we are more content for an adult woman to take her chances in that kind of risk than we are for someone on the threshold like Anne. In these ways, our own venturing and withholding of judgment on the issue are a bit similar to Anne's own.

Of course, we are never in any doubt that Anne made a disastrous mistake, and we cannot be satisfied to adopt the hindsight answer to the "right and wrong" of it that Anne finally gives to Wentworth. But it makes a big difference how we understand Anne's refusal: whether we see it as the timid yielding of someone whose feelings are weak enough to be easily diverted, or as the action of someone whose unusual maturity can admit many points of view apart from her own, but whose inexperience prevents her seeing through them. If we adopt the former view, then it becomes too easy thenceforth to see Anne as a willing doormat for all and sundry, a self-effacing, spineless convenience who didn't have enough courage to grasp her own life when it was handed to her on a plate. However, as the incident and situation are elaborated by Jane Austen, this view comes to seem unwarrantable. So while we are far from taking Lady Russell's part, we are not entirely of Wentworth's persuasion about the matter either. His own case might look like a compelling argument for trust in one's deepest impulses: "His genius and ardour had seemed to foresee and to command his prosperous path," but with no less genius and ardour, Anne's path is impeded by more factors than Wentworth understands. Wentworth should not have assumed that her situation was the same as his; indeed, as we look back on the whole episode, we cannot help seeing that his response was less mature and self-possessed than hers, closer to being "captiously irritable," even if we might not want to go that far. But certainly we cannot see Anne's refusal of Wentworth at the age of nineteen as a denial of her capacity to live according to her heart. If it were, her life and her story would be much simpler.

In its early chapters, then, the novel creates a world not reducible to terms of simple alternatives, especially simple moral alternatives. Indeed, the notion that the novel and the reader can easily fix on or derive any "system" of values seems to ignore most about Jane Austen's enterprise. The novel is not of that expository temper at all; it is much more interested in (and questioning of) the *process* by which Anne's happiness is secured than in attempts to make the outcome "signify" some moral generalization.

Jane Austen's viewpoint clearly overlaps with her heroine's, of course, but they are not identical: Anne is not "as right as her author," as is often thought. To take this view is to leave too much out of account, especially the way the prose so often works to place Anne's version of things. However, it is true that Anne is quite without illusions, either about her own decisive life's choice or about the capacities for life in the people around her, whether at Kellynch, Uppercross, or Bath. She is as quick to sense something fishy about Mr Elliot's appearing when there was "nothing to gain," for example, as she is to understand the nature of Mary's malady. People are always avowing the opposite of what they really want, thinly masking self-interest with a veneer of social forms, and material considerations are forever determining the most important human affairs. None of this escapes Anne's eye. Yet Anne's balance is not upset by the extent of duplicity and caprice she sees around her. Her vision is not clouded by bitterness or cynical resignation, although there are seductions for her in both modes of distancing. And of course this clarity and astringent judgment are even more characteristic of Jane Austen herself. "Mr Shepherd laughed, as he knew we must"; "A lady, without a family, was the very best preserver of furniture"; "His two other children were of very inferior value." The presence of this acerbic note in the novel, especially directed against the people who foil things, is perfectly gauged to correspond with the seriousness of the losses incurred for someone like Anne. This is not to say that Jane Austen's characteristic irony is absent or sour. The way characters like the Musgroves persuade themselves into their own attitudes, for example, is as amusing as the way they persuade themselves of others' attitudes.

Yet for Anne, as distinct from Jane Austen, merely to comment on and expose her world is not sufficient. She must make her own place in it as well. She has to exert all her energies to achieve a resignation to the emptiness her life holds out to her, to live in the world without expectations, and to make do with incentivess to action and gratifications which leave her heart in abeyance: "she had the satisfaction of knowing herself extremely useful there." To live this way, just about all the vital centres of her life must be shut down. The continual chafing abrasion of having her heart awakened in that world is something from which she must protect herself. The reappearance of Wentworth is to disturb that calm, however, and Anne's fevered apprehension of his arrival shows her to be quite riveted by the prospect, even though "soon she began to wish that she could feel secure even for a week." She is thankful that no one knows or would care about her former alliance to Wentworth, and we can only be thankful too. After Mary's first meeting with Wentworth, we have sufficient evidence to confirm the novel's intimations about this:

> "Henrietta asked him what he thought of you, when they went away; and he said, 'You were so altered he should not have known you again.'"
>
> Mary had no feelings to make her respect her sister's in a common way; but she was perfectly unsuspicious of being inflicting any particular wound.

As it is, what Anne has to suffer from Mary's coarse vanity is bad enough, but we know there are several who would not scruple to "inflict a peculiar wound" had they known the whole story. The novel does not see it as a perverse trifling with her best interests when Anne concludes about her removal to the same village as Wentworth that "this was against her."

Jane Austen gives full weight to such conclusions drawn by Anne, but she also maintains an ironic perspective on her. And here it is important that we notice how much the title of the novel gathers into itself, for the book is interested in the various modes and motives of *self*-persuasion—more, indeed, than in persuasion by others; and it is still more interested in what people are persuaded of and therefore what they will find to be persuaded by, and in the moral qualities involved in this to-and-fro process. Anne is certainly subjected to this kind of scrutiny, since persuasion is and has been one of the most obvious determinants of her life. But the way Jane Austen scrutinizes her, along with the other characters, involves a very delicate kind of irony and wit.

On the walk to Winthrop, Louisa Musgrove extorts from Wentworth an avowal which many readers have taken to be the novel's "position" on persuadability: "My first wish for all, whom I am interested in, is that they should be firm." As we soon see, however, Louisa's subsequent self-persuasion that she can win Wentworth by displays of "firmness" is precisely what leads her to reject his counter-persuasions to watch her step on the Cobb. The apparently simple, straightforward distinction between "persuasion" and "firmness" dissolves; in fact, the two episodes involving Louisa and Wentworth undercut any such notion, since involved in both episodes are contrary directions and levels of persuasion. Anne, we notice, has no such notion. What she sees in the incident on the Cobb is what she also mentally insists on against Wentworth: that, although she cannot articulate fully the complexities we see develop in her own life, "She thought it could scarcely escape him to feel, that a persuadable temper might sometimes be as much in favour of happiness, as a very resolute character." After all, reality is a great persuader—as Anne knows all too well and as Louisa, impelled by the romantic urgings of her heart, and with her sights set only on securing Wentworth—discovers.

But, of course, questions about what "reality" *is* to a person, and how much it *can* persuade him, and what it can persuade him of, all arise at the very beginning of the novel, with Sir Walter Elliot. His vanity, his obsession with the Baronetage, and his repulsive attitude to his wife's death are very much to the point: "Precisely such had the paragraph originally stood from the printer's hands; but Sir Walter had *improved* it . . . by *inserting most accurately* the day of the month on which he had lost his wife" (my italics). In Sir Walter's eyes, the more room one takes up in the Baronetage, the more firmly established one is as a person; births and deaths are equally grist to the mill of Sir Walter's lofty self-esteem, equally a source of satisfaction and diversion. Unlike Louisa, he is very attentive to facts; but it is an attentiveness that is chillingly falsifying just because it is negligent of the *human* facts. His meticulous addition to the record of his wife's death blandly ignores and erases any record of her existence as a wife. Can we say that the reality of the past is unaffected by such persuasion about it, especially as it is preserved in the present and guides action in the future? Against Sir Walter's we are clearly invited to put Anne's sense of and relation to her past: "With all these circumstances, recollections and feelings, she could not hear that Captain Wentworth's sister was likely to live at Kellynch, without a revival of former pain"; or "it was highly incumbent on her to clothe her imagination, her memory, and all her ideas in as much of Uppercross as possible." These life-lines to human meanings (which often feel, to Anne, like millstones around her neck) spell out just what Sir Walter lacks—recollections, feelings, imagination, memory, and ideas; and it is precisely these, we notice, that make the persuasiveness of *her* "reality" at once so powerful to her and so painful.

Nevertheless, the novel does not present the mere capacity to feel, to remember, to imagine, and to be persuaded accordingly, as a moral ideal, for the novel insists on the crucial difficulty: "How quick come the reasons for approving what we like!" This wry comment from the author is prompted by the plans to let Kellynch and remove the Elliots to Bath; but the same point is revealed again and again: the subtle but crucial difference between the legitimate claims of personal exigence, and the universal tendency to rationalize one's preference by selective attention, self-delusion, and evasion of the claims of others. Lady Russell on the desirability of moving to Bath is only one example of the process. So is the humourous episode, later on, when Charles and Mary Musgrove are dealing with their invitation to meet Captain Wentworth and the rival claims of their sick child: once again personal preference gradually turns into more obligation through manoeuvering facts and other people.

And yet even on this process the novel is anything but simpleminded, for it shows the process as also an everyday, tacitly understood, and mutually employed means of coming to an arrangement. The meeting of the owners and the tenants of Kellynch is a case in point: "This meeting of the two parties proved highly satisfactory, and decided the whole business at once. Each lady was previously well disposed for an agreement, and saw nothing, therefore, but good manners in the other." The amusement here goes with the recognition, the acceptance, of this rather questionable process of pre-disposing oneself and others as a necessary way of expediting important social transactions. There are many instances of this in the novel, and in none of them is anyone deliberately setting out to pull the wool over people's eyes. Rather, each of the characters is of some inner persuasion about grades of value—a persuasion that has a degree of wilfulness in it, and a certain dispositional, abiding quality, a characteristic leaning towards something. Because of this each finds himself being persuaded about certain possibilities in the world as though these things were pressed upon him for recognition. The sentence about the letting of Kellynch leaps in lightning sequence from the ladies' interests, to what they saw, conjoined by that very telling "there-fore." This highlights the potential danger as well as the humour in the readiness with which people construct reality according to purely private specifications. "Persuasion," it seems, has a lot to do with how one channels, amplifies, and distorts the truth—often through recounting versions of it, but always with the object of reconciling or aligning the conscious self and the rest of the world. The process is often tacit or unavowed, but of course is always likely to run up against resistance from somewhere or other.

It is no coincidence, I think, that hard on the heels of the letting of Kellynch and that telling "therefore," Anne undertakes her own self-persuasion about the prospects of going to Bath: "It would be most right, and most wise, and, therefore, must involve least suffering, to go with the others." Of course, Anne's reconciling of self and world here is in the reverse direction to other reconcilings we have witnessed or are soon to witness. She is trying to shape her deeper feelings and dispositions so as to conform with an apparently fixed external arrangement of things; and she is also attributing to that arrangement a weight of propriety and moral sanction to "justify" her accepting what, in reality, she cannot influence. The attempt is more futile than in some way reprehensible. The spare, tough word "suffering" is not overbalanced by the meagre suitability of the plan as Anne is invoking it, a suitability that looks all the more meagre for its having to be iterated so strongly as "*most* right, and *most* wise." This is a good example of how complex Jane Austen's attitudes are. She appreciates how little Anne is a person to leap to moralizing self-negation, and yet how much Anne's position makes the adoption of such self-protective measures necessary to her. The effort of control evinced in the rhythm of the first half of the sentence makes clear that this self-repression goes against the grain with Anne, just as it testifies to the unbudging resistance of that self which has the capacity to suffer. The bald statement of her "persuasion" here—that feelings order themselves (to *some* degree; it is only the "*least* suffering") according to external conveniences—ironically highlights the incongruity of placing the two kinds of consideration on the same plane. Indeed, the sentence works to refine this irony by placing the logic Anne tries to impose on these considerations against the real lack of logic we see in them (for how much logic is there in "therefore" here?). What we are made to realize is that the "persuasion" that accords this minor, relative role to feelings, is *not* right and *un*wise. Rather than being dissolved, the connection reverses itself. Anne cannot afford to see this.

This little example is more significant than it looks at first sight and not only because it is one of the earliest indications of Anne's rigorous, sober clarity in assessing the possibilities of life in her world, and her refusal to indulge in personal fantasies of thwarted or renewable prospects with a Prince Charming. This very unblinkering, we find, can tip over into another kind of blindness. If, as is often noted, Anne can see clearly in all directions, then an exception must be made for her vision of herself. It is true, of course, that what one sees does not delimit what is there, nor does it entirely and automatically determine what one experiences. In this case it is anything but reprehensible that Anne should often try to impose a certain vision on herself and over and over again, set about to "teach herself " or "persuade herself." And yet always present at these moments is a contrary impulse or invitation within her to lend herself to promptings that well up in her rather than to those that are borne in upon her. The course of the novel traces Anne's response to the challenge of admitting her own persuasion.

The most ineradicable persuasion Anne has she can admit because it seems to her a purely academic point now. It is simply this: that she would have been able to weather all sorts of trials had her heart asserted its attachment to Wentworth, and that "she should yet have been a happier woman in maintaining the engagement, than she had been in the sacrifice of it." Yet by this point (chapter 4) the novel has already suggested that the process of persuasion (especially self-persuasion) can actively narrow or expand one's world, not be a more passive matter of merely ignoring or recognizing it. So we may well start to wonder if this persuasion of Anne's is as academic as she supposes. As the novel unfolds, it becomes a testing of her on every detail of it—not now in the maintaining of a formal engagement, but in the maintaining of an engagement of her hopes. Her persuasion has to resist all the trials she could have anticipated, and more, since it now takes on the quality of a certain kind of faith or attestation. Clearly, that faith is very different from a naive trust that if one believes in something hard enough, then it will come true. What the novel presents in her, and tests, is the quality of her moral being; for, as I have been trying to suggest, the novel constantly insists that this depends in part on what a person expects from the world, and this influences in turn what the person partly creates, partly finds in his "persuasions" about the world and himself.

The continued engagement of Anne's hopes is signalled very early in the novel by a deduction she attempts to toss off: "She had only navy lists and newspapers for her authority, but she could not doubt his being rich;—and, in favour of his constancy, he had no reason to believe him married." The novel immediately takes up the crucial point about the "eloquence" of Anne's wishes, tying the essentially prospective nature of wishes (however they are cast) to the apparently finalized past. This "eloquence" already marks Anne off from anyone else in the novel; and for that to be the dominant quality of the story one tells oneself, of the way one rehearses things and hence acknowledges their reality, bespeaks a certain moral character akin to fidelity. It is finally her "eloquence" with Captain Harville about precisely the point of her firmest persuasion, evincing a deep adherence to what she is saying, that opens the way for Wentworth's return to Anne.

We realize quite early on that Anne's heart has always belonged to Wentworth, and realize moreover what an ardent and passionate attachment it is during the discussion on the letting of Kellynch, when it requires great effort before she can "harden her nerves sufficiently" to endure conversation about anything connected with him. Harden her nerves she might, harden her heart she cannot. In contrast to the world she has to live in, which is either shallow or heartless, Anne is a woman of very deep feeling: indeed, although it is uncommon to say so, a passionate woman. And against her will, her heart keeps asserting its demand for fulfilment. No one in the novel has any kinship with her in this capacity for deep and faithful feeling. Part of Jane Austen's exploration of different kinds of persuasion and persuadability is the juxtaposition of Anne's capacity with the incapacity of others. At one extreme there is Louisa Musgrove and Mary, with their self-indulgence and sentimentality; at the other is the rigid barrenness of Elizabeth's propriety, not admitting feeling at all. Anne is sharply distinguished from all these. Her lively, sensitive heart repeatedly dislodges her composure. Whenever her deepest emotions are touched into life, her only recourse is escape to solitude, for her world certainly allows her no way her feelings and needs can be expressed. To Anne herself, these moments of disruption are a repeated reminder of what cannot be repressed. To us, they are evidence of the resurgence and tenacity of hope in a life that seems to have no warrant for it. But of course the unacknowledged, involuntary reflexes of feeling to which she is subject early in the book hardly establish a solid and compelling "persuasion" about her life. The moral seriousness of the novel demands a more active assent and venturing by Anne for any happiness to be secured.

Jane Austen's sense of Anne's life and its prospects is a very delicately flexible one, and because of this she earns the right, at a certain point, to become uncompromising in her demands for and of her heroine. The first prospect author and heroine broach may seem to unite their voices in the plan to negotiate it: "With the prospect of spending at least two months at Uppercross, it was highly incumbent on her to clothe her imagination, her memory, and all her ideas in as much of Uppercross as possible." Yet if we attend to the metaphor, it will strike us as very odd indeed: the notion of these lively human faculties being "clothed," rather than spinning the fabric of life, is as ill-fitting as Uppercross is to Anne's capacities. Jane Austen is well aware of the incongruity, of course; the metaphor places Anne's proposal to clothe and tailor the yearnings of her heart in "house-keeping, neighbours, dress, dancing, and music" as insufficient to all it is trying to deal with; yet the metaphor also registers Jane Austen's sober sense of why it was "highly incumbent" on Anne to try. Still, the stress falls on the sluggishness of Anne's ruminations, and her over-willed compliance with what is borne in on her, which undermine what she is trying to believe: that "she must now submit to feel that another lesson, in the art of knowing our own nothingness beyond our own circle, was become necessary for her." There is certainly some truth to reality in this "lesson," but it cannot wholly persuade her because it denies the reality—the verve and "eloquence"—of her deepest wishes and desires. Jane Austen is fully aware of both elements of Anne's "reality"—which is a major reason why the novel avoids both sentimental wish-fulfilment and callousness. The sense of the intransigence of desire must not be compromised or weakened by any toning down of all it has to contend with.

One way of acknowledging but coping with the "nothingness" Anne's world holds out to her is for her to sink her energies into serving the needs of those round about. Jane Austen gives this impulse its due credit: "To be claimed as a good, though in an improper style, is at least better than being rejected as no good at all," although even here there is a hint of the self-pity into which it so easily slides and from which Anne barely retrieves herself a short time later: "as for herself, she was left with as many sensations of comfort, as were, perhaps, ever likely to be hers. She knew herself to be of the first utility to the child." In fact, to plead the promotion of others' welfare can be the most dangerous persuasion of all, because it seems to be so morally unimpeachable. Its value is brought under scrutiny very early, especially in regard to Anne's rejection of Wentworth:

> But it was not a merely selfish caution, under which she acted, in putting an end to it. Had she not imagined herself consulting his good, even more than her own, she could hardly have given him up.—The belief of being prudent, and self-denying principally for *his* advantage, was her chief consolation, under the misery of a parting—a final parting.

As the novel sees it, Anne's belief in self-abnegation and self-sacrifice is anything but despicable; but it is also seen to be at best a consoling distraction, and at worst an active destroyer of the chance to bestow herself where the gift can be most creative. Even Anne is led to place this persuasion against a persuasion of her value and legitimate needs as a woman, though this is not a matter of conscious debate but of catching herself expecting rather more from life than merely being useful to others—as, for example, in her pain in Wentworth's reaction to the foiling of his plan that she should nurse Louisa after the accident: "but his evident surprise and vexation . . . made but a mortifying reception of Anne; or must at least convince her that she was valued only as she could be useful to Louisa."

Anne's deeper self protests against her life being so cut back, and the spirit of the novel contains an even stronger protest. The thrust of the novel, like that of Anne's own life, is towards a belief in some possible fuller and deeper fulfilment. There is a vital trenchancy in the writing—in its urgings, admonitions, and injunctions, its distancing from Anne's attempts to cut back her expectations, or to moralize her way out of her feelings, or to take refuge in self-pity and self-censure. In this way a demand is made that Anne persuade herself of such a possibility of fulfilment and then act on the persuasion. Thus Jane Austen delights in any evidence of Anne's resurgent spirits. She is delicately amused, in a tender yet uncompromising way, at the extent to which Anne's reviving hopes are troublesome to her—rejoicing because they are the only avenue to renewed life and vigour for Anne, yet taking the pain and agitation seriously. Jane Austen's irony towards Anne has the same sober gentleness. On Mrs Croft's tantalizing conversation about one or other of her brothers, Anne leaps to the assumption that Frederick is in question until tipped off by the mention of marriage:

> She could now answer as she ought. . . . She immediately felt how reasonable it was, that Mrs Croft should be thinking and speaking of Edward, and not of Frederick; and with shame at her own forgetfulness, applied himself to the knowledge of their former neighbour's present state, with proper interest.

The contrast between the involuntary veering of Anne's thoughts and the reasoning she imposes on them produces a very characteristic kind of smile in the writing.

It is also characteristic of Jane Austen's attitude towards her heroine that she is most satisfied with Anne when Anne is most dissatisfied with herself. After the first meeting with Wentworth, Anne attempts to deal with her response: "Soon, however, she began to reason with herself, and try to be feeling less." The attempt to slump into a fact that won't be ignored: "Alas! with all her reasonings, she found, that to retentive feelings eight years may be little more than nothing." The control of tone is masterly here, for while maintaining the sense this has for Anne, Jane Austen conveys something on her own account altogether different, for that "Alas!" has a buoyancy that makes it sound like anything but commiseration. She is amused at Anne's "reasonings," knowing that her less rational wisdom of heart will assert itself and supplant her more guarded appraisals: "Now, how were his sentiments to be read? Was this like wishing to avoid her? And the next moment she was hating herself for the folly which asked the question." Yet clearly, Jane Austen is also loving her for the wisdom which asked the question, which she well knows to be a very foolish sort of wisdom indeed. The puny fortifications of Anne's "utmost wisdom" against the onslaught of what she hopes for from Wentworth are not in the least ridiculed by Jane Austen, or blown away by a puff of romantic fervour. They are presented as both poignantly naive and only too well apprised of the consequences she can expect if they are abandoned. Infused in all Jane Austen's irony about Anne is a deep care for her pain, as, in this section, there is no overlooking or dismissing of the "peculiar wound" inflicted on Anne or of the "silent, deep mortification" which is all she is left with from the upsurge of her need. On this occasion Anne's pang of misery is caused by Wentworth's thinking her "altered beyond his knowledge." The irony of his saying that, when she is centrally *un*altered in her need of him, has a touch of bitterness on Anne's behalf because it sees how powerful is his kind of knowledge and how ineffectual is hers. Anne attempts to talk herself out of her feelings again: "Yet she soon began to rejoice that she had heard [his words]. They were of sobering tendency; they allayed agitation; they composed, and consequently must make her happier." The very uncomposed rhythm and logic of these reflections, and the clear sense and feeling of Anne's pain, prevent any comfortable superiority to her evasion. On another level, it is as difficult for us to demand that Anne abandon this safeguarding refuge as it is for Anne to venture beyond it.

And this, I think, is partly Jane Austen's point about the value of such "persuasions" as Anne's. Because Anne loves Wentworth the way she does (and he has his reality in the book through her loving him), she cannot help herself venturing her hopes again and again. By the time she discovers him to be in Bath, she has fully embraced her real persuasion of her life's true home. She no longer tries to subject her feelings to a false persuasion of self-abnegation or denial, but respects their unmanageability. On the discovery that Wentworth's attachment to Louisa has been dissolved, "She had some feelings which she was ashamed to investigate. They were too much like joy, senseless joy." She has now learned that her feelings and hopes are not to be sacrificed and cannot be sacrificed, no matter how perilous the course of action they oblige her to follow. Jane Austen remains very clear-eyed about this. Against Anne's developments, she places Benwick, for whom such a respect and cherishing of feeling plunges into self-indulgence as he complacently hugs his grief, feeding off it and risking nothing. But Jane Austen underlines Anne's realism in other ways. By the time Anne catches a glimpse of Wentworth out of the shop window, for example, she is so firmly reconciled to the direction her life is taking, that she is able to laugh at her own paltry and token gestures to divert it:

> She now felt a great inclination to go to the outer door; she wanted to see if it rained. Why was she to suspect herself of another motive? Captain Wentworth must be out of sight. She left her seat, she would go, one half of her should not be always so much wiser than the other half, or always suspecting the other of being worse than it was. She would see if it rained.

Anne's self-teasing and irony here are as lively as Jane Austen's; and she is aware, too, that the questions of where suspicion and trust should lie, where wisdom and folly apportioned—in venturing or in restraining herself?—have been answered long ago, counter to the apparent direction of these rhetorical denials. Anne's ability to have a joke on herself is one of the strongest clues to the vigour of her orientation. If Anne "learned romance as she grew older," it certainly has nothing of the melting mood about it.

The attitude of readiness for fulfilment that Jane Austen develops in Anne has none of the manipulative calculation with which other characters set about securing what they want. The novel is too subtle to see this as a simple opposition, however, of self-assertion versus deference or doormat behaviour. The kinds of assertion open to and pursued by all the characters in the novel vary enormously, but there is very little unabashed declaration of need to those from whom they hope to gain. Anne chooses instead to expose her self and its needs, with all the risks that involves. Thus at the concert in Bath, she finally steels herself against the coldness of her father and sister, against her own misgivings and uncertainty about the state of Wentworth's heart, and makes a deliberate approach to him, offers an invitation to change the terms of their relationship. In this situation Anne decisively fulfills her potentiality to answer to the world with whole-hearted, self-venturing vigour, at the same time abandoning those defences against hurt which have supported her for so long.

This is the point of greatest vulnerability for Anne. However, Wentworth recognizes and responds to her venturing, making it for her the moment of supreme self-establishing. As we discover, he has been undergoing a testing of his own heart's orientation. So how does this happy ending sit with the rest of the novel? Is it merely a fairy-tale ending, which ignores the moral complexity elaborated so far?

This is an obvious question, especially if we grasp the seriousness of the story up to the ending, but not altogether a simple one to answer. If we find the ending somehow insufficient, as I think we do, it is not because we want to protest that such stories do not have happy endings, that it would have been in some way more honest or unflinching for Jane Austen to have left Anne's prospects barren, thereby affirming that desires and needs such as hers do not have much chance of affecting the world. But on the other hand, we are not inclined to say that the novel only makes sense if Anne and Wentworth are reunited. In fact, on this point the novel seems to take the least indulgent, the least absolute and tendentious course, by insisting that such endings *can* happen (but not often), and can efface *some* (but not all) of the pain and injury that has gone before. The price exacted by those eight long years can never be fully restored. No, the ending is unsatisfactory not because Jane Austen chose the wrong one out of several possible outcomes, but because it suggests that Anne's venturing is morally justified only by its consequences. But how valid a principle is this applied to Anne's case? Just as there was no external reason, or promise, or calculation of likely consequences, sufficient to prompt Anne's self-persuasion, so we do not judge her self-persuasion "good or bad only as the event decides." For the force of the novel's thinking about persuasion does not hinge on any such general principle of judgment, any more than the value of Anne's morally self-creating actions depends on what those actions can secure. Although Jane Austen does not get it quite clearly into focus, the fact is that her subtle, dramatic, evaluative sense of Anne cannot be reduced to any such general moral principle or calculation. The course of the novel has been making this clear in its delicate shaping of demands on and within Anne, always through the power of its dramatization rather than through any crude assertions. A case in point is the novel's clear recognition, in the way it elaborates and juxtaposes different episodes, that self-sacrifice, however appealing psychologically, may not be of much moral value. Many critics lament that Jane Austen has not explained how we should judge whether persuasion and persuadability are good or bad. Yet if there is anything unsatisfactory about the ending, it is precisely that it seems to offer, or at least suggest, just such an explanation. For what the novel embodies in the fortunes of Anne Elliot is a different kind of insight: that the life that cannot be repressed has only the assurance of its own pulse to rely upon, a pulse that cannot be reduced to "reasonable" calculations or expectations, or to pious principles, or to self-exaltation. To accept this pulse—an acceptance that is the heart of any persuasion—is both a kind of victory and a kind of surrender. When all is said and done and achieved, *Persuasion* is about Anne Elliot's belief *in* her self rather than her belief *that* her self can win through. The kind of moral intelligence required for this venture is as honest, courageous, and fine as Jane Austen has created in any character—or shown in any of her writing.

MARTIN PRICE

Austen: Manners and Morals

*Let us imagine a picture story in schematic pictures, and thus more
like the narrative in a language than a series of realistic pictures. . . .
Let us remember too that we don't have to translate such pictures into
realistic ones in order to "understand" them, any more than we ever
translate photographs or film pictures into coloured pictures, although
black-and-white men or plants in reality would strike us as unspeaka-
bly strange and frightful.*

—LUDWIG WITTGENSTEIN

Jane Austen's novels present a world more schematic than we are accustomed to find in more recent fiction. The schematism arises in part from her
"vocabulary of discrimination," those abstract words which classify actions
in moral terms. Wittgenstein's remarks recall the adaptability of our responses, the readiness of our minds to discover how a literary work conveys
its meanings and to make insensible adjustments to the forms its signs may
take. Black-and-white photography can make discriminations and tonal gra-
dations that cannot be achieved by color, just as, in another case, an en-
graving can define a structure through line that a painting renders with less
precision in its fuller range of effects. Translation into a new medium or
language sharpens our awareness of certain elements and of the functions
they serve. Our initial question is to ask what Jane Austen's mode of fiction
is designed to reveal.

Let us consider a passage (in *Sense and Sensibility*) in which Elinor and
Marianne Dashwood accompany Lady Middleton to a party in London:

From *Forms of Life: Character and Moral Imagination in the Novel.* © 1983 by Yale
University. Yale University Press, 1983.

They arrived in due time at the place of destination, and as soon
as the string of carriages before them would allow, alighted, as-
cended the stairs, heard their names announced from one landing-
place to another in an audible voice, and entered a room splen-
didly lit up, quite full of company, and insufferably hot. When
they had paid their tribute of politeness by curtseying to the lady
of the house, they were permitted to mingle in the crowd, and
take their share of the heat and inconvenience, to which their
arrival must necessarily add.

Much that might be shown is not. (One may think of the ball Emma Bovary
attends at Vaubyessard or the Moscow ball at which Kitty loses Vronsky to
Anna Karenina.) We trace the rituals of entry with the Dashwood sisters,
reaching the goal only to find it acutely oppressive. At this point the irony
becomes firmer and the diction more abstract ("their tribute of politeness")
as they observe the required forms, and are "permitted" to participate in
the mutual affliction that such a party too easily becomes. The pattern of
the experience, not least the ironic pattern of the final clause, takes the place
of particular detail.

Another ball is that held at the Crown in *Emma*:

The ball proceeded pleasantly. The anxious cares, the incessant
attentions of Mrs. Weston, were not thrown away. Every body
seemed happy; and the praise of being a delightful ball, which is
seldom bestowed till after a ball has ceased to be, was repeatedly
given in the very beginning of the existence of this. Of very important, very recordable events, it was not more productive than
such meetings usually are.

(chapter 38)

One can say of either scene that Jane Austen presents it for recognition rather
than seeks to imagine it anew. It is meant to recall a world we know or at
least know about, and there is little effort to catch its sensory qualities or
evoke it pictorially. Instead, we have, in John Bayley's words, "the negligent
authority of a world that is possessed without being contemplated." It is
seen from the inside of its physical and moral structure. What Jane Austen
stresses in the first case is the tissue of ceremony and protocol that shrouds
an unpleasant reality. In the second, a scene of comparative informality where
all the guests are known to each other, we see the social machine run
smoothly and comfortably.

In a world of recognition, people are defined less by isolated features than by their total address. We see characters in Jane Austen's novels as we see many people in life, recognizing them as familiar but hardly able to enumerate their features. We may recognize a friend at a distance by stance or gait, by the way he enters traffic or passes others on the street. The process of recognition is composed of a series of small perceptions which, if their combination is right, bring along a familiar total form. In some cases, a very small number of perceptions (or, for the novelist, specifications) will serve. Jane Austen's introduction of characters tends to stress qualities that are not directly visible but will shape and account for the behavior that follows.

> The Musgroves, like their houses, were in a state of alteration, perhaps of improvement. The father and mother were in the old English style, and the young people in the new. Mr. and Mrs. Musgrove were a very good sort of people; friendly and hospitable, not much educated, and not at all elegant. Their children had more modern minds and manners. There was a numerous family; but the only two grown up, excepting Charles, were Henrietta and Louisa, young ladies of nineteen and twenty, who had brought from a school at Exeter all the usual stock of accomplishments, and were now, like thousands of other young ladies, living to be fashionable, happy, and merry. Their dress had every advantage, their faces were rather pretty, their spirits extremely good, their manners unembarrassed and pleasant; they were of consequence at home, and favorites abroad.
>
> (*Persuasion*)

Here Jane Austen provides us with representative members of a social class, its two generations exhibiting change without conflict. The Musgroves look toward modernity as warmly as Sir Walter Elliot retraces his lineage in his favorite book. The Musgroves are representative, even undistinguishable from most others of their age and class; yet happy, assured, comfortable in their world, all that Anne Elliot is not. In the sentences that follow, we have an explicit report of Anne's thoughts, but here too the author imposes her own ironic presence:

> Anne always contemplated them as some of the happiest creatures of her acquaintance; but still, saved as we all are by some comfortable feeling of superiority from wishing for the possibility of exchange, she would not have given up her own more elegant and cultivated mind for all their enjoyments; and envied them nothing but that seemingly perfect good understanding and agreement

together, that good-humoured mutual affection, of which she had known so little herself with either of her sisters.

(Persuasion, chapter 5)

We can be sure that the narrative voice supplies the characterization of Anne's mind, serving up, so to speak, the reasons for the superiority that Anne probably thinks she feels as mere difference.

We have so far considered a world given us for recognition but an action that is ingeniously directed toward a happy ending. We are never in serious doubt, as we read Jane Austen's novels, that they will take a comic form and find a bright resolution. There are countless indications of this as we read. They come from the narrative control, its brisk judgments and ironic asides, and the cool tone which in almost every case keeps us from that self-forgetful immersion in a scene that a literature of sentiment demands. There is only a small distance between a narrative voice that orders events pointedly, describing them in terms which are full of implicit judgment, and a voice that, becoming self-conscious, calls attention to the artifice of the whole narrative process.

The comic frame of these novels permits us to scrutinize the world they present with detachment and to observe its incongruities with great precision. It is in manners that Jane Austen's world exhibits greatest density, for manners are concrete, complex orderings, both personal and institutional. They are a language of gestures, for words too become gestures as they are used to sustain rapport. Such a language may become a self-sufficient system: polite questions that expect no answers, the small reciprocal courtesies of host and guest, or elder and younger; the protocol and management of deference. The code provides a way of formalizing conduct and of distancing feeling. We need not feel the less for giving our feeling an accepted form; yet of course we may, for the code of manners provides disguise as readily as expression.

The control that manners provide is made clear in *Emma.* All the company at Hartfield have been invited to spend an evening with the Westons at Randalls. John Knightley is outraged at the imposition:

"here are we . . . setting forward voluntarily, without excuse, in defiance of the voice of nature, which tells man, in every thing given to his view or his feelings, to stay at home himself, and keep all under shelter that he can;—here are we setting forward to spend five dull hours in another man's house, with nothing to say or to hear that was not said and heard yesterday, and may not be said and heard again tomorrow."

(chapter 13)

In contrast we have the effusive Mr. Elton:

> "This is quite the season indeed for friendly meetings. At Christ-
> mas every body invites their friends about them, and people think
> little of even the worst weather. I was snowed up at a friend's
> house once for a week. Nothing could be pleasanter. I went for
> only one night, and could not get away till that very day se'nnight.

We may shudder in behalf of Mr. Elton's friend and as much in behalf of
John Knightley's hosts. But in fact both men must adjust to the social scene.

> Some change of countenance was necessary for each gentleman as
> they walked into Mrs. Weston's drawing-room;—Mr. Elton must
> compose his joyous looks, and Mr. John Knightley disperse his
> ill-humour. Mr. Elton must smile less, and Mr. John Knightley
> more, to fit them for the place.—Emma only might be as nature
> prompted, and shew herself just as happy as she was. To her, it
> was real enjoyment to be with the Westons.
>
> (chapter 14)

One could perhaps speak of John Knightley's initial attitude toward this
society as "unregulated hatred," which undergoes regulation as he enters
the drawing room. His charges are accurate enough so far as they go. Yet
the standard of conversation upon such occasions need not be demanding;
clearly the warmth of having "friends about them" (in Mr. Elton's words)
is sufficient for most, and the conversation of friends may be an occasion,
above all, for recognition and reaffirmation, for pleasures that are only in-
cidentally registered in the words spoken. "The happiest conversation," Dr.
Johnson once remarked, "is that of which nothing is distinctly remembered
but a general effect of pleasing impression"; and elsewhere he spoke of it as
"a calm quiet interchange of sentiments."

While manners may be a self-sufficient code, at their most important
they imply feelings and beliefs, moral attitudes which stand as their ultimate
meaning and warrant. Both passion and principles are stable. When they
change, the change is slow and massive. When they are in conflict, the conflict
is sharp and convulsive. In the middle range, that of manners, change is
frequent, less momentous, and less costly; we call it accommodation. To the
extent that manners allow us to negotiate our claims with others, they become a system of behavior that restrains force and turns aggression into wit
or some other gamelike form of combat.

So at least we may say of manners in the ideal sense. Yet Jane Austen's
concern is not simply with good manners but with manners of all kinds,

boorish, insolent, graceful, rigid, pompous, or easy. Manners have considerable suppleness and ambiguity. We may see in them a comic incongruity: the failure of behavior to realize intention, the use of the conventions of courtesy to express cold distaste or angry resentment. The novelist must always recognize the conflict between the code of a society and the code of moral principle; manners may become a code of socially acceptable immorality. David Lodge has stated the issue with admirable clarity:

> In brief, Jane Austen creates a world in which the social values which govern behaviour at Mansfield Park are highly prized . . . but only when they are informed by some moral order of value which transcends the social. . . .
>
> A code of behaviour which demands such a delicate adjustment of social and moral values is by no means easy to live up to. It demands a constant state of watchfulness and self-awareness on the part of the individual, who must not only reconcile the two scales of value in personal decisions, but, in the field of human relations, must contend with the fact that an attractive or unexceptionable social exterior can be deceptive.

Lodge provides us with two codes, one of terms that establish "an order of social or secular value" (for example, agreeable, correct, fit, harmony, peace, regularity) and another of terms that suggest "a more moral or spiritual order of value" (for example, conscience, duty, evil, principle, vice). The former code tends to assert "the submission of the individual to the group," the latter "the possibility of the individual having to go against the group." The two codes overlap; they are not "unambiguously distinguished or opposed," and their interpretation requires, therefore, considerable power of discrimination.

There are, moreover, times when the moral, as much as the social, order can itself become a refuge from self-awareness. To live entirely by principle, as Mrs. Norris persuades herself she does, or as Fanny Price in a quite different way would like to do, may be almost as destructive as to remain oblivious of a moral order. What seems most important to Jane Austen is a mind that has range and stretch, an unconstricted consciousness that can make significant choices. This is not to suggest that Jane Austen's characters must engage in vice to know its import, nor is it to deny that Fanny Price, even when she is all but imprisoned in fears of doing wrong, earns our sympathy.

One of the most original and influential critics of Jane Austen was Lionel

Trilling, and he was never sharper than in his discussion of the "chief of-fence" of *Mansfield Park* for the modern reader:

> This lies . . . in the affront it offers to an essential disposition of
> the modern mind, a settled and cherished habit of perception and
> judgment—our commitment to the dialectical mode of appre-
> hending reality is outraged by the militant categorical certitude
> with which *Mansfield Park* discriminates between right and
> wrong. This disconcerts and discomfits us. It induces in us a
> species of anxiety. As how should it not? A work of art, notable
> for its complexity, devotes its energies, which we cannot doubt
> are of a very brilliant kind, to doing exactly the opposite of what
> we have learned to believe art ideally does and what we most love
> it for doing, which is to confirm the dialectical mode and mitigate
> the constraints of the categorical. *Mansfield Park* ruthlessly rejects
> the dialectical mode and seeks to impose the categorical con-
> straints the more firmly upon us.

There is often a moment, however, recognized only in retrospect, when a great "offence" becomes a new orthodoxy. We may have reached a mo-ment—to judge by recent books on Jane Austen—when moral rigor has a renewed attraction, even a romantic appeal; and it is not to question the praise *Mansfield Park* has been given to see it as a telling symbol of what we may miss in our lives and prize all the more when we find it in a novel. The leech-gatherer of Wordsworth's poem appears on the moor just when the poet's delight has turned to despair, and the aged pedestrian has a mean-ing for the poet he hardly has for himself: "Such a figure, in such a place, a pious self-respecting, miserably infirm . . . Old Man telling such a tale!"

If we are to disencumber Jane Austen of the role of moralist, we must distinguish between moral assertion and moral imagination. Let me present an instance from *Sense and Sensibility*. Mrs. Ferrars, who is an imperious and vain mother, fond of her least worthy children, disinherits her son Ed-ward when he announces his intention to marry Lucy Steele. But Lucy breaks the engagement in order to marry the new heir, his brother Robert, and frees Edward in turn to marry Elinor Dashwood, whom he genuinely loves. Ed-ward turns to his mother for forgiveness:

> After a proper resistance on the part of Mrs. Ferrars, just so
> violent and so steady as to preserve her from that reproach which
> she always seemed fearful of incurring, the reproach of being too

amiable, Edward was admitted to her presence, and pronounced
to be again her son.

Her family had of late been exceedingly fluctuating. For many
years of her life she had had two sons; but the crime and annihilation of Edward a few weeks ago, had robbed her of one; the
similar annihilation of Robert had left her for a fortnight without
any; and now, by the resuscitation of Edward, she had one again.

In spite of his being allowed once more to live, however, he did
not feel the continuance of his existence secure, till he had revealed his present engagement; for the publication of that circumstance, he feared, might give a sudden turn to his constitution,
and carry him off as rapidly as before.

(chapter 56)

In the first of these sentences we see a mock-rationale such as alone can
explain Mrs. Ferrars's behavior in any terms but the true one, willfulness.
In the second paragraph, the irrational vigor of that will is felt in the fluctuating fortunes of her family, as members in turn suffer "annihilation" and
"resuscitation." And finally this fiction of her godlike power to crush and
restore is assumed with literal mock-solemnity. The comic energy expands
in the course of the passage: Mrs. Ferrars's fantasies are recognized as her
reality, as well they may be, since her will is almost matched by her power;
and the narrative quietly accepts her vision, by a method that is akin to free
indirect discourse.

Clearly Jane Austen means us to see the tyranny and the failure of love,
but these are too obvious to demand our full attention; they are the sub-
stratum upon which the fantastic edifice of will is erected, and the elabo-
ration of that edifice commands our wonder. Or to change the metaphor,
we can see the singular tenacity with which character is sustained, the formidable genius of the passions to find pretexts and saving illusions or, somehow, at any rate, to generate an idiom of respectability. We can see this even
more in the brilliant second chapter of the novel, where John and Fanny
Dashwood collaborate in casuistry. They pare away his obligations to his
sisters ("related to him only by half blood, which she considered as no
relationship at all"). They magnify the value of what they might surrender
("How could he answer it to himself to rob his child, and his only child too,
of so large a sum?"). They reduce the claims of others upon them ("They
will be much more able to give *you* something"). And at last they cultivate
resentment to dissolve any obligation to fulfill his father's request ("Your
father thought only of *them*"). The projected settlement of three thousand

pounds contracts at last to officious advice and (perhaps) an occasional small gift. What is dazzling is not merely the selfishness of the Dashwoods, formidable as that is, but the brilliant efficiency and ease of their self-justification.

It is here that one sees Jane Austen's moral imagination shaping comic invention, as it so often had in Henry Fielding before her. For the progressive contraction of the Dashwoods' spirit is caught with that splendid assurance of movement we can see in Lady Booby's resolution to call back Joseph Andrews once she has dismissed him. The movement defeats all scruple with a splendid show of moral righteousness.

It is by such deftness that one can best identify comic movement. It eludes scruple just as it eludes physical obstacles; the comic decision has much in common with the comic chase in films; there is the same miraculous evasion of every blocking force, whether the strictures of reason or the traffic ahead. In the comic hero such movement becomes the deft avoidance of threatening intrigues, of blocking elders, of false rigidities and narrow conventions. In such fools as the Dashwoods or Mrs. Ferrars, the deftness lies in prompt obedience of their consciousness to their passion; and what it eludes is not a false restriction but the censorship of decency. So of Lucy Steele, the author writes that her intrigue and its success "may be held forth as a most encouraging instance of what an earnest, an unceasing attention to self-interest, however its progress may be apparently obstructed, will do in securing every advantage of fortune, with no other sacrifice than that of time and conscience" (chapter 61).

It may, of course, be said that Jane Austen uses her comic celebration of ingenious villainy as a way of insisting all the more, through ironic understatement, upon its evil. The hard egoism that makes these characters imperturbable provides a striking contrast to the vulnerability and pathos that both Elinor and Marianne at times exhibit. The moral insight which the irony evokes and reinforces lives deep in the conception of the novel and informs all its parts. Yet the insight is not what the novel seeks to create, but is rather that upon which it draws. Such comic characters as the John Dashwoods may be morally discredited, but they survive admirably. The novel rests not so much upon their satiric exposure as upon their comic performance.

We can see this most clearly in *Pride and Prejudice*. Whatever his deficiencies as a father, Mr. Bennet has a superb relish for folly; the fools, as Rachel Trickett observes, are "all funnier for his comments on them, and he thus sustains and increases the comic force." He plays Jaques, with all his "irresponsible detachment," to Elizabeth's Rosalind, and he sets off all the more Elizabeth's growth beyond detachment. "He sets the scale of criticism though he is criticized himself, and it is in the relation to him that we recognize the heroine's good sense and her real feelings." We are struck with the continuity, at the close, of the comic pattern. Mrs. Bennet remains as she was at the outset, and this is "perhaps lucky for her husband, who might not have relished domestic felicity" if she were not "still occasionally nervous and invariably silly." Mr. Bennet has made his accommodation; and while he has missed the luxury of having Collins as a son-in-law, he can be content with the outrageous Wickham. The brief crisis of moral assertion and self-reproach has passed, and the Bennets are restored to the climate of comedy.

There may be an element of pathos in a comic character, as is the case with Miss Bates. Her compulsive talking awakens us to the narrow life that finds fulfillment in this kind of release. We need not keep in focus the emptiness that finds vicarious existence in gossip or the ardor for attachment that intensifies and distends each minute detail of commonplace encounters. In short, our sense of all the displaced feeling that floods into silly words does not overweigh the impression of their silliness, nor does our sense of motive distract our attention from the resourcefulness of the motive power, the alacrity with which all experience is translated into an obsessive idiom. We retain enough comic detachment for the most part to regard Miss Bates with amusement, and it is significant that our own surprise at her modest expression of pain after Emma's insult marks a shift in our awareness of Miss Bates somewhat as, through Knightley's comments, it marks an epoch in Emma's "development of self" (chapter 47).

For those who are themselves self-absorbed, such bores as Miss Bates may become very irksome. The attention they fail to give makes the attention they demand all the more troubling. Screened from others by their volubility, needing only the pretext of an audience, they yield little of what one feels is owed one; and for one with claims so large as Emma's, they represent a peculiar affront. So that we find Emma chafing under the strain, while Knightley is sufficiently his own man to be detached and liberal: he can endure the nonsense, see the pathos and warmth, and recollect above all the duties of consideration.

Miss Bates is a special case of the bores and fools we find throughout Jane Austen's novels. Some are aggressively sociable, like Sir John Middleton; others archly prying like his mother-in-law, Mrs. Jennings; some pretentious and alternately servile or smug like Collins, some oppressively rude and patronizing like Augusta Elton. What they all share is deficiency of awareness, indifference to others' feelings or privacy, obtuseness about their own motives. They tend to be great talkers, talking not so much for victory, like Dr.

Johnson, as for survival; they retain their stable existence, their life of un-
troubled repetition, by blocking off reality with talk.

The comic limitations remain in those characters who are at once more
plausible and treacherous. They seem, at first, to be of the very spirit of
comedy themselves, for they are dedicated to play. And they help to remind
us that Jane Austen's novels have themselves provided the materials of a game
of allusions for generations of "Janeites." Games have every charm until they
are used to displace broader awareness and deeper feelings. It is this charm
we see in such figures as Frank Churchill or the Crawfords. Frank has
"smooth, plausible manners," but he wins Mr. Knightley's criticism, even
before he arrives, for his failure to visit his father. Knightley's words are like
the more peremptory moral assertions that Jane Austen herself adopts at
times. Of Tom Bertram she writes, at the close of *Mansfield Park,* "He
became what he ought to be, useful to his father, steady and quiet, and not
living merely for himself " (chapter 48). So in *Emma,* she writes of Mrs.
Weston: "She was happy, she knew she was happy, and knew she ought to
be happy" (chapter 36). Knightley speaks in similar vein about Frank Churchill: " 'There is one thing, Emma, which a man can always do, if he chuses,
and this is, his duty; not by manoeuvring and finessing, but by vigour and
resolution. It is Frank Churchill's duty to pay this attention to his father. He
knows it to be so, by his promises and messages; but if he wished to do it,
it might be done' " (chapter 18). Frank Churchill is essentially a young man
who cannot resist "manoeuvring and finessing." His love of games comes
out in his readiness to foster Emma's unpleasant conjectures about Jane.
Frank knows the truth and cannot reveal it; but he gains enormous pleasure
from helping Emma to imagine scandal that permits her the comfort of
superiority to Jane. Frank in turn can enjoy his superiority to Emma: he is
playing a game of his own in which she participates unknowingly and to her
ultimate shame. Even if we credit his belief that Emma has guessed the truth,
the game he thinks he is playing with Emma and the game she, in her
ignorance, thinks she is playing with him are both of them little less shameful
than the actual ones, and we see their culmination at Box Hill. In fact,
Knightley sees in Frank's professed belief a further sign of his disingenuous-
ness:

> "Always deceived in fact by his own wishes, and regardless of
> little besides his own convenience.—Fancying you to have fath-
> omed his secret. Natural enough!—his own mind full of intrigue,
> that he should suspect it in others.—Mystery; Finesse—how they
> pervert the understanding! My Emma, does not every thing serve

to prove more and more the beauty of truth and sincerity in all
our dealings with each other?''

(chapter 51)

Emma, in her recovery, recognizes Frank's motives as all too much like her
own: "I am sure it was a source of high entertainment to you, to feel that
you were taking us all in. . . . I think there is a little likeness between us."
But what distinguishes Frank from Emma is his reluctance to give up the
game. As he dwells lovingly upon his memories of others' deception, Jane
says "in a conscious, low, but steady voice, 'How you can bear such recollections, is astonishing to me!—They *will* sometimes obtrude—but how you
can *court* them!'" (chapter 54).

Frank Churchill's games strike us as immature; they are games of exclusion and superiority. Henry Crawford's games are a more radical part of
his nature and far more painful in their consequences. As he is first introduced in *Mansfield Park* we learn of his lighthearted intention to make the
Bertram sisters like him. "He did not want them to die of love; but with
sense and temper which ought to have made him judge and feel better, he
allowed himself great latitude on such points" (chapter 5). The Bertram
sisters are "an amusement to his sated mind," but one feels that the satiation
is as much with himself as with familiar pleasures. Henry's love of role-
playing seems a search for distraction, from a self he indulges but hardly
respects. The accounts that William gives of naval service fire Henry's fancy:
the "glory of heroism, of usefulness, of exertion, of endurance, made his own
habits of selfish indulgence appear in shameful contrast" (chapter 24). And
later with Edmund he imagines himself a clergyman preaching, only to recognize shewdly enough his need even in such a fancy to exercise power over
an audience and to coerce an eager response. But it is significant that Henry
reveals his unsteadiness and does so with no cynical pleasure. Fanny, once
he has planned to win her heart, awakens in him a deeper purpose.

Henry has "moral taste enough" to respond to her sensibility and her
capacity for feeling. His decision to make her his wife is in some sense what
Shaftesbury saw in the awakening of taste, the beginning of an ascent from
the aesthetic to the moral, from gallantry to a love of the Good. These are
large terms to bring to this text, but it seems clear that Henry Crawford
would wish to be saved from a self that wearies him and to find a new order
of life in marriage to Fanny. He had, we are told, "too much sense not to
feel the worth of good principles in a wife, though he was too little accustomed to serious reflection to know them by their proper name"; and so, in
his praise of her firmness of character, he has unknowingly "expressed what

was inspired by the knowledge of her being well principled and religious." There is considerable subtlety in this identification of an attraction that Henry Crawford feels but cannot recognize. His relapse is a failure not of consciousness but of will: "the temptation of immediate pleasure was too strong for a mind unused to make any sacrifice to right." Henry acts as he does with no love for Maria, and "without the smallest inconstancy of mind" toward Fanny, the one woman "whom he had rationally, as well as passionately loved" (chapter 48).

Henry Crawford's relapse is more interesting and moving than his sister's self-betrayal. Throughout the novel, Mary carries herself with great style, if not always with delicacy. She accepts her own outrageousness disarmingly: "Selfishness must always be forgiven, you know, because there is no hope of a cure," or, "Nothing ever fatigues me, but doing what I do not like." In a world where the worst are hypocritical and the best inhibited, this seems fresh and natural—except of course that it also seems calculated to gain its end. Mary is insincere only in assuming that sincerity alone—and it is often courageous—should acquit her. Her sincerity loses its spontaneity. As we hear it too often, it seems calculated. And it vanishes altogether in the painful exposure of that last "saucy playful smile" which seems held by the text as in a frozen film sequence, its futility turning to grimace.

There is a troubling moment at the close of *Mansfield Park*. Edmund has seen Mary's limitations and avowedly rejected her, but Fanny can see that the choice is not yet a firm resolve. At that moment, as if to administer a dose of truth that will cure or kill, Fanny tells him that the prospect of his brother's death and of his own inheritance may have restored him to eligibility in Mary's eyes (chapter 47). It is a cruel revelation but perhaps a necessary one. Edmund is seldom seen without irony during the last part of the book; and it is appropriate that by demanding Fanny as a confidante of his grief, he find himself in love with her. "She was of course only too good for him; but as nobody minds having what is too good for them, he was very steadily earnest in pursuit of the blessing." As for Fanny herself, she "must have been a happy creature in spite of all that she felt or thought she felt, for the distress of those around her" (chapter 48).

The larger irony that informs all of Jane Austen's comic art is a sense of human limitation. This is not a cynical vision; it may be affectionate enough, even a tribute to those feelings we value warmly. In *Sense and Sensibility* Elinor and Edward wait impatiently for the parsonage to be refurbished in time for their marriage: "after experiencing, as usual, a thousand disappointments and delays, from the unaccountable dilatoriness of the workmen, Elinor, as usual, broke through the first positive resolution of not marrying till every thing was ready" (chapter 50). The use of "as usual" catches the typicality both of their situation and of Elinor's decision. That they sense their situation as unique is equally clear; they are understandably self-absorbed and impatient with workmen who seem, through some strange indifference, "unaccountably" dilatory. There is gentle amusement with the irrationality, so little typical of Elinor but so generally typical of brides. One is reminded of Gibbon's account of his parents' marriage: "Such is the beginning of a love tale at Babylon or at Putney," or even more of his account of his own coming to an awareness of love: "it less properly belongs to the memoirs of an individual than to the natural history of the species."

Jane Austen constantly insists upon the limitations of our feelings. Does Henry Tilney love Catherine Morland? Yes, but the narrator "must confess that his affection originated in nothing better than gratitude; or, in other words, that a persuasion of her partiality for him had been the only cause of giving her a serious thought. It is a new circumstance in romance . . . and dreadfully derogatory of an heroine's dignity" (chapter 30). Is Willoughby a rake? No, he genuinely loves Marianne. "But that he was for ever inconsolable, that he fled from society, or contracted an habitual gloom of temper, or died of a broken heart, must not be depended on—for he did neither. He lived to exert, and frequently to enjoy himself " (chapter 50). So, too, Henry Crawford might well have won Fanny Price's love, for "her influence over him had already given him some influence over her" (chapter 48). And Colonel Brandon wins all of Marianne's love in time, for Marianne "could never love by halves" (chapter 50). The endings of the novels insist upon the capacity for self-repair and recovery; they provide the consolation of the finite for those who are easily deluded. Mrs. Grant's words to Mary Crawford on marriage are apt: "'You see the evil, but you do not see the consolation. There will be little rubs and disappointments every where, and we are all apt to expect too much; but then, if one scheme of happiness fails, human nature turns to another; if the first calculation is wrong, we make a second better; we find comfort somewhere'" (chapter 5).

"I purposely abstain from dates," we read at the close of *Mansfield Park*, "that every one may be at liberty to fix their own, aware that the cure of unconquerable passions, and the transfer of unchanging attachments, must vary much as to time in different people.—I only intreat every body to believe that exactly at the time when it was quite natural that it should be so, and not a week earlier, Edmund did cease to care about Miss Crawford, and became as anxious to marry Fanny, as Fanny herself could desire" (chapter 48).

This pleasure in human absurdity gives us, in Charles Lamb's words, "all that neutral ground of character, which stood between vice and virtue; or which in fact was indifferent to neither, where neither properly was called in question; that happy breathing-place from the burthen of a perpetual moral questioning"; it allows us to "take an airing beyond the diocese of the strict conscience." It is one thing to see men and women as fallible, another to insist that they are corrigible. If nature can be trusted to correct what men cannot, if man is never quite so good or evil as he intends or imagines, we are freed of the stringency of the moral passions, which, as Lionel Trilling has remarked, can be "even more willful and imperious and impatient than the self-seeking passions." Our moral judgments are at once necessary and dangerous; they exercise our deepest passions, but they terminate our free awareness. The commitment they require brings an end to exploration and openness. In that sense, among others, the moral passions are "not only liberating, but also restrictive," and the subtlest task of "moral realism" is "the perception of the dangers of the moral life itself." It is the sense of the problematic that we must preserve, a sense of the difficulty of such judgments, of their cost and of the dubious gratification they often provide.

The comic sense is compatible with moral imagination if not moral passion; its awareness of limitation need not provide a surrender of all judgment, and in fact the idea of limitation is itself a judgment. Yet it is also a recognition that the moral passions cannot trespass beyond certain limits. The effort to sustain moral consciousness at the same level of intensity in all our experience becomes a form of destructive anxiety. We may sense the consequences of the imperceptible choice and insist upon the fact of choice; yet we cannot always be bringing scruple and moral vigilance to each gesture of our lives or even, easier though it may prove, of the lives of others. There is at last a residual innocence we must grant to experience, a power to absorb us, to awaken curiosity, to claim our attention and affections with simple immediacy. We can see this best in the detached and free observation an otherwise busy mind like Emma's can achieve on the village street:

> Harriet, tempted by every thing and swayed by half a word, was always very long at a purchase; and while she was still hanging over muslins and changing her mind, Emma went to the door for amusement.—Much could not be hoped from the traffic of even the busiest part of Highbury;—Mr. Perry walking hastily by, Mr. William Cox letting himself in at the office door, Mr. Cole's carriage horses returning from exercise, or a stray letter-boy on an obstinate mule, were the liveliest objects she could presume to

expect; and when her eyes fell only on the butcher with his tray, a tidy old woman travelling homewards from shop with her full basket, two curs quarrelling over a dirty bone, and a string of dawdling children round the baker's little bow-window eyeing the gingerbread, she knew she had no reason to complain, and was amused enough; quite enough still to stand at the door. A mind lively and at ease, can do with seeing nothing, and can see nothing that does not answer.

(chapter 27)

It is not often, however, that we find Emma's mind both "lively" and "at ease." Its liveliness is usually a form of "eagerness" or self-assertion, such as we find in different ways in Marianne Dashwood or in Mary Crawford, to whom Edmund Bertram would grant the "rights of a lively mind." This "eagerness" betrays impatience with the limits of the actual: it may take the form of a wishful shaping of reality with self-gratifying fantasy or (in the case of Mary) more deliberate cultivation of outrageous assertions as much for their effect as for their partial truth. Those who are fully "at ease" may achieve something of what Wordsworth celebrated as a "wise passiveness," that is, an openness to experience that restrains the shaping will and allows oneself to be confronted by whatever is unpredictably there. We may see this receptiveness as opposed to both the moral passions and the self-seeking passions, for in both we find a closing of the mind to the variety of experience, an assumption of superiority, whether in the name of principle or in the name of wit. Marianne's impatience with the vulgarity of Mrs. Jennings, Mary Crawford's impatience with the dull conventionalities of the pious, and Emma's impatience with Miss Bates have this much in common.

Once Emma has been reproached by Mr. Knightley for being so "unfeeling" and "insolent" in her wit, she begins to be freed of the force of self-seeking passions and to undergo a true "development of self." By the time she is ready to receive Knightley's proposal, she has achieved something like the receptiveness Wordsworth celebrated: "Never had the exquisite sight, smell, sensation of nature, tranquil, warm, and brilliant after a storm, been more attractive to her. She longed for the serenity they might gradually introduce" (chapter 49). Not the least significant word in that passage is "gradually." We think of Anne Elliot's walk to Winthrop: "where the ploughs at work, and the fresh-made path spoke the farmer, counteracting the sweets of poetical despondence, and meaning to have spring again" (chapter 10).

ROBIN GROVE

Austen's Ambiguous Conclusions

"Jane Austen is by common consent an author remarkably sure of her values," one recent book begins, before going on to say what those values were and how they stood in the War of Ideas. Another speaks of her "authentic commitment to a social morality," while a third is concerned with her "moral certainties" as they make for the "inevitable resolution" of the ending. The wish to find firm absolutes in her work continues to be strong, for few of us like to feel we have wasted our time—as we may appear to have done, unless we can specify what's been learnt in the course of our reading. Perhaps the visibly nonproductive nature of the occupation has something to do with this. A man sitting reading *may* be advantageously employed, but you never can tell; and Coleridge was famously severe on the subject:

> I will run the risk of asserting, that where the reading of novels prevails as a habit, it occasions in time the entire destruction of the powers of the mind.
> (*Lectures on Shakespeare and Milton,* 1811, First Lecture)

So since novel-reading, if at all attentively done, absorbs so many private hours, the conscientious reader of fiction naturally wants to believe that he or she has profited from time so extravagantly spent. We owe it to ourselves, as the saying goes, to get something out of the music we listen to, the conversations we have, the novels we enjoy, when the very term "worthwhile"

From *The Critical Review* (Australia), no. 25 (1983). © 1983 by Robin Grove.

reminds us that a while *is* worth something and ought to be made the most of. "He that is prodigal of his Hours," wrote Benjamin Franklin, "is, in effect, a Squanderer of Money" (*Poor Richard's Almanack,* 1751); while, for Wesley, even more momentous issues were at stake, Christians being duty-bound to redeem the time, buying it back as our Saviour bought us, and snatching "every fleeting moment out of the hands of sin and Satan, out of the hands of sloth, ease, pleasure, worldly business" (quoted in E. P. Thompson, "Time, Work-Discipline, and Industrial Capitalism," *Past and Present,* no. 38). The way "pleasure" slips into that combination, as obviously a dangerous thing, is indicative of the suspicions the reader of novels still has to lay to rest—in himself amongst others, maybe.

The assumptions buried here are a product of history, of course—a piece of puritan-commercial life. But the history in question helped to shape the English novel in the first place, along with formative ways of thinking about it. No exploration of eighteenth- or nineteenth-century life gets far before colliding with ideas about conscience, responsibility, and so on. And partly because the novels themselves (partly) embody middle-class beliefs, a traditional criticism sharing many of the same beliefs continues to illuminate the works. It illuminates them, though, only from its particular angle, which necessarily casts shadows as well as light. And because literary criticism grew professional in a mercantile age, it is no wonder if motifs of accountability, profit, growth, are so often thrown up. Even now, to judge from the commentaries one comes across, among the first things a serious reader will look for in plays and novels is that the characters should learn their lessons. This makes experience worthwhile. Thus, Lear is blind to start with, but, through suffering, comes to see; the scales fall from Dorothea's eyes; Emma realizes her mistakes: in every case, enlightenment and self-improvement. The possibility that Lear learns nothing, or that Emma remains herself, no wiser or more mature, is alarming precisely because it seems to deny the works a reason for being written or read at all. (And poetry, in which few characters profit by experience, is especially hard to see the point of when attended to this way.) So naturally we look to endings, where we may expect to find how far the characters or author got. Half-forgetting the Aristotelian dictum that the end inheres in the beginning, we take the difference between the hero of the opening chapters and the same hero at the close as proof of insights achieved, goals won, lessons learned. One can rest on the fact that in most works of literature change occurs, and, being change, must tend in some direction—preferably towards a last state better than the first.

In the case of the early nineteenth-century novel many of our assumptions really are borne out by Jane Austen. She helped to form them, after all, so our finding in her books what they themselves taught us to see is a fine example of the self-referring nature—the proper circularity—of discourse. And indeed the fact that literary criticism is an activity of this sort, with circularities and self-referrals from which it cannot escape, is no cause for dismay. Rather, it provides a new energy with which to extend ourselves into the works, and thereby the works into ourselves, by attending the more to the patterns we form from what we read, and the disparity between those patterns as we see them now, and what we predicted, guessed at, hazarded, or had been led to expect.

Jane Austen's finales, for example, are just what they seem to be—happy endings where fortunes are handed out and partners are disposed. But they have a notable trick of dissolving the formulae which constitute them, so that, whether we are first-time readers looking forward to the marriages we knew would happen all along, or experienced commentators enthusiastic to be supported in a theory of our own, we are prompted to shape for ourselves "conventions" which actually the endings don't obey. What we see, because we were looking for it, may change on reflection under our gaze, till not only general summaries, but even established familiar terms are liable to sound suddenly inept. "Subtle . . . dramatic . . . evaluative . . . moral intelligence . . . complexity . . . attitudes . . . irony": it is perfectly possible to realize that that vocabulary constricts as well as sharpens one's understanding, but it is far more difficult to talk about Austen without settling into some other, equally confining mode. No need to point to interpretative thesis-books like Alastair Duckworth's *The Improvement of the Estate*; even quite open-meshed formulations have the effect, often, of netting the sinker rather than the fish:

> The form of Jane Austen's novels is . . . a dramatic action in which one of the leading characters learns something important enough about reality and his own nature to experience a deep change of mind or heart.
> (Robert Garis, "Learning Experience and Change," in *Critical Essays on Jane Austen,* ed. B. C. Southam, London, 1968)

Similar (sensible) descriptions of the books could be duplicated a dozen times without achieving either more relevance or less. The living thing we all try to grasp at simply isn't there.

It would be bold for me to pretend I can now produce it out of my bag. Perhaps the best one can hope for is to watch it in action; and even that is asking a lot. So to make things easier I too begin where Austen comes to a stop: the final pages of the books.

Usually, you'd gather, she happily just winds up the plot, and some readers admire her lightness of touch, while others detect in these marriages and settlements not her mastery but rather her subservience to conventional values: a giving-in to the optimism of bad faith. Either way, however, the endings are thought to bring the accidentals of the action to a halt. "Jacke shall have Jill, nought shall goe ill, / The man shall have his Mare againe, and all shall bee well." But that is, if anything, even less true a summing-up of Austen's endings than of the close of *A Midsummer Night's Dream*. Her heroines end joyfully in marriage; yet in the *way* their marriages are settled quite unsettling second thoughts and unaccommodated possibilities glance in. Because Anne Elliot glories in being a sailor's wife, "the tax of quick alarm" gets into the final sentence of *Persuasion*; and the final paragraph keeps us still measuring the certain good of prosperity, when we think of Mrs. Smith, against the realization that prosperity, like every good we can rely on, will not be enough: "She might have been absolutely rich and perfectly healthy, and yet be happy." What sort of comedy is this? To have every good thing, and still, for all that, *possibly* gain happiness: no simple culmination is arrived at here, any more than at the end of *Emma,* where true feeling takes one as far as it can—Mr Knightley has declared himself, Emma has accepted—yet this cannot change conditions. "She hesitated—she could not proceed," and the wedding is indefinitely postponed. In the end, it is not self-knowledge, or a reformed nature, or a loving heart, but turkeys that make her marriage possible—and, in doing so, commit her poor husband to life under the Woodhouse roof. "They were befriended," in other words, "not by any sudden illumination of Mr Woodhouse's mind, or any wonderful change of his nervous system, but by the operation of the same system in another way." Exactly. Right in the midst of the fun and happiness of the closing chapter, "the same system," because it cannot do otherwise, prevails, and Austen's joke points up its operations, for better, for worse, one must say. The nervous system by which Mr Woodhouse has long protected himself from life is not a reason for less joy in these closing pages; on the contrary, being part of the life it has sought to deny, it becomes the very ground from which the happy ending is, unpredictably, raised.

Austen's endings, though, tend to be even more delightedly thoughtful than single details can suggest. There is their sceptical turn, for instance, whereby the fiction, admiring its own contrivance, holds itself mockingly up to the light. Thus "perfect happiness" is regularly offered—the point being that that *is* what a novelist can arrange, and so in her pages we will have destinies settled, unions achieved, knots untied, with all the satisfying rightness of style that Life can never provide. It is very fine indeed to be disillu-

sioned on such a scale. But even this recurrent pleasure is not formulaic, but occurs in unique, unrepeatable resolutions.

> The anxiety, which in this state of their attachment must be the portion of Henry and Catherine, and of all who loved either, as to its final event, can hardly extend, I fear, to the bosom of my readers, who will see in the tell-tale compression of the pages before them, that we are all hastening together to perfect felicity.
>
> (*Northanger Abbey*)

> I purposely abstain from dates on this occasion, that every one may be at liberty to fix their own, aware that the cure of unconquerable passions, and the transfer of unchanging attachments, must vary much as to time in different people.—I only intreat every body to believe that exactly at the time when it was quite natural that it should be so, and not a week earlier, Edmund did cease to care about Miss Crawford, and become as anxious to marry Fanny, as Fanny herself could desire.
>
> (*Mansfield Park*)

As we hasten forward through the sentence from *Northanger Abbey*, urged yet delayed by the syntax and modulated from "anxiety" through "fear" to the "perfectly felicity" of the end, more and more enjoyment is given, till "tall-tale compression of the pages" releases a last upsurge of wit—namely, that unblemished happiness really is waiting for Henry and Catherine, for whom, inside the world of the novel, the present claim is no mockery but rather a statement of happy truth. By contrast, the sentences from *Mansfield Park* gather much more complicated feelings. What begins as open burlesque ("the cure of unconquerable passions") changes to a genuinely unsettling note—unsettling, because we're not able to divide what is comic from what is pitiful in Fanny's final reward: an Edmund as anxious to marry her as she herself could desire. One unchanging attachment switches off, and, the current running the other way, another switches on; "exactly at the time," moreover, "when it was quite natural that it should be so." That it should be "natural," as it is, is perhaps the saddest and funniest touch together, and a real sign that the wit of the passage is addressed to painful truths. For, far from being ensconced by her author in the Pamela-position (Virtue Rewarded), Fanny seems the most vulnerable of Austen's heroines—humorously and generously presented as vulnerable, both to her superiors at Mansfield Park and, indeed, to *us* if we want to treat her so. The novel keeps her assailability before us right to the end.

We might not hear it doing so to start with. "The happiness of the married cousins," the second-last paragraph begins, "must appear as secure as earthly happiness can be." That sounds smug enough. But inflect it whichever way we will, to stress one part of speech or the other—"married cousins," "earthly happiness," what "appears" or what really is—however we read it, it gives something other than the "perfect felicity" Catherine and Henry Tilney are allowed to enter upon. Nor do robust forms of humour, critically edged, fall silent: completing "the picture of good" is Dr Grant bringing on his apoplexy and death by three great institutionary dinners in one week.

> On that event they removed to Mansfield, and the parsonage there, which under each of its former two owners, Fanny had never been able to approach but with some painful sensation of restraint and alarm, soon grew as dear to her heart, and as thoroughly perfect in her eyes, as every thing else, within the view and patronage of Mansfield Park, had long been.

Yes, married to her cousin and brought back to the scenes of past distress, Fanny is one of the family at last, and "patronage" (the last words of the book don't permit us to forget) has been instrumental in her seeing and feeling as she does. She is *more* than Sir Thomas or Edmund or anyone else at Mansfield could have made her; but she is also *what* they made her, and there is an ineradicable sadness (amongst other things) in that.

It is sad-comic, if only because one of the diconcertingly open effects of Austen's endings is to bring into sight, for a moment or two, other feasible conclusions to the tale. Here, Fanny marries Edmund, and that is as "natural" as it's been shown to be. But the Fanny who engages Edmund ("most endearing claims of innocence and helplessness," "depending on his kindness," "soft light eyes," "timid, anxious, doubting"; he doesn't concern himself much with her strength of principle now) is very different from the Fanny of, say, chapter 44, reacting to his news of Mary Crawford:

> "He is blinded, and nothing will open his eyes, nothing can, after having had truths before him so long in vain.—He will marry her, and be poor and miserable. . . ." 'So very fond of me!' 'tis nonsense all. She loves nobody but herself and her brother. Her friends leading her astray for years! She is quite as likely to have led *them* astray. They have all, perhaps, been corrupting one another. . . . 'The only woman in the world whom he could ever think of as a wife.' I firmly believe it. It is an attachment to govern

> his whole life. . . . Oh! write, write. Finish it at once. Let there
> be an end of this suspense. Fix, commit, condemn youself."

That is a splendid outburst of bad temper, and an authentic voice—one which
only the Fanny Price of this particular set of circumstances has. Edmund, we
may be sure, will never hear it, because, circumstances having altered, so
too has Fanny. But the woman capable of rubbing her resentment into the
wound really did exist in the novel, quite as much as the docile self-sup-
pressor of whom we see far more.

One way and another, in fact, a willingness to unmake the very solidities
she has been at pains to establish is typical of Austen's mind. So Henry
Crawford, despite his worst intentions, does fall in love with Fanny—one
reversal of himself—and then despite that seduces Maria Bertram after all.
Likewise Catherine Moreland, brought out of one library-coloured existence,
only to be confirmed in another—that of "true romance": "for there are
some situations of the human mind in which good sense has very little
power." Or again, *Persuasion* is one long fugue on the theme that hope and
happiness are irrecoverably gone—although, as it turns out, they're not. In
each case, the novel proposes one reading of reality, and engrafts us into it,
practically in order (it seems) to surprise us out of it again. And something
similar happens in *Sense and Sensibility*. Elinor's care for Marianne, and the
elder sister's good judgment, are vigorously portrayed; they stand, whatever
else is laughed at in the book. Yet when the climax comes, it is she, not
Marianne, who receives the shocking revelation of how liable the mind is to
feelings it cannot approve or control.

> Willoughby, he, whom only half an hour ago she had abhorred
> as the most worthless of men, Willoughby, in spite of all his faults,
> excited a degree of commiseration for the sufferings produced by
> them—

his sufferings, that is: for once, Elinor is too crowded in upon by passions
of her own "to think even of her sister"—

> which made her think of him as now separated for ever from her
> family with a tenderness, a regret, rather in proportion, as she
> soon acknowledged within herself—to his wishes than to his mer-
> its. She felt that his influence over her mind was heightened by
> circumstances which ought not in reason to have weight; by that
> person of uncommon attraction, that open, affectionate, and
> lively manner which it was no merit to possess; and by that still

ardent love for Marianne, which it was not even innocent to indulge.

I am surely not the only reader who, coming to that final clause, has stretched
his eyes and focused again in momentary disbelief. The devastating truth is
that it is Willoughby's love for Marianne which makes her sister find him
the more fascinating, and the ardent attraction "which it was not even innocent to indulge" applies both to him and to her. Sense, in Austen's handling of it here, turns into something more dangerous than Sensibility while
we watch.

II

Austen's novels themselves seem to have been the result of admitting
and then making the most alternative versions of their own final form—other
possible novels, that is, which they might have been. Incidents and characters
of which not much was made in the 1790s when Austen employed them first,
turn up again, transposed, in compositions twenty years on: so the materials
of *Love and Freindship* or *Lady Susan* are redistributed into a variety of
more fruitful plots. And the interest to be drawn from investigations into it
all is perhaps that the experience of creating characters this way suggested
to Austen that character itself (as the novelist is concerned with it, I mean)
is scarcely more than a congeries of plausible effects. It may *look* consistent
and solid, but that is the improvisation of the moment. And if such an insight
is ironic—essentially, radically, so—it goes well beyond the usual province
of irony, "style." The whole substance of the novels is involved, though style
all the same may be the gate through which to approach.

To start with the simple case, there are times when Austen's irony is
not much more than a saying one thing while meaning another. So Elizabeth
Bennet, forced to observe her family at the Netherfield ball, mortifies her
feelings, but simultaneously relieves them, by calling vulgarity and misde-
meanour by opposite names:

> had her family made an agreement to expose themselves as much
> as they could during the evening, it would have been impossible
> for them to play their parts with more spirit, or finer success.

Her mother especially has been very fine indeed, and to call her so focuses
in one word the daughter's shame and the outsider's scorn: imagining what
the Bingleys and Darcy think, Elizabeth's cheeks burn.

More frequently, though, a sentence tells just the truth its context was not expecting to hold—thus liberating amusement, instead of turning it in on itself as sarcasm. So, of Edward IV in her "History of England," the young historian notes:

> This Monarch was famous only for his Beauty and his Courage, of which the Picture we have here given of him, and his undaunted Behaviour in marrying one Woman while he was engaged to another, are sufficient proofs.

Her "sufficient," capping the joke, is pleased with itself for being able to be so prim and yet so accurate, and already something of the enigmatic reserve into which her mature ironies will point is beginning to appear. So far, however, the ironist is still self-consciously in control.

What signals a more exploratory, less manipulative kind of wit is, often, the opening into larger, more varied rhythms. Epigrammatic flourishes—"It is a truth universally acknowledged, that a single man in possession of a good fortune," and so on—are of principal interest no longer. Instead, in a paragraph like this from *Sense and Sensibility* the couplet-like movement of the first few lines gives way as one listens to a different rhythm and a different comedy both at once:

> Mrs Ferrars was a little, thin woman, upright, even to formality, in her figure, and serious, even to sourness, in her aspect. Her complexion was sallow; and her features small, without beauty, and naturally without expression; but a lucky contraction of the brow had rescued her countenance from the disgrace of insipidity, by giving it the strong characters of pride and ill nature. She was not a woman of many words: for, unlike people in general, she proportioned them to the number of her ideas.

From presenting her as an automaton, moved by stylistic devices in the prose ("upright, even to formality . . . serious, even to sourness"), the writer gradually allows the figure a fortune of its own: a fortune of a kind, that is. Sentimentalists are keen to hear that novelists' characters get away from them—that being the mark of a Great Novelist, it appears; but what I mean is something else. Jane Austen does shape the figure of Mrs Ferrars; there is no getting away from that. But just when the novelist's pattern seems set to proceed according to the programme already announced, new factors make themselves felt. A "lucky contraction of the brow" rescues Mrs Ferrars's features from nullity, to make them (actually) worse. Luck, though, is something writers know about, and share with their creations, since the very act of finding words (which in turn *are* characters and incidents: these being

nothing more) can never be guaranteed or arranged-for in advance. A fortunate, chance-come phrase brings any of us, struggling to write, the height-
ened vitality of feeling that what we are trying to say has become more
real—as it has; for, transmitting our own luck as writers to the ideas, characters, arguments we are in the midst of evoking, we pass on that vitality as
well. So "Mrs Ferrars" is no longer to be summed up in parallelisms which,
opening and shutting in their regular way, imply that everything needful to
the figure is being neatly displayed. Instead, the final sentence carefully skirts
definition; if Mrs Ferrars proportions her words to the number of her ideas,
we cannot scoff at the chance that she has no ideas to articulate, without
admiring the discretion that keeps that possibility concealed. To read the
three sentences in sequence, therefore, is to move from external witticisms
at the character's expense, to an irony much further in. When deep irony is
in question, Jane Austen, like Mrs Ferrars, chooses not to say too much;
and in her not-saying the best comedy of the paragraph resides.

It must seem paradoxical, to praise so marvellously vocal a novelist for
leaving things to declare themselves unsaid. But I think that's what Austen
does. Of course, the things she leaves to speak for themselves were put there
by her in the first place. The prose did not write itself; but brought to the
fine pitch that hers is kept at, it seldom needs an overlay of authorial opinions
or extra weight. It "means" exactly what it says: as when a letter to her
niece, Fanny Knight, avers: "I am by no means convinced that we ought not
all to be Evangelicals, & am at least persuaded that they who are so from
Reason and Feeling, must be happiest and safest." The scrupulous filtering
of the sentence through double and triple negatives deposits the last word
with a force that leaves it up to the reader to decide what to do with so
much security. "Do not be frightened from the connection by your Brothers
having most wit," she goes on. "Wisdom is better than Wit." Well, if only
the sentence had ended there, we could have thought we knew Jane Austen's
views on the serious subject; but it's continued in such a fashion as to undo
what it just seemed to clinch: "Wisdom is better than Wit, & in the long
run will certainly have the laugh on her side." The elements in that joke, like
the slip-knot in Buckminster Fuller's rope, form a self-interfering pattern.
You can tighten it or loosen it, you can slide other strands of material
through; but the only way in which the knot will cease to tug against itself
is if you finally take it apart.

The underlying process here, to quote a seminal essay by George Whalley, is true metaphor—that is,

the collision of elements none of which will give up any part of its integrity. .... In this, we are considering not simply a verbal locution or "figure of speech" but a commanding process radical to poetry itself—the metaphorical process that secures and enriches the interaction not only of single words, but of elements within sentences, of sentences within paragraphs, and the collisive interaction of elements of much larger scale if they can be constructed with strong enough identity.

> ("Jane Austen: Poet," in *Jane Austen's Achievement,*
> ed. Juliet McMaster, London, 1976)

This takes us at a stride beyond the whole terminology of "attitudes" and "values," of novelists "endorsing" this, or "undercutting" that, and so on. The writer does not adopt a "stance," so much as achieve felicities. That last, somewhat old-fashioned word is in danger of sounding merely affected when used by a twentieth-century critic. I return to it, though, because I can think of no other which better conveys the work of the novelist-as-poet whom Professor Whalley has brought to light. Thus, to praise Wisdom by giving *it* the laugh in the long run is a felicity, a well-founded joke, made possible by the lucky chance which gave English the cliché to start with, then brought it renewed into Jane Austen's hand. It is a real *trouvaille.* In one sense, therefore, there was nothing for her do—nothing, except to be as alert as any writer has been to the nuances and possibilities, the lucky strikes, of the language of her day. And so she was, supremely. She listened, and heard in the most innocuous phrases possibilities she could improve. Mr Yates comes to Mansfield "on the wings of disappointment"; Edmund strives that Fanny should get a horse "against whatever could be urged by the supineness of his mother, or the economy of his aunt"; Tom quietens a bad conscience, when Dr Grant turns out to be in hearty middle-age, with the reflection that "no, he was a short-neck'd, apoplectic sort of fellow, and, plied well with good things, would soon pop off." We read prose like this, says one critic, as we read the verse of *The Dunciad.*

Its effects are not always satiric, though. They may give genial comedy one moment, immediately after a passage of mordant attack, then something more allusive the next. I called some of the ironies "enigmatic" a moment ago, but not even that suggests how far they range. One of the most splendid passages in English fiction is surely the sense of the Crofts driving Anne Elliot home and debating as openly as if they were by their own fireside the chances of Captain Wentworth marrying one of the Musgrove girls:

> "And very nice young ladies they both are; I hardly know one from the other."

"Very good humoured, unaffected girls, indeed," said Mrs
Croft, in a tone of calmer praise, such as made Anne suspect that
her keener powers might not consider either of them as quite
worthy of her bother; "and a very respectable family. One could
not be connected with better people.—My dear admiral, that
post!—we shall certainly take that post."

But by coolly giving the reins a better direction herself, they
happily passed the danger; and by once afterwards judiciously
putting out her hand, they neither fell into a rut, nor ran foul of
a dung-cart; and Anne, with some amusement at their style of
driving, which she imagined no bad representation of the general
guidance of their affairs, found herself safely deposited by them
at the cottage.

(Persuasion)

It is not just the Admiral's altogether proper inability to tell Musgrove females
apart, nor the timely hand Mrs Croft lends the reins, which gives such pleasure here, but the writing's unboastfully poetic vigour. Without straining
towards imagery or metaphor, the phrasing achieves what it wants of their
power: thus it observes that, whereas one merely falls into a rut, dung-carts
would be run foul of. Quite. And at the very moment Mrs Croft agrees "One
could not be connected with better people," she must alert her husband to
the realities they *are* in danger of being connected with: "—My dear admiral,
that post!—we shall certainly take that post." The imaginative chance presented by the turn of the phrase has been gratefully seized. A happy accident
for the English-speaking.

What makes it genuine felicity, though, is that, once grasped, it is allowed to go free. Experimental scientists, I am told, have made it possible
for rats to pleasure themselves by pressing a button in the cage. Once they
get the hang of it, they cannot stop; most rats pleasure themselves to death.
I take it that this, though physiologically happiness, is its opposite in fact.
Deprived of chance and luck and hazard, all that is left is excitation on
demand; whereas happiness, as the word itself conveys, is not to be had for
the asking. It comes and goes free; Shakespeare says as much in an ordinary
pun:

> Wish me partaker in thy happinesse,
> When thou do'st meet good hap.
> (*The Two Gentlemen of Verona*, I.i.14)

It is a deep thing about Jane Austen's art that it should be so responsive to
the passing chance of joy, and so in more than one sense have the grace to
take, and relinquish, lightly.

IAN WATT

Jane Austen and the
Traditions of Comic Aggression

I've long been intending to develop some things that were omitted from *The Rise of the Novel* to make it shorter and clearer in structure. It is to be called *Gothic and Comic: Two Variations on the Realistic Tradition*. As regards the comic tradition, one of the central arguments is that when Jane Austen began to write there was no established narrative tradition that would serve her turn. More specifically, earlier writers of English comic novels, such as Fielding, Smollett, and Fanny Burney, had in different ways adopted the polar opposition between good and bad characters which is typical of stage comedy from the Greeks on. Through the finer and more detailed psychological calibration of her narrative, Jane Austen made the hero and heroine psychologically complex, and therefore capable of internal and external development. By this means the traditional conflict of "good" and "bad" characters in comedy was internalised as a conflict within and between the "good" characters; and this enabled Jane Austen to discover the answer to Horatio Bottomley's prayer—"I pray that the bad be made good, and the good nice, and the nice, interesting."

The prayer is very rarely answered—alas!—either in life or in art; but one can surely say about Elizabeth Bennet and Emma Woodhouse that they are not only good and nice, but interesting. They are made interesting be-

From *Persuasions: Journal of the Jane Austen Society of North America* 3 (December 16, 1981). © 1981 by Ian Watt. Since this address was prepared in haste, and for a very particular occasion and audience (The Jane Austen Society of North America), Ian Watt wishes it to be considered not as a "publication" but merely as a printed souvenir.

cause they are idiosyncratic mixtures of character traits, mixtures by no means limited to the good and unexceptionable qualities. For the purposes of comedy there remained a further task—the protagonists had to take over many of the aggressive functions which stage comedy has traditionally allotted to other actors—to the witty helpers, blocking characters, and villains. It is this, I think, that constitutes Jane Austen's greatest originality as an artist; and I would add that this literary originality is based on her psychological and moral realism, which gave the aggressive impulses a role which went far beyond the thought of her time, and, in some ways, of ours.

I will first illustrate the general idea by looking at *Emma* and *Pride and Prejudice*; and then I will consider *Sense and Sensibility* as an early stage in Jane Austen's development of the treatment of aggression.

Jane Austen's novels contain three main types of comic aggression, and all of them involve the "good" characters as well as the others. The first category—which I will call the social—is concerned with how people have different ways of hitting back at the restraints which social life exacts.

Most of the social gatherings described by Jane Austen provide illustrations. In the first social occasion in *Emma,* for instance, the party at the Westons' is dominated by the dialectic of constraint and hostility, and it thus serves as symbolic prelude to the novel's climactic scene on Box Hill. On the one hand, there are the positive, outgoing feelings, however strained, which are directed towards congeniality and sociability, and are expressed through compliments, jesting, and amiability; on the other hand, there are the contrary negative impulses of resentment at whatever threatens or inhibits the individual's status, habits, or convictions.

Every topic of conversation, we notice, evokes some note of hostility. For instance, Isabella Knightley's maternal zeal leads her to an odiously gratuitous pretence of benevolence in connections with Mrs. Churchill: "What a blessing that she never had any children! Poor little creatures, how unhappy she would have made them!" Then Mr. John Knightley comes in to give an alarmist account of the snow, "Concluding with these words to Mr. Woodhouse: 'This will prove a spirited beginning of your winter engagements, sir. Something new for your coachman and horses to be making their way through a storm of snow.'"

Others try to comfort poor Mr. Woodhouse, but his tormentor is "pursuing his triumph rather unfeelingly," and continues sardonically: "I admired your resolution very much, sir . . . in venturing out in such weather, for of course you saw there would be snow very soon. Every body must have seen the snow coming on. I admired your spirit; and I dare say we shall get home very well. Another hour or two's snow can hardly make the road impassable;

and we are two carriages; if *one* is blown over in the bleak part of the common field there will be the other at hand."

John Knightley's gleeful malice towards poor Mr. Woodhouse's timidity is authorised by his ideology; he is unkind only in the pursuit of a higher truth. The truth is the pointless folly of social life in general, and it has as its primary axiom that dinner-parties are "in defiance of the law of nature"— an axiom which strikes a death blow at two of the cardinal values of comedy—laughter and feasting.

Here, as in most of the social gatherings in *Emma*, harmony only prevails when the group is happily engaged in the malicious criticism of third parties. The most intransigent and socially-destructive manifestation of aggression occurs when some challenge arises to the imperative need of the individual ego to maintain its own image of itself in the face of the outside world. This need produces the cruellest deliberate act in *Emma*, when Mr. Elton refuses to dance with Harriet Smith at the ball in the Crown; his pride has been offended, and seeks revenge. In Jane Austen, however, unconscious cruelty is much commoner, and most often arises from a mere refusal or inability to understand other people. Mr. Woodhouse, for instance, is genuinely kind in his way; but, lacking the controls of intelligence or awareness, his phobias often lead him into the milder forms of cruelty, invective and lying. Thus his tyrannical valetudinarianism leads him to disappoint Mrs. Bates's eager anticipation of a "delicate fricassée of sweetbread and asparagus," on the grounds that the latter were not "quite boiled enough"; the same phobia emerges in a more rancorous verbal form when the arrival of gruel in his family circle becomes the occasion for "pretty severe Philippics upon the many houses where it was never met with tolerable."

It would certainly be wrong, I must observe, to infer that Jane Austen condemns all social forms of aggression. For one thing, it is manifested by every character in *Emma* about whom we can make a judgment, except for two, and they are the exceptions which prove the rule: I mean Mrs. Bates and Harriet Smith—good people no doubt, but intellectually null, with one of them—Harriet—not yet arrived at maturity, and the other—Mrs. Bates— long past it.

I come now to the other two kinds of comic aggression—the interpersonal and the internal—as they are manifested in *Pride and Prejudice*. The personal relations between Elizabeth and Darcy are dominated by the aggressive elements in their characters; these alone replace the roles of the villains, the blocking characters, and the mistaken identities in traditional comedy. This replacement depends on two narrative techniques: first, the aggressive impulses at play in the comic arena are psychologised in the "courtship" of the protagonists; and they are also psychologised as conflicts inside the egos of both the lovers.

These conflicts in the personalities of Elizabeth and Darcy provide the mechanism of the main plot. At first the aggressive aspects of their characters block their separation even before they are actually acquaintances. Darcy's pride leads him to reject Bingley's suggestion that he dance with her—"She is tolerable; but not handsome enough to tempt *me*; and I am in no humour at present to give consequence to young ladies who are slighted by other men." Elizabeth overhears him, and her offended pride, exacerbated by Meryton gossip and Wickham's lies, insulates her from Darcy's rapidly changing feelings. The whole of their relationship is thus presented as an adaptation and recombination of one of the most standard modes of comic aggression, invective, to the purposes of psychological and moral realism. Elizabeth and Darcy begin by insulting the other to third parties; later their acquaintance develops almost exclusively through bouts of contemptuous raillery which are as close to the verbal combats of Greek comedy as the manners of Regency England allowed.

The reason for the tradition of invective in comedy is presumably that it offers a symbolic release from the constraints on which civilisation depends; as Freud put it, "The man who first flung a word of abuse at his enemy instead of a spear was the founder of civilisation." But in the kind of novel which Jane Austen wrote the invective and the wit-combats cannot be treated as they usually are in stage comedy, in Aristophanes, for example; they cannot merely stop, and be succeeded by a quick change to feasting, song, dance, and marriage. For in *Pride and Prejudice* the substance of the debate between the two lovers is very real—it expresses the deepest divisions in the way the protagonists see the world and experience the circumstances of their place in it. Jane Austen's moral solution to these divisions is exactly what the solution, if any, would be in real life: the pains of self-education— the realisation of the errors, the delusions, and the prejudices of the self. In narrative terms Jane Austen brings the pattern of invective to a climax by a dual psychological transformation: interpersonal aggression is internalised in both hero and heroine.

In Darcy's case we do not see the process of self-punishment at work; but we can surmise that nothing else would lead him to propose marriage to Elizabeth. Then her insulting rejection apparently causes Darcy to take his self-punishment much further and he writes his abject explanatory letter. Now it is Elizabeth's turn. At first reading she is sure that "it was all pride and insolence," as regards Jane, while as regards Wickham, "she wished to discredit it entirely." Elizabeth then protests "that she would never look in (the letter) again," and we are already expecting the quick change of mind which the comic reversal requires. It soon comes: "in half a minute the letter was unfolded again." Elizabeth faces "the mortifying perusal of all that related to Wickham." From this second perusal there slowly emerges the deep personal humiliation of having to recognize how completely she has been taken in by this handsome scoundrel. From this traditional comic discovery of having been deceived, Elizabeth's negative emotions, which had previously all been directed outwards against Darcy, rapidly now alter their course and are directed inwards in a self-discovery of unflinching psychological rigour:

> "How despicably have I acted!" she cried.—"I who have prided myself on my discernment!—I, who have valued myself on my abilities! who have often disdained the generous candour of my sister, and gratified my vanity, in useless or blameable distrust— How humiliating is this discovery!—Yet, how just a humiliation!—Had I been in love, I could not have been more wretchedly blind. But vanity, not love, has been my folly.—Pleased with the preference of one, and offended by the neglect of the other, on the very beginning of our acquaintance, I have courted prepossession and ignorance, and driven reason away, where either were concerned. Till this moment, I never knew myself."

Now Elizabeth must come to terms with the fact that in many matters she shares with Darcy the same moral impulses, of which the most basic is to face the truth, even when it is deeply mortifying to the self. As a result Elizabeth joins Darcy in emerging from her deepest humiliation with a salutary increment of self-knowledge: they both undergo a parallel process of education through mortification.

Sense and Sensibility offers many examples of social, interpersonal, and internalised aggression. At the same time *Sense and Sensibility* is also, as one would expect from an earlier work, much closer than *Pride and Prejudice* or *Emma* to the classical tradition of comedy, and to Fanny Burney. The characters in *Sense and Sensibility*, for instance, tend to be more simply good or bad; the plot develops almost entirely through external events rather than inward changes in the protagonists; and although at the end Marianne and Edward Ferrars blame themselves for their past actions, they do so in spoken apologies to Elinor, and so there is no real analogy to the mortification scenes of Elizabeth or Emma.

First, social aggression. In *Sense and Sensibility* the battlefields of civility are littered with casualties. The most openly hostile characters are those who are wholly concerned with improving their financial and social condition; the way that John and Fanny Dashwood treat Mrs. Dashwood, Elinor, and Marianne is as gratuitous and persistently malicious as the behaviour of any stage villain. Having forced her husband to betray his promise, and his father's last wishes, Fanny Dashwood persuades herself—and John—that it is they who have been wronged; in the last tortuous extravagances of aggressive projection, John and Fanny even come to the persuasion that Elinor is as falsely designing as they are, and that she is trying to ensnare Fanny's brother, Edward Ferrars, in marriage. So, we observe, Fanny's observations of Edward's affectionate manner to Elinor give rise to her rudest outburst: "it was enough . . . to make her uneasy; and at the same time, (which was still more common), to make her uncivil. She took the first opportunity of affronting her mother-in-law on the occasion, talking to her so expressively of her brother's great expectations, of Mrs. Ferrars's resolution that both her sons should marry well, and of the danger attending any young woman who attempted to *draw him in*; that Mrs. Dashwood could neither pretend to be unconscious, nor endeavour to be calm."

Jane Austen pursues her theme remorselessly; and we see manipulative aggression becoming compulsive in the best stage traditions of the miser's monomania. The parallel hostility of Lucy to Elinor is expressed in false pretences of friendship which make it merely a polite variation on the same theme of ruthless social competitiveness. For example, when she meets the Dashwood sisters in London, Lucy gushes: "'I should have been quite disappointed if I had not found you here *still*,' said she repeatedly, with a strong emphasis on the word. 'But I always thought I *should*. I was almost sure you would not leave London yet awhile, though you *told* me, you know, at Barton, that you would not stay above a *month*. But I thought, at the time, that you would most likely change your mind when it came to the point. It would have been such a great pity to have went away before your brother and sister came. And now to be sure you will be in no hurry to be gone. I am amazingly glad you did not keep to *your word*.'" Lucy's attempts at poisoned badinage are as unsatisfactory as her grammar; a fatal garrulity betrays her intentions long before she has finished, and thus reveals her unwitting violation of the first law of sarcasm—a rapidity that leaves no time for a riposte, let alone a yawn.

Lucy Steele, like John and Fanny Dashwood and Mrs. Ferrars, is a one-dimensional comic villain; she evokes unremitting dislike from the reader and the narrator alike. The other main group in the cast of *Sense and Sensibility* are also one-trait comic characters whose function is to be the butt of the narrator's running joke. Whenever they appear, we are asked to join in mocking Sir John Middleton's smothering hospitality, his wife's bored egocentricity, Mrs. Jenkins's misguided preoccupation with matchmaking, Mr. Palmer's boorish rudeness, and Mrs. Palmer's silly laugh.

Mr. Palmer cannot be denied the honour of being the ancestor of John Knightley; he never says anything that is *not* aggressive, and utterly refuses the slightest concessions to social civility. At Barton Park he draws even that most minimal of conversational counters, the weather, into his aggressive symbolic system: "'How horrid all this is!' said he. 'Such weather makes every thing and every body disgusting. Dullness is as much produced within doors as without, by rain. It makes one detest all one's acquaintance. What the devil does Sir John mean by not having a billiard room in his house? How few people know what comfort is! Sir John is as stupid as the weather!'" Elinor, astonished at Mrs. Palmer's forbearance at her husband's rudeness, observes him closely, and decides that he is not "so genuinely and unaffectedly ill-natured or ill-bred as he wished to appear ... It was the desire of appearing superior to other people."

The nearest parallel in *Sense and Sensibility* to the wit combats of Darcy and Elizabeth are—I suppose—the dialogues between Elinor and Marianne. There are, of course, many important differences: for one thing, the fairly strict dichotomy in the novel between good and bad characters means that Elinor and Marianne are often the victims of unprovoked social aggression from the rest of the world, so that the reader usually sympathises with them against all the unfair, unjust, and hostile circumstances in which they find themselves; secondly, Elinor comes to us as a person having, unlike Marianne, nothing to learn, so that there is a built-in asymmetry in the relations between the two sisters; and thirdly, their dialogue does not lead to change or permanent understanding. *Sense and Sensibility* was originally entitled "Elinor and Marianne"; and this would have been appropriate in a way that "Elizabeth and Darcy" would not have been, because although Elinor and Marianne have some of both qualities they function as symbolic and permanent opposites as far as their relationships to each other are concerned.

Marianne never has a hostile thought which she forces herself to repress; she openly attacks Edward for his reserve, speaks very rudely to Mrs. Ferrars in defense of Elinor, and is openly indignant at John Dashwood's account of Mrs. Ferrars's disinheriting Edward. In each case, Marianne's anger is justified, but Elinor's obtrusively different behavior brings into question her openness in expressing it.

Whenever Elinor's criticism has ethical foundations and she believes that speaking may be useful or is morally obligatory, she gives her view openly and earnestly. Thus Elinor cautions Mrs. Jenkins against her gossiping about

Marianne and Willoughby: "you are doing a very unkind thing"; and she upbraids Miss Steele for listening at a keyhole and reporting what she has overheard. Under other conditions, and if her target is sufficiently dense, Elinor voices her opinion ironically; for example, when John Dashwood complains to her about his financial difficulties, we are told that Elinor, recalling how much cash he has withheld from her family, at first "could only smile." But when John presses his demand for her sympathy, saying "'You may guess, after all these expenses, how very far we must be from being rich, and how acceptable Mrs. Ferrars' kindness is,'" Elinor responds with adroitly ironic duplicity: "'Certainly,' said Elinor; 'and assisted by her liberality, I hope you may yet live to be in easy circumstances.'" She has read the barometer of complacent self-importance correctly, and her sarcasm goes right over John's head: "'Another year or two may do much towards it,' he gravely replied."

However, when John goes on to tell Elinor of his having pulled down all the walnut trees on the Dashwoods' beloved old property, Elinor in the best tradition of Mrs. Radcliffe's Emily de St. Aubert and Goethe's Werther, is really angry: but, we note, "Elinor kept her concern and her censure to herself; and was very thankful that Marianne was not present, to share the provocation." There is the same reserve when she watches the hopelessly duped Mrs. Ferrars being kind to Lucy Steele: "while (Elinor) smiled at a graciousness so misapplied, she could not but reflect on the mean-spirited folly from which it sprung, nor observe the studied attentions with which the Miss Steeles courted its continuance, without thoroughly despising them all four." As Robyn Housley has observed, "Elinor at her angriest is Elinor at her most silent"; Elinor knows that in her circumstances discretion is the best weapon which sense supplies for the defence of sensibility.

Compared to her behavior in public, Elinor's responses to her sister are much less reserved. From the beginning Elinor teases Marianne about the imprudence and danger of her excessive sensibility. Thus Elinor attempts to caution Marianne against her fast-growing friendship with Willoughby: "'You know what he thinks of Cowper and Scott, you are certain of his estimating their beauties as he ought, and you have received every assurance of his admiring Pope no more than is proper. But how is your acquaintance to be long supported, under such extraordinary dispatch of every subject for discourse? You will soon have exhausted each favourite topic. Another meeting will suffice to explain his sentiments on picturesque beauty, and second marriages, and then you can have nothing farther to ask'—." Marianne rejects the warning and counterattacks by asserting her superior sensitivity: "But I see what you mean . . . I have erred against every commonplace notion of decorum; I have been open and sincere where I ought to have been re-served, spiritless, dull, and deceitful:—had I talked only of the weather and the roads, and had I spoken only once in ten minutes, this reproach would have been spared."

Later, when Marianne has received Willoughby's letter, Elinor's advice becomes passionately serious: " 'Exert yourself, dear Marianne, if you would not kill yourself and all who love you. Think of your mother; think of her misery while *you* suffer; for her sake you must exert yourself.' " Marianne remains blind to Elinor's efforts and responds with self-indulgent insult: " 'I cannot, I cannot,' cried Marianne; 'leave me, leave me, if I distress you; leave me, hate me, forget me! but do not torture me so. Oh! how easy for those who have no sorrow of their own to talk of exertion!' "

Marianne's willful ignorance would remain invincible but for a com-bination of further accidents—the discovery of Edward's engagement to Lucy Steele, and Marianne's recovery. On both of these occasions, Marianne cer-tainly voices bitter self-accusation, and her words certainly sound like at-tempts at self-mortification. But her change of heart surely lacks inwardness and depth.

> "Oh! Elinor," she cried, "you have made me hate myself for ever.—How barbarous have I been to you!—you, who have been my only comfort, who have borne with me in all my misery, who have seemed to be only suffering for me!—Is this my gratitude!— Is this the only return I can make you? Because your merit cries out upon myself, I have been trying to do it away."

The ensuing commentary suggests that the narrator, at least, is not wholly persuaded that Marianne's remorse may not be yet another form of high emotional self-indulgence:

> In such a frame of mind as she was now in, Elinor had no dif-ficulty in obtaining from her whatever promise she required; and at her request, Marianne engaged never to speak of the affair to any one with the least appearance of bitterness:—to meet Lucy without betraying the smallest increase of dislike to her;—and even to see Edward himself, if chance should bring them together, without any diminution of her usual cordiality.—These were great concessions;—but where Marianne felt that she had injured, no reparation could be too much for her to make.

The listing of Marianne's promises builds up to a climax that is surely one of tolerant irony; and it suggests that there is still a residue of self-dramatising emotionalism in Marianne: her prime need is still to make herself interesting to herself. Of course, we don't really know if we are dealing with a reliable narrator or not, or what she is reliable about. Is it a prediction, coming out of authorial foreknowledge of the future, that Marianne will never change her ways? Or is it just the persistently ironic tone that everyone except Elinor evokes from the narrator? We do not know, and so, although we are not persuaded that Marianne undergoes the mortification of internal aggression, as we are with Elizabeth and Emma, neither are we persuaded that we know *how* we should see her.

At this point, having tried, in the small hours of the night, to bring my argument to some sort of a conclusion, and having failed, I fell asleep. Happily, for the narrator of *Sense and Sensibility* appeared and claimed the right to speak in her own defence. When I woke up, however, I was unfortunately unable to recall her exact words, except for the first sentence:

I see what you would be at, Mr. Watt,—and, yes, I suppose I am in my own way what you call modern—disgusting word! I first thought about this two generations ago when a copy of *Abinger Harvest* arrived in Heaven. I noticed that E. M. Forster wrote about T. S. Eliot's "The Love Song of J. Alfred Prufrock": "The author was irritated by tea-parties, and not afraid to say so." It set me thinking: "What's so new about that? And why should people be afraid to say so? But I suppose we are, and I was." Perhaps that's why my family tried to cover up the role of aggression in my novels when they put up that memorial brass to me in Winchester Cathedral, in 1872, that ends with the quotation from Proverbs (31:26): "in her tongue is the law of kindness." Surely they should have noticed from my novels, if they looked nowhere else, that the law of kindness is a very complicated one to obey especially if you also try to obey the law of truth. I think I did that battle rather well in *Emma*.

Of course it was more difficult, in my day, at least, for a woman: they were supposed to be all kindness, and truth was left to the men, like the right to anger. Men were entitled to have what the psychologists called "pugnacity," as long as most of it was whipped out of them at school; but women weren't supposed to have any, or at least not to show it. It wasn't easy for me when I started writing because I knew I wasn't like that at all. In *Northanger Abbey* I gave the "wrong" side of myself, the one that did not always think nice thoughts, to a man, Henry Tilney: and I'm afraid that later on I did the same thing a good deal in the other novels. In a way I wish Emerson's "Self-Reliance" had been written then, at least the beginning, when he says: "In every work of genius we recognise our own rejected thoughts."

I started trying to do more with my "own rejected thoughts" in *Sense and Sensibility,* but I was timid: I hid behind Elinor, and let her hide behind me. Of course, we had a lot of fun together—when we collaborated, for instance, when, after one of Robert Ferrars's interminable vapid pomposities we wrote: "Elinor agreed to it all, for she did not think he deserved the compliment of rational opposition." I do believe that it's no good pretending that society isn't just what we see it is; and I don't think my novels make aggression any commoner or more brutal than it is in ordinary life. That's why I thought that the article by D. W. Harding—"Regulated Hatred: An Aspect of the Work of Jane Austen"—is unfair. He understands my writing very well, I think, and gives me one good clue about why people have been admiring my novels more and more over the years. But why does he use the word "hatred"? That denies the normality of most of the aggressive feelings and actions which I show in my novels because I observe them in the real world. Does Mr. Harding really think that it would be dangerous to eat the Donwell Abbey strawberries out of fear that Mrs. Elton might have poison hidden away in "all her apparatus of happiness"? Of course, in your century as in mine, the passions take a much less extreme form than those which animated the wars of Troy. But isn't there still, expressed in different manners, the same flux and reflux of aggressive motives as once inspired Homer, and as still animate the crowd when they laugh to see Punch and Judy trying to knock each other's brains out?

It is surely misunderstanding of kindness to think it should blind us to society's lack of it. Shouldn't we attack those who pretend to ignore that lack? Surely that's what comedy is for? After all, when intelligent, sensitive and principled people meet, what better thing is there for them to do than share their assurance that they are seeing the same world. Isn't it bracing to face together our recognition of irremediable truths? And what better use can there be of our wit and experience than to write novels which make people who understand them laugh in liberated complicity at all the foolish and dangerous manifestations of aggression that are there in the world and in ourselves?

But I've talked too long. You seem quite gentleman-like, so I'm sure you'll keep this talk as secret as Elinor kept Lucy Steele's about her engagement to Edward Ferrars. Oh, no, thank you, don't get up, I can see myself to the door. In fact, I don't use doors any more. I'm much freer than I was in the old days.

DEBORAH KAPLAN

Achieving Authority: Jane Austen's First Published Novel

"I should like to see Miss Burdett very well," Jane Austen wrote her sister in 1813, "but that I am rather frightened by hearing that she wishes to be introduced to *me*.—If I *am* a wild Beast, I cannot help it." Miss Burdett had evidently heard that Jane Austen was the author of *Sense and Sensibility* and *Pride and Prejudice,* for, while Austen had been trying to keep her authorship secret, her brother Henry kept giving the secret away. As Austen wrote to another brother: "Henry heard P. & P. warmly praised in Scotland, by Lady Robt Kerr & another Lady;—& what does he do in the warmth of his Brotherly vanity & Love, but immediately tell them who wrote it! A Thing once set going in that way—one knows how it spreads!—and he, dear Creature, has set it going so much more than once." The portrait provided here— of the exhibiting brother and reserved sister—does not exaggerate the gender difference revealed in responses to fame in the late eighteenth and early nineteenth centuries. Austen's attitude was typical of women writers. In 1810, for example, another novelist, Mary Brunton, declared with similar vehemence about the prospect of literary fame, "I would sooner exhibit as a rope-dancer."

What women like Austen and Brunton wished to avoid was not simply fame but the attribute of assertiveness or authority implicit in novel-writing and recognized with fame. Both Austen and Brunton reach for creatures in an exhibition to convey the vanity of fame as well as the oddity or uncon-

From *Nineteenth-Century Fiction* 37, no. 4 (March 1983). © 1983 by the Regents of the University of California.

ventionality of authority. Austen associates a seemingly oxymoronic feminine authority with wild aggression; Brunton conjures up sexual immodesty. To avoid the ignominy of fame, late eighteenth- and early nineteenth-century women writers frequently adopted anonymity. A similar public gesture was made by women who would not put their names on the title pages of their books but signed their prefaces or who presented humble, dependent self-images in their prefaces. But such gestures of feminine modesty solved only the social and not the personal problem of female authorship. Women writers knew they were transgressing their culture's gender codes even if their readers did not. How did they justify to themselves their assertiveness—what Austen derogated as the "thing once set going in that way"—in a culture which denied authority to women?

As a psychological achievement of writers, authority has increasingly interested psychoanalytic critics who see the writer's struggles to assume the authority to write inscribed in the text. Most such investigators suggest that authors use images of the family—of genealogy or generational succession—in the novel to convey their experience of authority. And such images are also said to serve as a metaphor for the authority of narrative—its intentionality, temporal continuity, and the proliferation of narrative "events" or even, at times, of plots. Just as a parent produces a child, so one event or plot "gives birth" to another. This critical perspective is important because it makes possible discussions of literary works in relation to biographical issues without recourse to mimetic correlations between a writer's life and his or her art.

Unfortunately, this method avoids an old-fashioned reductionism at the cost of introducing a new male bias. Most practitioners of this method find the authority of authorship expressed in variants of the Oedipal conflict. Writing is viewed as a bid by the son for the father's authority and a record of the success or failure of that bid. For example, Edward Said's paradigm of authority and molestation, advanced in *Beginnings,* is not identified as an Oedipal conflict but nonetheless evokes it. According to Said, novelists compare their works with reality and become conscious of the secondary order of their creations. Through what is implicitly a contest with God, novelists discover that their authority "is a sham," confined "to a fictive, scriptive realm." Their failure to achieve authority is expressed in "a character's experience of disillusionment during the course of a novel."

The work of subsequent critics has been more explicitly psychoanalytic. Eric Sundquist's *Home as Found: Authority and Genealogy in Nineteenth-Century American Literature,* for example, adopts Freud's *Totem and Taboo* as a heuristic in order to argue that the kind of authority achieved by the act of writing will not only locate its own power in rebellion and seizure but also paradoxically augment the power of the ancestor whose downfall has become the subject of the sacrament of writing. Mockery and tribute will be fused in the craft of narrative, and the authority a writer's own performance implements will be sanctioned by violence at the same time it is hedged by his unconscious invocation and veneration of the ancestors whose place he has usurped.

David Wyatt's *Prodigal Sons: A Study in Authorship and Authority*, though just as focused on the Oedipal conflict, applies yet a different version to the study of writers' careers:

> My interest . . . is less in the occurrence of the paradigm *within* individual works than *across* a developing body of them. In each essay I search for a decisive turn in a career, the moment when an author makes his accommodation with authority and ceases wrestling with his role as a son. . . . If every son experiences an Oedipal conflict, these prodigal sons find themselves especially engaged in defining themselves within the terms of this conflict.

Because these critical studies uncritically assume that authoring is a male endeavor, because they insist that a male-oriented paradigm expresses the development of authority, they cannot adequately treat women writers. Indeed, with the exception of a few brief references to female writers in Said's *Beginnings* none of them tries to do so. These studies, however, do justly remind us that the novel, like the psychoanalytic models applied to it, emerged in patriarchal cultures and that it is itself a patriarchal genre—one which explores and celebrates bourgeois family life under the rule of the father. [By patriarchal, I mean the assumption that heads of households owned the women and children of their families as property and thus had complete command over them. . . . By patrilineal, another key term in this study, I mean the European aristocratic kinship organization which emerged in the tenth century with the appearance of family names, primogeniture, and the depreciation of the rights of women. Patrilineal practices maintained the continuity of the aristocratic family.] Were the figure of the father not consistently crucial in English and American novels, Wyatt or Sundquist could not, after all, find the rich textual evidence that they do for their accounts. That female writers have lived within patriarchal cultures, however, does not mean that they have had the same relations to paternal authority as their male counterparts. And we are going to have to open our theories of authority to social and historical considerations—not only of gender, but also of time, location, class, or ideologies—in order to understand how women dared to assert themselves in a society and a literature which allocated that act to men.

In the following essay I propose to examine Jane Austen's first published novel, *Sense and Sensibility,* as a means of discovering her particular accommodation of femininity and authority. I have chosen this novel because it marks a turning point in Austen's writing history. Jane Austen was born in 1775 to a rural Hampshire clergyman and his wife. The seventh of eight children, she entered a family which had already developed an avid interest in literature. At about the age of twelve Austen began writing burlesques—many of which she left unfinished—to amuse her family. In her early twenties she attempted full-length novels, though she also continued to produce short, humorous, and sometimes incomplete sketches. The few references to the novels which appear in her letters show only that they circulated among family members and close friends. We do know, however, that her father attempted to find publishers for two of these works. In 1797 he offered "First Impressions" to the firm of Cadell but was refused, and in 1803 he sold "Susan" to Crosby for ten pounds, though Crosby never published the manuscript. What is different about *Sense and Sensibility,* however, is not its publication but its preparation. Though we have little evidence of the relations between Austen and her publishers (her brother Henry often served as an intermediary), we do see, for the first time in the period from the spring of 1809 through 1810, evidence of Austen's own interest in publishing. In April 1809 she wrote under an assumed name to Crosby, inquiring after the manuscript "Susan." She offers to send him another copy of the manuscript, supposing the original lost, and threatens to seek another publisher: "Should no notice be taken of this address," she insists, "I shall feel myself at liberty to secure the publication of my work, by applying elsewhere." In the same period, she also chose not to write a new novel but to rework a draft of *Sense and Sensibility* written several years earlier. The serious intention revealed by these efforts is unmistakable.

We will probably never know what gave Austen the desire to publish, but we can learn from *Sense and Sensibility* her justification for doing so. The novel which resulted from this period of preparation displays her contemplation and adjustment of the concept of authority. *Sense and Sensibility* expresses authority with the metaphor of paternity, and the novel does so in two modes: first, its characters render the metaphor dramatically. Indeed, the novel depicts not simply fathers who control their children but patrilineages which regulate the social identities and inheritances of subsequent generations. Though their members may be male or female, these lineages are, nonetheless, masculine institutions. They focus on and control eldest sons, who inherit and transmit in their turn their families' status and fortune. Second, the novel's narrative structure expresses the metaphor. *Sense and Sensibility* provides, really, two narratives. The narrator's account is prefigured, "fathered" by the story which Colonel Brandon tells of his cousin Eliza.

While *Sense and Sensibility* expresses metaphors of masculine authority, it also presents, through character representations, the possibility of a feminine authority. Austen draws on a social and literary code of the second half of the eighteenth century—Sensibility—in order to explore female assertiveness in a world already organized by the institution of patrilineage. Though sensibility was by no means espoused only by women, Austen attributes it in this novel primarily to female characters as a way of establishing a gender-specific opposition to conventional authority. The one exception is Colonel Brandon, a character intermittently shown to be a man of sensibility. But he is a younger son within a patrilineage which places him structurally in the same position as a daughter. *Sense and Sensibility* suggests, however, that the results of maintaining the code of sensibility are devastating to women. Like so many of her contemporaries, Austen insists that its effects are antisocial. Exponents of sensibility in the novel bear children out of wedlock, and thus identify feminine authority as illicit and immoral. As an indication of Austen's attitudes towards authority, such dramatic renderings suggest only the dangers of novel-writing. Female assertiveness constitutes a transgression.

But while Austen's novel shows metaphors of masculine authority to be socially sanctioned and metaphors of feminine authority to be illegitimate, it also subjects both kinds of tropes to a moral critique and, in the process, shows them to bear common characteristics. In both, reproduction creates resemblance—parents beget children in their own image—and such resemblances are evidence of narcissism. The novel, then, ultimately registers disapproval not just of feminine authority but of all its human forms however conventional. But as it expresses this position, *Sense and Sensibility* also reveals a way to avoid not simply female assertiveness but all self-preoccupied versions of authority. Using the resources of her own culture, Austen, as we shall see, creates a new metaphor to express authority for the self-effacing. She provides a trope not of reproduction and resemblance but of revision and difference. The trope is rendered by experiences or narratives, conveying self-preoccupied illusions, which authorize opposite and morally improved ways of life or story versions. Austen was able to achieve authority not in assertions but in the modification, the correction of such assertions. She did so literally in sitting down to rework *Sense and Sensibility* and metaphorically in formulating the aesthetic patterns the text now bears.

II

In *Sense and Sensibility* Austen begins with a vision of authority in which the relationship of resemblance is crucial. The test of authority is the ability not just to produce but to produce in one's own image. This notion is expressed in Austen's rendering of the trope of paternity. Reproduction is repetition in mimetic representations of parents in the novel who have children very like themselves and, more abstractly, in the novel's dual narratives. A prior or parent story is duplicated in a succeeding account.

The most explicit depiction of resemblance in images of parents and children is advanced in the story that Colonel Brandon tells Elinor Dashwood about his cousin Eliza. The story goes like this: Several years earlier, Brandon's father pressed his orphaned cousin Eliza to marry his elder son—not Colonel Brandon but his older brother. He urged the marriage on Eliza because she had a large fortune and the Brandon estate was "much encumbered." Eliza and Colonel Brandon, very much in love, tried to elope, but her maid betrayed them. As a consequence, Brandon's father locked Eliza up until she consented to marry his elder son. She gave in only to find marriage unendurable. Her husband was neither loving nor faithful, and Eliza had a "warmth of heart" and an "eagerness of fancy and spirits" which made resignation impossible. She allowed herself to be seduced, had a child by her seducer, and then accepted other lovers. Divorced and impoverished, she died of consumption, but not before she handed her illegitimate daughter, also named Eliza, into Colonel Brandon's care. He sent the daughter to school. At sixteen she went with a friend and her father to Bath. There, she met a young man, Willoughby, who seduced and abandoned her, pregnant.

The story reveals a conflict between romantic and patrilineal principles. The father wishes to preserve the family identity, the patronym, through mercenary marriages and primogeniture, and the young woman wishes only to marry a man she loves. The story also suggests that the coercion produced by patrilineal principles, however cruel, is socially sanctioned. By contrast, the feeling heart or "sensibility" produces behavior which while pathetic is also dangerously antisocial. In her quest both to relieve and satisfy her feelings, Eliza breaks the legal and moral codes of her society.

The conflicting codes—one masculine, the other feminine, one socially acceptable, the other immoral and illicit—are, in this story, each authoritative. They are figured in a father and son and a mother and daughter and in the resemblances of parents and children. Likeness is manifested in the transmission of names. The son inherits his father's patronym while the daughter, in an act which underscores the antisocial character of feminine authority, receives only her mother's first name, Eliza. And likeness is expressed in the transmission of fates. The son is heir to his father's estate, the daughter to her mother's passion. By complying with his father's plans, the son conforms to his father's model of a status-conscious, calculating landowner. By running off with Willoughby, the daughter reveals that, like her mother, feelings dominate in her nature.

Generational resemblance conveys the ability to render continuous a point of view, a conduct, and thus expresses authority. At the same time, however, it also expresses narcissism. Authority is measured by the success of self-duplication over time, by the conversion of others—of children—into the self. Though Austen calls our attention to the differences between romantic and patrilineal principles, she stresses at the same time, through generational resemblance, what they, indeed what all authorities, have in common.

The imagery of authority advanced in this story is also expressed by the novel's structure of similar narratives. Though literally an interpolation, Colonel Brandon's story is temporally situated "before" the main narrative, that told by Austen's impersonal narrator. Its distance from the time of the novel's characters is indicated by the skeletal nature of the plot, by the falling away of detail and dramatization which occurs with the telescoping of events by memory. By alluding to his story long before he actually recounts it, Colonel Brandon brings to our attention this "prior" narrative, and in scenes both before and after he tells it, his dull, depressed appearance always reminds us of the existence of his story. He is a man with a "past." Indeed, he is the past situated in the narrator's account to foreshadow the future. But the presence of Colonel Brandon in the narrator's account does not just remind us of his past, his story, for he calls our attention to the resemblance between it and the narrator's account in abrupt and halting references. "I once knew a lady," he tells Elinor Dashwood early in the novel, "who in temper and mind greatly resembled your sister, who thought and judged like her," and then, according to the narrator, "he stopt suddenly." As he watches Marianne, the experience of the heroine of his story, Eliza, keeps coming to his lips. He wants but fears to tell the parent-story of sensibility which precedes the narrator's rendering of Marianne's conflicts with patrilineal values and which may make her experience not an original but a disastrous repetition.

But I want to turn now to the second story, the child of this parent, to trace the likeness between the two stories which Colonel Brandon's aborted comments render thematically. The main narrative, like Colonel Brandon's story, does pit romantic against patrilineal principles, feminine against masculine authorities. The narrator introduces us to patrilineal authority not with a single family but with a world organized entirely by a cluster of patrilineages: the Dashwoods, Ferrars, Middletons, Palmers, Smith/Willoughbys. Though not every character in the novel world is an immediate family member, no character enters this narrative without some kinship tie, however distant, or can stay in it unless hosted by one of these lineages. The authority of these masculine institutions is expressed in their ability to reproduce the social world through the organization of marriages, procreation, and the transmission of property, and in the similarity of the new generation, the new world—with its indulged little Middletons, spoiled Baby Palmer, and the selfish, cunning, and noisy Harry Dashwood—to the old.

We are also introduced to women—Mrs. Dashwood and her daughters—at the moment when their lineage rejects them. The head of their immediate family dies, and the head of their lineage and the possessor of the Dashwood estate at Norland essentially bypasses them in his will. The rejection which first separates and individualizes them from the "family of Dashwood" also indicates the nature of femaleness in this novel as a whole. Women are objects of masculine determinations. Though they are assimilated in marriage as well as excluded in inheritances—patrilineages take them *and* leave them—women are never wholly free to determine their own lives. But if in Colonel Brandon's story, patrilineal attempts at assimilation provide the context for Eliza's sensibility, in the narrator's account it is exclusion from the lineage which provides the impetus for Marianne Dashwood's devotion to feelings. Sensibility, of course, is not the only possible response to a world organized and authorized by patrilineages, and it is precisely because there are diverse responses available to women that Marianne reminds Colonel Brandon so much of his cousin Eliza.

In a society which makes no provisions for genteel women independent of marriage into a husband's patrilineage, the desire of women to marry cold-bloodedly into status and wealth is understandably widespread. The world depicted by the narrator of *Sense and Sensibility* is dotted with young women in search of husbands—like the Steele sisters—and with their matchmakers—like Mrs. Jennings, Mrs. Palmer, and Sir John Middleton. But the Dashwoods are no fortune-hunters. Mrs. Dashwood makes the declaration which characterizes this family of women's attitude toward mercenary marriages. "I do not believe," she informs Sir John early in the novel, "that Mr.

Willoughby will be incommoded by the attempts of either of *my* daughters towards what you call *catching him*. It is not an employment to which they have been brought up. Men are very safe with us, let them be ever so rich." But while neither Elinor nor Marianne wants to "catch" a husband, their views of what is possible for women differ. Elinor, though unwilling to pursue men, realizes their power and the power of patrilineal organization as well as the dependence of women with an income as small as her own. That is her "sense." Marianne, as I have already suggested, proposes an alternative form of authority to patrilineages on which she determines to rely, that of sensibility.

Her code of sensibility determines the kind of man Marianne wishes to meet. She imagines, in effect, the hero of a romance. "He must enter into all my feelings," she tells her mother. "The same books, the same music must charm us both. . . . and his person and manners must ornament his goodness with every possible charm." Indeed, so detailed is her portrait of the perfect man that Willoughby's first appearance in the narrative seems both miraculous—he fits her fantasy image—and belated. If her code determines her choice of a man, it also governs her conduct towards him. She is open, expressive, and extremely attentive to Willoughby because it is enjoyable to be so. Criticized by Elinor for making pleasure the guide to conduct, Marianne offers her creed. Pleasure, she claims, is an excellent guide because one is "sensible" of impropriety. "We always know when we are acting wrong," she tells Elinor, "and with such a conviction I could have . . . no pleasure." Thus, at Barton Cottage she and Willoughby "read . . . talked . . . sang together," and at social gatherings "she had," the narrator tells us, "no eyes for any one else." And "if dancing formed the amusement of the night, they were partners for half the time; and when obliged to separate for a couple of dances, were careful to stand together and scarcely spoke a word to any body else."

Led on by delight, Marianne exhibits indifference to her society, and in such behavior we see intimations of an Eliza. Marianne's sensibility justifies obliviousness to people who do not evoke pleasure. As expressive as she can be, she is just as given to silence or retreat. She daydreams in the presence of the vulgar or dull or goes to her bedroom when they come to call. And sensibility justifies condemnation of those who cause unhappiness. Marianne is capable of despising an entire neighborhood for causing her discomfort. "We could not be more unfortunately situated," she tells Edward when he inquires about her neighbors. Elinor, of course, is quick to correct her: "How can you say so? How can you be so unjust? . . . Have you forgot . . . how many pleasant days we have owed to them?" "No," Marianne replies, "Nor how many painful moments." Sensibility not only makes Marianne uncivil but also reveals the extent to which "good manners" are gestures of accommodation between members of patrilineages and their dependents, between men and women, and between hosts and guests. It is Elinor, of course, so quick to see and accept power relations in her social world, who champions "manners."

If Marianne's uncivil behavior evinces a potential for antisocial acts, so do her energy and attractiveness. The fate of Colonel Brandon's cousin reveals the sexuality of sensibility, a sexuality which appears latent in the narrator's heroine of sensibility as well. "Her form," we are told, "though not so correct as her sister's" is "more striking." And even the coldhearted John Dashwood testifies to the special appeal of her beauty. It is very "likely to attract the men," he notes. There is "something in her style of beauty, to please them particularly." Her love of dancing, long walks in the country, fantasies of horseback riding in an age which viewed vigorous exercise for women as a sexual stimulant also suggest a latent eroticism. And, finally, so does her unchaperoned trip with Willoughby to his cousin's estate at Allenham, since a woman who went anywhere alone with a man, so contemporary opinion held, willingly risked seduction. Though Marianne does not, in fact, elope with Willoughby and have an illegitimate child, the similarity which Brandon sees between the two Elizas and Marianne, between their story and hers, is based on an understanding of the dangerous potential of sensibility. In telling his story, Colonel Brandon shows what could easily have happened to Marianne. "Who can tell," he says of Willoughby and Marianne, after describing the second Eliza's seduction by the same man, "what were his designs on her?"

And yet, important elements of Marianne's history belie the resemblance which Colonel Brandon establishes. Though Marianne is uncivil, though she has erotic appeal, her sensibility does not fundamentally challenge her society, that is, the lineages which authorize it. Marianne assumes that marriage is the necessary social confirmation of romantic love, just as she takes for granted the existence of a "moderate" family fortune—two thousand pounds a year—to support it. The narrator's story shows that sensibility encourages Marianne not to oppose society as it is but to believe that she can get what she wants within it. In a world in which women are chosen by men, sensibility provides Marianne with fantasies of agency. When Willoughby suddenly leaves for London, Marianne's sensibility summons him back. She expects him "in every carriage which drove near their house." Because she wants him to be delighted with her arrival in London, she writes him notes informing him of his pleasure: "How surprised you will be, Willoughby, on receiving this; and I think you will feel something more than surprise, when you know that I am in town." And because she expects him to call, she seems to hear his knock on the door, or his foot on the stairs. Indeed, sensibility has married her to Willoughby. "I felt myself," she says about the weeks she devoted to Willoughby at Barton, "to be as solemnly engaged to him, as if the strictest legal covenant had bound us to each other." "Unfortunately," her sister comments, "he did not feel the same."

For despite Marianne's fantasies, men are the initiators in this world, and Willoughby has retreated from Marianne at Barton and in London because he needs to marry an heiress in order to pay his debts, to capitalize his estate, and to live in the ostentation to which he is accustomed. The "blackest art," Marianne believes, has lost her Willoughby's affections, but in fact it is only her lack of a fortune. The romantic hero is at heart also prudent, even mercenary. Unaccompanied by wealth, Marianne's sensibility is powerless to attract, much less determine. Though her sensibility is narcissistic—she has, after all, mistaken Willoughby's character because, as she tells Elinor, "he talked to me only of myself "—it does not acquire the dubious status of an authority. Marianne's sensibility shows only the impossibility of authority for women in a world organized by patrilineages.

If the sensibility of the two Elizas leads to illicit sexuality, Marianne's points her toward celibacy. Her narrative gradually reveals that she is nurturing a never-to-be-realized fantasy of romantic love and, in the process, withdrawing from life. Marianne's inability to channel desire towards the concrete, the available world when in London, is revealed, for example, on a shopping trip in Bond Street: "Her mind was equally abstracted from every thing actually before them, from all that interested and occupied the others. Restless and dissatisfied every where, her sister could never obtain her opinion of any article of purchase, however it might equally concern them both; she received no pleasure from any thing." At the same time, her appearance begins to dramatize not eroticism but the impotence of sensibility. She loses color, grows thin, becomes ill. And on recovering from her illness her first plans for the future are in keeping with what she now understands to be the sterile nature of the sensible quest. She plans a life of "retirement and study" in a society limited to women—her mother and sisters.

While Colonel Brandon's story, then, shows the danger of women's feelings, the possibility that they will establish an illicit and immoral feminine authority, the narrator's account shows the powerlessness of women's feelings in a male-dominated world. That the narratives are not duplicates but

rather point in opposite directions is nowhere more clearly evident than when
Colonel Brandon sees in Marianne, recovering from her illness, his cousin
Eliza:

> His emotion in entering the room, in seeing her altered looks,
> and in receiving the pale hand which she immediately held out to
> him, was such, as, in Elinor's conjecture, must arise from some-
> thing more than his affection for Marianne, or the consciousness
> of its being known to others; and she soon discovered in his
> melancholy eye and varying complexion as he looked at her sister,
> the probable recurrence of many past scenes of misery to his
> mind, brought back by that resemblance between Marianne and
> Eliza already acknowledged and now strengthened by the hollow
> eye, the sickly skin, the posture of reclining weakness, and the
> warm acknowledgment of peculiar obligation.

How are we to read this passage? The resemblance which Colonel Brandon once again asserts is undermined by the plots of the two narratives.
Marianne, merely the victim of her own fantasies, is on the mend, nursed
by a loving family and friends; Eliza, subject to her guardian's oppression,
her husband's disinterest, her own passions, has died an outcast. The narrator is presenting Colonel Brandon ironically as someone whose "melan-
choly eye" sees, like Marianne's, only what it wants. After all, he too,
according to his own story, has been a person of sensibility, willing to defy
his father and his patrilineal interests in order to elope for love. And in his
inability to recover from the failure of the elopement and the death of his
cousin, in his propensity to see her and her death in the appearance and
experience of another, we see hints of the same narcissism so typical of
women of feeling. Like the parent-child mimetic representations which have
served as a metaphor for a morally tainted authority, the narrative structure
of repetition, established by Colonel Brandon, is now also called into question
and shown to be the result of self-preoccupied illusions.

The clearest indication of an ironic handling, not only of Colonel Brandon but of the narrative structure of resemblance, is in Austen's explicit
efforts to reform the trope of authority and in a way consistent with a
narrative structure not of resemblances but of opposites. She replaces the
metaphor of generational succession with the figure of discrete life histories
which undergo dramatic change. The change is indicated by the doing of
something again—but differently. Characters, towards the end of the narrator's account, select second loves, second marriages, second occupations,
or second sets of principles which are unlike and better than their first

choices. Marianne, for example, relinquishes her fantasy of a romantic hero in favor of marriage to a man for whom she has "no sentiment superior to strong esteem and lively friendship." "She was born," according to the narrator, "to discover the falsehood of her own opinions, and to counteract, by her conduct, her most favourite maxims." Edward Ferrars's life similarly demonstrates change. The position of eldest son in a wealthy family provides him with a preestablished social role. Edward is supposed to inherit a large estate, marry an heiress, make important and powerful friends, and spend his days riding around London in a barouche. He becomes, however, by his own choice and by his mother's decision to disinherit him, a clergyman with a modest living, married to a woman with only a few thousand pounds. Even Colonel Brandon, though he marries the woman who has resembled his Eliza, must stop grieving and learn to be happy: "In Marianne he was consoled for every past affliction;—her regard and her society restored his mind to animation, and his spirits to cheerfulness."

If similarity or repetition indicates self-love, difference or reversal reveals both self-effacement and self-improvement. An initial assertion is not repeated but instead gives way to its opposite. A first bad choice or false direction authorizes a second choice, seen in the novel not as assertion but as the correction of assertion. A character's romantic love authorizes a relationship based on esteem; a story of adultery authorizes the impersonal narrator's tale of differences. These patterns in *Sense and Sensibility* reveal Austen's resolution of the problem of authority. She circumvented narcissistic or unfeminine assertion by writing revisions.

III

In producing the metaphor of revision, Austen gave authority a sense radically different from that conveyed by the trope of paternity. As proponents of the trope of paternity—critics like Said, Sundquist, or Wyatt—suggest, paternal authority is power. Said, for example, maintains that the meanings of authority are "all grounded in the following notions":

> (1) that of the power of an individual to initiate, institute, establish—in short, to begin; (2) that this power and its product are an increase over what had been there previously; (3) that the individual wielding this power controls its issue and what is derived therefrom; (4) that authority maintains the continuity of its course.

Though writers or fictional characters recognize that their powers are illusory, this recognition, Said's "molestation," does not undermine or transform the notion of authority as power. Indeed, molestation occurs, according to Said, when writers measure their own works against what they see as the greater work, reality. Though writers or fictional characters ultimately experience defeat in disillusionment, doing so testifies implicitly to the existence of a superior, very potent Authority. By contrast, when Austen's fictional characters realize that their powers are insufficient or illusory, they are in the process of achieving real authority, rather than accepting a tragically reduced version of themselves.

For Austen, authority belongs to the self-consciously powerless. It is achieved by recognizing the fallacy of personal power in the material world. The ability to do or determine is shown to be the ability to err. And authority is achieved by counteracting in revisions the mistaken efforts which such "doing" constitutes. Not only *Sense and Sensibility* but several of Austen's early drafts ("First Impressions" and "Susan" are only two of the most famous) were corrected by later versions. So too, "first impressions," false steps, and fanciful and distorting narratives are revised in the careers of characters like Marianne Dashwood, Elizabeth Bennet, and Catherine Morland, as well as Sir Thomas Bertram, Emma Woodhouse, and Frederick Wentworth. Perceptiveness, humility, a willingness to alter—these traits ultimately replace "power" among Austen's characters and are also necessary to reflexive, not other-directed or pioneering activity. The particular moral scope of Austen's authority is revealed by the trope which represents it. In *Sense and Sensibility,* and in Austen's other novels, characters who gain authority are able to modify themselves. By contrast, the authority ideal espoused by Said and others is represented by the creation, the fathering of another, a new self.

In characterizing Austen's representation of authority in this way, I have not wished to replace a stereotypically masculine with a stereotypically feminine aesthetic but rather to suggest the need for more specificity in approaches to the problem of authority. If we connect our theories of authority with the historical circumstances of an author's production, as Said in another context has urged Harold Bloom to do, we will no doubt be in a position to discover a multiplicity of metaphors, or representational strategies, for the expression of authors' diverse experiences of authority.

Austen's version of authority is attributable not simply to her sense of herself as a woman but to the social and cultural context which provided resources for the expression of her gender identity. A crucial resource was Austen's Anglicanism, which reinforced paternalism in its depiction of humble, grateful worshippers and an almighty, beneficent Father. Austen drew her version of authority from the submission to a spiritual Father, which gentry Anglicanism prescribed. She fashioned an authority rooted not in power and dominance but in dependence. Anglicanism contributed in general to Austen's view of personal authority, and it also provided, in the experience of the sinner, a specific analogue for the authority of revision or reversal. Austen expressed the conventional notion of repentance in one of the prayers she composed for household worship: "Look with mercy on the sins we have this day committed and in mercy make us feel them deeply, that our repentance may be sincere, & our resolution steadfast of endeavouring against the commission of such in future."

Although she expresses and affirms the virtue of dependence in her metaphor of authority, Austen was acutely aware of how much more dependent women were than men in her society. The smaller gentry largely relied on wealthier, more socially prominent relatives or friends for legacies and professional advancement. But while men like Austen's father and brothers had opportunities to move from the position of patronized to that of patron, women like Austen, her mother, and sister remained dependent. Her father and brothers became, through the assistance of others, benefactors in their turn of Austen, her mother, and sister. In the process they not only reinforced their gender authority over their female relations but also acquired economic, political, and spiritual authority over tenants, sailors, and parishioners.

If Austen turned to Anglicanism for her rendering of authority, her sensitivity to the extreme, the irrevocable dependence that was women's "situation" also led her to draw on her religion for the critique she directs at the institutionalization of masculine authority in the worlds of her novels. In effect, she judges a social form of paternal authority against the standard of spiritual paternity. For Austen the authority of the "maker" was inaccessible because it was paternal *and* because it was not a human possession. All social forms of it are sinful or, in the secularized terms of Austen's novels, indicative of pride, greed, self-love. She ridicules patrilineal structures because the kind of authority they attempt to enforce is usurped. Patrilineages or their representatives—Mrs. Ferrars or the elderly bachelor Dashwood in *Sense and Sensibility,* but also Lady Catherine in *Pride and Prejudice* or Sir Walter Elliot in *Persuasion*—are shown to have as much right to govern the next generation's marital partners, careers, or fortunes as they do to determine the weather, a feat, by the way, which Lady Catherine does not hesitate to attempt.

Nevertheless, if Anglicanism influenced Austen's formulation of a viable version of authority and helped her to criticize masculine social authority, it also inhibited a direct probe of the role of gender in her society. *Sense and*

Sensibility finds fault with the institution of patrilineages for underwriting the expression and satisfaction of immoral impulses at the expense of identifying outright its favoring of male heirs. It is this structural feature that historically made women into dependents and objects of exchange. Nothing more clearly reveals the shortcomings of Austen's analysis, the limitations of what we can only loosely call her feminism, than the close of *Sense and Sensibility*. The narrator moves characters whose lives have undergone reversals away from patrilineal rule, a shift figured in a flurry of geographic relocations. While Mrs. Ferrars, John and Fanny Dashwood, Robert and Lucy Ferrars are left to enjoy their family fortunes and social importance in the hell of one another's company, Marianne and Colonel Brandon, Edward and Elinor Ferrars become neighbors in the country and devote themselves to the quiet comforts of domestic life. The narrator suggests that these two families are sexually egalitarian. Presumably, equality is ensured by the moral reversals which so many of these characters—male and female—have undergone. And yet it is only their individual experiences of revision which stand between egalitarian households and patriarchal rule, between, say, the growing, mutual love and respect of Colonel Brandon and Marianne, and her domination by a man who despite his romantic past is, as Marianne herself once complained, "old enough to be *my* father." Is the experience of revision sufficient to prevent the practice of another form of paternal authority?

It was, at least, sufficient to justify for Austen a writing career within a patrilineal and patriarchal social context. Austen began to rework *Sense and Sensibility* soon after moving with her mother, sister, and friend, Martha Lloyd, into a cottage at Chawton. The house was a present from Edward, the brother who was adopted as a boy by wealthy and childless relatives. With estates both at Chawton and Godmersham, he had cottages to spare. The Austen family biographers like to find in Edward's gift, in his "male protection," the impetus for, the very making of, Austen's career. "As soon as she was fixed in her second home [at Chawton]," J. E. Austen-Leigh suggests, "she resumed the habits of composition which had been formed in her first [at Steventon]." W. and R. A. Austen-Leigh add: "In this tranquil spot, where the past and present even now join peaceful hands, she found happy leisure, repose of mind, and absence of distraction, such as any sustained creative effort demands." But it is not to Edward's benevolence but to her own tactics of revision—enacted literally when she took out *Sense and Sensibility* and rewrote it, and imaginatively, within the novel—that Austen owed her career. Edward may have provided the house, but it is her own metaphor of authority which enabled her to write within it.

Chronology

1775 Jane Austen is born on December 16 in the village of Steventon, Hampshire, to George Austen, parish clergyman, and Cassandra Leigh Austen. She is the seventh of eight children. She and her sister Cassandra are educated at Oxford and Southampton by the widow of a Principal of Brasenose College, and then attend the Abbey School at Reading. Jane's formal education ends when she is nine years old.

1787–93 Austen writes various pieces for the amusement of her family (now collected in the three volumes of *Juvenilia*), the most famous of which is *Love and Freindship*. She and her family also perform in the family barn various plays and farces, some of which are written by Jane.

1793–95 Austen writes her first novel, the epistolary *Lady Susan*, and begins the epistolary *Elinor and Marianne*, which will become *Sense and Sensibility*.

1796–97 Austen completes *First Impressions*, an early version of *Pride and Prejudice*. Her father tries to get it published without success. Austen begins *Sense and Sensibility* and *Northanger Abbey*.

1798 Austen finishes a version of *Northanger Abbey*.

1801 George Austen retires to Bath with his family.

1801–2 Jane Austen probably suffers from an unhappy love affair (the man in question is believed to have died suddenly) and also probably becomes engaged for a day to Harris Bigg-Wither.

1803   Austen sells a two-volume manuscript entitled *Susan* to a publisher for £10. It is advertised, but never printed. This is a version of *Northanger Abbey,* probably later revised.

1803–5 Austen writes ten chapters of *The Watsons,* which is never finished.

1805   George Austen dies. Jane abandons work on *The Watsons.*

1805–6 Jane Austen, her mother, and her sister live in various lodgings in Bath.

1806–9 The three Austen women move to Southampton, living near one of Jane's brothers.

1809   The three Austen women move to Chawton Cottage, in Hampshire, which is part of the estate of Jane's brother Edward Austen (later Knight), who has been adopted by Thomas Knight, a relative. Edward has just lost his wife, who died giving birth to her tenth child, and the household has been taken over by Jane's favorite niece, Fanny.

1811   Austen decides to publish *Sense and Sensibility* at her own expense and anonymously. It comes out in November, in three volumes.

1811–12 Austen is probably revising *First Impressions* extensively, and beginning *Mansfield Park.*

1813   *Pride and Prejudice: A Novel. In Three Volumes. By the Author of 'Sense and Sensibility'* is published in January. Second editions of both books come out in November.

1814   *Mansfield Park* is published, again anonymously, and in three volumes. It sells out by November. Austen begins *Emma.*

1815   Austen finishes *Emma,* and begins *Persuasion. Emma* is published in December anonymously, in three volumes, by a new publisher.

1816   A second edition of *Mansfield Park* is published.

1817   A third edition of *Pride and Prejudice* is published. Austen begins *Sanditon.* She moves to Winchester, where she dies, after a year-long illness, on July 18. She is buried in Winchester

Cathedral. After her death, her family destroys much of her correspondence, in order to protect her reputation.

1818   *Persuasion* and *Northanger Abbey* are published posthumously together; their authorship is still officially anonymous.

Contributors

HAROLD BLOOM, Sterling Professor of the Humanities at Yale University, is the author of *The Anxiety of Influence, Poetry and Repression,* and many other volumes of literary criticism. His forthcoming study, *Freud: Transference and Authority,* attempts a full-scale reading of all of Freud's major writings. A MacArthur Prize Fellow, he is general editor of five series of literary criticism published by Chelsea House.

JOEL WEINSHEIMER is Assistant Professor of English at Texas Tech University. He is the editor of *Jane Austen Today* and coeditor with Barry Roth of a bibliography of Jane Austen studies.

ALICE CHANDLER is President of the State University of New York, College at New Paltz, where she is also Professor of English. She is the author of *Dream of Order: The Medieval Ideal in Nineteenth-Century English Literature.*

RUTH apROBERTS is Professor of English at the University of California, Riverside, and the author of *The Moral Trollope.*

GENE W. RUOFF is Associate Professor of English at the University of Illinois at Chicago. He has published many articles on Jane Austen.

SANDRA M. GILBERT is Professor of English at Princeton University. SUSAN GUBAR is Professor of English at Indiana University. Together they have written *The Madwoman in the Attic,* and edited *The Norton Anthology of Women's Literature* and *Shakespeare's Sisters: Feminist Essays on Women Poets.*

JULIA PREWITT BROWN is the author of *Jane Austen's Novels: Social Change and Literary Form.*

SUSAN MORGAN is Assistant Professor of English at Stanford University and the author of *In the Meantime: Character and Perception in Jane Austen's Fiction*.

GARY KELLY is Associate Professor of English at the University of Alberta. He is the author of *The English Jacobin Novel, 1780–1805* and *Learning about Sex: The Contemporary Guide for Young Adults*.

ANN MOLAN teaches at Australian National University.

MARTIN PRICE is Sterling Professor of English at Yale University. His books include *To the Palace of Wisdom* and *Forms of Life*.

ROBIN GROVE is Senior Lecturer in English at the University of Melbourne. He has published on Emily Brontë and on Pope, and is on the editorial staff of *The Critical Review*.

IAN WATT is Professor of English at Stanford University. He is the author of *The Rise of the Novel* and the forthcoming *Gothic and Comic: Two Variations on the Realistic Tradition*.

DEBORAH KAPLAN is Assistant Professor of English at George Mason University in Fairfax, Virginia.

Bibliography

Adams, Timothy Dow. "To Know the Dancer from the Dance—Dance as a Metaphor of Marriage in Four Novels of Jane Austen." *Studies in the Novel* 14, no. 1 (1982): 55–65.

Armstrong, Nancy. "Inside Greimas's Square: Literary Characters and Cultural Constraints." In *The Sign in Music and Literature,* edited by Wendy Steiner, 52–66. Austin: University of Texas Press, 1981.

Auerbach, Nina. "O Brave New World: Evolution and Revolution in *Persuasion.*" *ELH* 39 (1982): 112–28.

Babb, Howard. *Jane Austen's Novels: The Fabric of Dialogue.* Columbus: Ohio State University Press, 1962.

Banfield, Ann. "The Moral Landscape of *Mansfield Park.*" *Nineteenth-Century Fiction* 26 (1971): 1–24.

Barfoot, C. C. "Choice Against Fate in *Sense and Sensibility* and *Pride and Prejudice.*" *Dutch Quarterly Review of Anglo-American Letters* 10 (1980): 176–98.

Berger, Carole. "The Rake and the Reader in Jane Austen's Novels." *Studies in English Literature 1500–1900* 15 (1975): 531–44.

Bloom, Harold, ed. *Modern Critical Interpretations: Jane Austen's* Emma. New Haven: Chelsea House Publishers, 1987.

———, ed. *Modern Critical Interpretations: Jane Austen's* Mansfield Park. New Haven: Chelsea House Publishers, 1986.

———, ed. *Modern Critical Interpretations: Jane Austen's* Pride and Prejudice. New Haven: Chelsea House Publishers, 1987.

Boles, Carolyn G. "Jane Austen and the Reader: Rhetorical Techniques in *Northanger Abbey, Pride and Prejudice,* and *Emma.*" *Emporia State Research Studies* 30, no. 1 (1981): 152–67.

Bowen, Elizabeth. "Jane Austen." In *The English Novelists,* edited by Derek Verschoyle, 101–13. New York: Harcourt, Brace & Co., 1936.

Bradbrook, Frank. *Jane Austen and Her Predecessors.* Cambridge: Cambridge University Press, 1967.

Bradbrook, M. C. "A Note on Fanny Price." *Essays in Criticism* 5 (1955): 289–92.

Bradbury, Malcolm. "*Persuasion* Again." *Essays in Criticism* 18 (1968): 383–96.

Branton, C. L. "The Ordinations in Jane Austen's Novels." *Nineteenth-Century Fiction* 10 (1955): 156–59.

Brown, Carole O. "Dwindling into a Wife: A Jane Austen Heroine Grows Up." *International Journal of Women's Studies* 5, no. 5 (1982): 460–69.

Brown, Julia Prewitt. *Jane Austen's Novels: Social Change and Literary Form.* Cambridge: Harvard University Press, 1979.

Brown, Lloyd. *Bits of Ivory: Narrative Techniques in Jane Austen's Fiction.* Baton Rouge: Louisiana State University Press, 1973.

Burgan, Mary H. "Mr. Bennet and the Failures of Fatherhood in Jane Austen's Novels." *Journal of English and Germanic Philology* 74 (1975): 536–52.

Burroway, Janet. "The Irony of the Insufferable Prig: *Mansfield Park*." *Critical Quarterly* 9 (1967): 127–38.

Burrows, J. F. "A Measure of Excellence: Modes of Comparison in *Pride and Prejudice*." *Sydney Studies in English* 5 (1979–80): 38–59.

Bush, Douglas. *Jane Austen.* New York: Macmillan Co., 1975.

Butler, Marilyn. *Jane Austen and the War of Ideas.* Oxford: Oxford University Press, 1975.

Carroll, David R. "*Mansfield Park, Daniel Deronda,* and Ordination." *Modern Philology* 62 (1965): 217–26.

Cecil, David. *A Portrait of Jane Austen.* New York: Hill & Wang, 1980.

Chabot, C. Barry. "Jane Austen's Novels: The Vicissitudes of Desire." *American Imago* 32 (1975): 288–308.

Chapman, R. W. *Jane Austen: Facts and Problems.* Oxford: Clarendon Press, 1948.

Colby, R. A. *Fiction with a Purpose.* Bloomington: Indiana University Press, 1967.

Collins, Barbara B. "Jane Austen's Victorian Novel." *Nineteenth-Century Fiction* 4 (1949): 175–85.

Copeland, Edward. "What's a Competence? Jane Austen, Her Sister Novelists, and the 5%'s." *Modern Language Studies* 9, no. 3 (1979): 161–68.

Cowart, David. "Wise and Foolish Virgins (and Matrons) in *Mansfield Park*." *South Atlantic Bulletin* 44, no. 2 (1979): 76–82.

Craik, W. A. *Jane Austen: The Six Novels.* London: Methuen & Co. Ltd., 1966.

DeRose, Peter. "Hardship, Recollection, and Discipline: Three Lessons in *Mansfield Park*." *Studies in the Novel* 9 (1977): 262–78.

————. "Marriage and Self-Knowledge in *Emma* and *Pride and Prejudice*." *Renascence* 30 (1978): 199–216.

Devlin, David. *Jane Austen and Education.* New York: Barnes & Noble Books, 1975.

Donohue, Joseph W., Jr. "Ordination and the Divided House at Mansfield Park." *ELH* 32, no. 2 (1965): 169–78.

Donovan, Robert. *The Shaping Vision: Imagination in the English Novel from Defoe to Dickens.* Ithaca: Cornell University Press, 1966.

Draffan, R. A. "*Mansfield Park:* Jane Austen's Bleak House." *Essays in Criticism* 19 (1969): 371–84.

Duckworth, Alistair. *The Improvement of the Estate: A Study of Jane Austen's Novels.* Baltimore: The Johns Hopkins University Press, 1971.

Duffy, Joseph M., Jr. "Moral Integrity and Moral Anarchy in *Mansfield Park*." *ELH* 23 (1956): 71–91.

————. "The Politics of Love: Marriage and the Good Society in *Pride and Prejudice*." *University of Windsor Review* 11, no. 2 (1976): 5–26.

Edge, C. E. "*Mansfield Park* and Ordination." *Nineteenth-Century Fiction* 16 (1961): 269–74.

Edge, Charles. "*Emma:* A Technique of Characterization." In *The Classic British Novel,* edited by Howard M. Harper, Jr. and Charles Edge, 51–64. Athens: University of Georgia Press, 1972.

Ehrenpreis, Anne Henry. "*Northanger Abbey:* Jane Austen and Charlotte Smith." *Nineteenth-Century Fiction* 25, no. 3 (1970): 343–47.

Ehrenpreis, Irvin. "Jane Austen and Heroism." *The New York Review of Books,* February 8, 1979, 37–43.

Fergus, Jan. *Jane Austen and the Didactic Novel:* Northanger Abbey, Sense and Sensibility, *and* Pride and Prejudice. Totowa, N.J.: Barnes & Noble Books, 1983.

Fleishman, Avrom. *A Reading of* Mansfield Park: *An Essay in Critical Synthesis.* Minneapolis: University of Minnesota Press, 1967.

Fowler, Marian. "'Substance and Shadow': Conventions of the Marriage Market in *Northanger Abbey.*" *English Studies in Canada* 6 (1980): 277–91.

Frazer, June M. "Stylistic Categories of Narrative in Jane Austen." *Style* 17, no. 1 (1983): 16–26.

Fry, Paul H. "Georgic Comedy: The Fictive Territory of Jane Austen's *Emma.*" *Studies in the Novel* 11, no. 2 (1979): 129–46.

Gilbert, Sandra M., and Susan Gubar. *The Madwoman in the Attic: The Woman Writer and the Nineteenth-Century Literary Imagination.* New Haven: Yale University Press, 1979.

Gillie, Christopher. *A Preface to Jane Austen.* London: Longmans, Green & Co. Ltd., 1975.

Giuffre, Giula. "The Ethical Mode of *Pride and Prejudice.*" *Sydney Studies in English* 6 (1980–81): 17–29.

———. "Sex, Self, and Society in *Mansfield Park.*" *Sydney Studies in English* 9 (1983–84): 76–93.

Gold, Joel J. "The Return to Bath: Catherine Morland and Anne Elliot." *Genre* 9 (1976): 215–29.

Gould, Gerald. "The Gate Scene at Sotherton in *Mansfield Park.*" *Literature and Psychology* 20 (1970): 75–78.

Gullans, C. B. "Jane Austen's *Mansfield Park* and Dr. Johnson." *Nineteenth-Century Fiction* 27 (1972): 206–8.

Halperin, John. "Jane Austen's Anti-Romantic Fragment: Some Notes on *Sanditon.*" *Tulsa Studies in Women's Literature* 2, no. 2 (1983): 183–91.

———. *The Life of Jane Austen.* Sussex: Harvester Press, 1984.

———, ed. *Jane Austen: Bicentenary Essays.* Cambridge: Cambridge University Press, 1975.

Hardy, Barbara. *A Reading of Jane Austen.* New York: New York University Press, 1976.

Hardy, John. *Jane Austen's Heroines: Intimacy in Human Relationships.* London: Routledge & Kegan Paul, 1984.

Heath, William, ed. *Discussions of Jane Austen.* Boston: D. C. Heath & Co., 1961.

Hilliard, Raymond F. "*Emma:* Dancing Without Space to Turn In." In *Probability, Time, and Space in Eighteenth-Century Literature,* edited by Paula R. Backscheider, 272–98. New York: AMS Press, 1979.

Hochman, Baruch. "Jane Austen and the Development of the Novel." *Hebrew University Studies in Literature* 7 (1979): 161–81.

Hopkins, Robert. "General Tilney and Affairs of State: The Political Gothic of *Northanger Abbey*." *Philological Quarterly* 57 (1978): 213–24.

Hummel, Madeline. "Emblematic Charades and the Observant Woman in *Mansfield Park*." *Texas Studies in Literature and Language* 15 (1973): 251–66.

Ireland, K. R. "Future Recollections of Immortality: Temporal Articulation in Jane Austen's *Persuasion*." *Novel* 13 (1980): 204–20.

Johnson, Claudia L. "The 'Operations of Time, and the Changes of the Human Mind': Jane Austen and Dr. Johnson Again." *Modern Language Quarterly* 44, no. 1 (1983): 23–38.

———. "The 'Twilight of Probability': Uncertainty and Hope in *Sense and Sensibility*." *Philological Quarterly* 62, no. 2 (1983): 171–86.

Johnson, Judy Van Sickle. "The Bodily Frame: Learning Romance in *Persuasion*." *Nineteenth-Century Fiction* 38, no. 1 (1983): 43–61.

Jones, Myrddin. "Feelings of Youth and Nature in *Mansfield Park*." *English* 29, no. 135 (1980): 221–32.

Kelly, G. "The Art of Reading in *Pride and Prejudice*." *English Studies in Canada* 10, no. 2 (1984): 156–71.

Kennard, Jean E. *Victims of Convention*. Hamden, Conn.: Archon Books, 1978.

Kestner, Joseph A., III. *Jane Austen: Spatial Structure and Thematic Variations*. Salzburg: Institut für Englischen Sprache und Literatur, University of Salzburg, 1974.

Kilroy, G. J. F. "Ironic Balance in *Persuasion*." *Downside Review* 96 (1978): 305–13.

Kirkham, Margaret. *Jane Austen: Feminism and Fiction*. Totowa, N.J.: Barnes & Noble Books, 1983.

Kissane, James. "Comparison's Blessed Felicity: Character Arrangement in *Emma*." *Studies in the Novel* 2, no. 2 (1970): 173–84.

Knight, Charles A. "Irony and Mr. Knightley." *Studies in the Novel* 2, no. 2 (1970): 185–93.

Koppel, Gene. "The Role of Contingency in *Mansfield Park*: The Necessity of an Ambiguous Conclusion." *Southern Review* (Adelaide) 15, no. 3 (1983): 306–13.

Kroeber, Karl. *Styles in Fictional Structure: The Art of Jane Austen, Charlotte Brontë, George Eliot*. Princeton: Princeton University Press, 1971.

Lascelles, Mary. *Jane Austen and Her Art*. Oxford: Oxford University Press, 1939.

Lauber, John. "*Sanditon*: The Kingdom of Folly." *Studies in the Novel* 4 (1972): 353–63.

Lee, David. "Modality, Perspective, and the Concept of Objective Narration." *Journal of Literary Semantics* 11, no. 2 (1982): 104–11.

Lenta, Margaret. "Androgyny and Authority in *Mansfield Park*." *Studies in the Novel* 15, no. 3 (1983): 169–82.

———. "Jane Fairfax and Jane Eyre: Educating Women." *Ariel* 12, no. 4 (1981): 27–41.

Lerner, Laurence. *The Truthtellers: Jane Austen, George Eliot, D. H. Lawrence*. New York: Schocken Books, 1967.

Liddell, Robert. *Novels of Jane Austen*. London: Longmans, Green & Co. Ltd., 1963.

Litz, A. Walton. *Jane Austen: A Study of Her Artistic Development*. New York: Oxford University Press, 1965.

Lock, F. P. "The Geology of *Sense and Sensibility*." *Yearbook of English Studies* 9 (1979): 246–55.

Lodge, David, ed. *Jane Austen:* Emma: *A Casebook*. Nashville, Tenn.: Aurora Publishers, 1970.

McKeon, Richard. "*Pride and Prejudice:* Thought, Character, Argument, and Plot." *Critical Inquiry* 5 (1979): 511–27.

McMaster, Juliet. *Jane Austen on Love*. Victoria, B.C.: University of Victoria Press, 1978.

————, ed. *Jane Austen's Achievement*. London: Macmillan & Co., 1976.

Mansell, Darrel. *The Novels of Jane Austen: An Interpretation*. London: Macmillan & Co., 1973.

Marshall, Sarah L. "Rationality and Delusion in Jane Austen's *Emma*." *University of Mississippi Studies in English* 9 (1968): 57–67.

Merrett, Robert James. "The Concept of Mind in *Emma*." *English Studies in Canada* 6 (1980): 39–55.

Mews, Hazel: *Frail Vessels: Woman's Role in Women's Novels from Fanny Burney to George Eliot*. London: Athlone Press, 1969.

Moler, Kenneth L. *Jane Austen's Art of Illusion*. Lincoln: University of Nebraska Press, 1968.

Monaghan, David. *Jane Austen: Structure and Social Vision*. London: Macmillan & Co., 1980.

————, ed. *Jane Austen in a Social Context*. London: Macmillan & Co., 1981.

Moore, E. Margaret. "Emma and Miss Bates: Early Experiences of Separations and the Theme of Dependency in Jane Austen's Novels." *Studies in English Literature 1500–1900* 9 (1969): 573–85.

Morgan, Alice. "On Teaching *Emma*." *Journal of General Education* 24 (1972): 103–8.

Morgan, Susan. *In the Meantime: Character and Perception in Jane Austen's Fiction*. Chicago: University of Chicago Press, 1980.

Mudrick, Marvin. *Jane Austen: Irony as Defense and Discovery*. Princeton: Princeton University Press, 1952.

Nardin, Jane. *Those Elegant Decorums: The Concept of Propriety in Jane Austen's Novels*. Albany: State University of New York Press, 1973.

Newton, Judith Lowder. *Women, Power, and Subversion: Social Strategies in British Fiction, 1778–1860*. Athens: University of Georgia Press, 1981.

Nineteenth-Century Fiction 30, no. 3 (December 1975). Special Jane Austen issue.

Odmark, John. *An Understanding of Jane Austen's Novels*. Oxford: Basil Blackwell, 1981.

O'Neill, Judith. *Critics on Jane Austen*. Miami, Fla.: University of Miami Press, 1970.

Page, Norman. *The Language of Jane Austen*. Oxford: Basil Blackwell, 1972.

Paris, Bernard. *Character and Conflict in Jane Austen's Novels*. Detroit: Wayne State University Press, 1979.

Parrish, Stephen M. *Jane Austen:* Emma. New York: W. W. Norton & Co., 1972.

Patterson, Emily H. "Family and Pilgrimage Themes in Austen's *Mansfield Park*." *CLA Journal* 20, no. 1 (1976): 14–18.

Person, Leland S., Jr. "Playing House: Jane Austen's Fabulous Space." *Philological Quarterly* 59, no. 1 (1980): 62–75.

Persuasions: Journal of the Jane Austen Society of North America, 1979–.

Phillips, K. C. *Jane Austen's English.* London: Andre Deutsch Ltd., 1970.

Piggott, Patrick. *The Innocent Diversion: A Study of Music in the Life and Writings of Jane Austen.* London: Douglas Cleverdon, 1979.

Polhemus, Robert. *Comic Faith: The Great Tradition from Austen to Joyce.* Chicago: University of Chicago Press, 1980.

Poovey, Mary. *The Proper Lady and the Woman Writer: Ideology as Style in the Works of Mary Wollstonecraft, Mary Shelley, and Jane Austen.* Chicago: University of Chicago Press, 1984.

Reinstein, P. Gila. "Moral Priorities in *Sense and Sensibility.*" *Renascence* 35, no. 4 (1983): 269–83.

Rees, Joan. *Jane Austen: Woman and Writer.* New York: St. Martin's Press, 1976.

Roberts, Warren. *Jane Austen and the French Revolution.* New York: St. Martin's Press, 1979.

Ross, Mary Beth. "Jane Austen as a Political Novelist: Class Consciousness in *Emma.*" *The Mary Wollstonecraft Newsletter* 1, no. 1 (1972): 8–12.

Roth, Barry, and Joel Weinsheimer, eds. *An Annotated Bibliography of Jane Austen Studies, 1952–1972.* Charlottesville: University Press of Virginia, 1973.

Rothstein, Eric. "The Lessons of *Northanger Abbey.*" *University of Toronto Quarterly* 44 (1975): 14–30.

Rubinstein, E., ed. *Twentieth-Century Interpretations of* Pride and Prejudice: *A Collection of Criticism.* Englewood Cliffs, N.J.: Prentice-Hall, 1969.

Rumrich, John Peter. "The Importance of Being Frank." *Essays in Literature* 8, no. 1 (1981): 97–104.

Ruoff, Gene W. "The Sense of a Beginning: *Mansfield Park.*" *The Wordsworth Circle* 10, no. 2 (1979): 174–86.

Ryals, Clyde. "Being and Doing in *Mansfield Park.*" *Archiv* 206 (1970): 345–60.

Scott, P. J. M. *Jane Austen: A Reassessment.* Totowa, N.J.: Barnes & Noble Books, 1982.

Sherry, James. "*Pride and Prejudice:* The Limits of Society." *Studies in English Literature 1500–1900* 19, no. 4 (1979): 609–22.

Sherry, Norman. *Jane Austen.* London: Evans Brothers, 1966.

Sieferman, Sylvia. "*Persuasion:* The Motive for Metaphor." *Studies in the Novel* 11, no. 3 (1979): 283–301.

Siefert, Susan. *The Dilemma of the Talented Heroine: A Study in Nineteenth-Century Fiction.* Montreal: Eden Press, 1977.

Smith, LeRoy W. *Jane Austen and the Drama of Woman.* London: Macmillan & Co., 1983.

Southam, B. C. *Jane Austen.* Essex: Longman Group Ltd., 1975.

———, ed. *Critical Essays on Jane Austen.* London: Routledge & Kegan Paul, 1968.

———, ed. *Jane Austen: The Critical Heritage.* London: Routledge & Kegan Paul, 1968.

Spacks, Patricia Meyer. "The Difference it Makes." *Soundings* 64, no. 4 (1981): 343–60.

———. *Gossip.* New York: Alfred A. Knopf, 1985.

Spence, Jon. "The Abiding Possibilities of Nature in *Persuasion.*" *Studies in English Literature 1500–1900* 21, no. 4 (1981): 625–36.

Steele, Pamela. "In Sickness and In Health: Jane Austen's Metaphor." *Studies in the Novel* 14, no. 2 (1982): 152–60.

Steeves, Harrison. *Before Jane Austen.* New York: Holt, Rinehart & Winston, 1965.

Stone, Donald D. "Sense and Semantics in Jane Austen." *Nineteenth-Century Fiction* 25, no. 1 (1970): 31–50.

Studies in the Novel 7, no. 1 (1975). Special Jane Austen issue.

Tamm, Merike. "Performing Heroism in Austen's *Sense and Sensibility* and *Emma.*" *Papers on Language and Literature* 15 (1979): 396–407.

Tave, Stuart M. *Some Words of Jane Austen.* Chicago: University of Chicago Press, 1973.

Taylor, Mary Vaiana. "The Grammar of Conduct: Speech Act Theory and the Education of Emma Woodhouse." *Style* 12 (1978): 357–71.

Ten Harmsel, Henrietta. *Jane Austen: A Study in Fictional Conventions.* The Hague: Mouton & Co., 1964.

Todd, Janet, ed. *Jane Austen: New Perspectives. Women & Literature* n.s. 3. New York: Holmes & Meier, 1983.

Watson, J. R. "Mr. Perry's Patients: A View of *Emma.*" *Essays in Criticism* 20 (1970): 334–43.

Watt, Ian, ed. *Critical Jane Austen: A Collection of Essays.* Englewood Cliffs, N.J.: Prentice-Hall, 1963.

Weinsheimer, Joel. "Theory of Character: *Emma.*" *Poetics Today* 1, nos. 1–2 (1979): 185–211.

———, ed. *Jane Austen Today.* Athens: University of Georgia Press, 1975.

Welty, Eudora. "A Note on Jane Austen." *Shenandoah* 20, no. 3 (1969): 3–17.

White, E. M. "A Critical Theory of *Mansfield Park.*" *Studies in English Literature 1500–1900* 7 (1967): 659–77.

White, Edward M. "Freedom is Restraint: The Pedagogical Problem of Jane Austen." *San Jose Studies* 2, no. 1 (1976): 84–90.

Whitten, Benjamin. *Jane Austen's Comedy of Feeling: A Critical Analysis of* Persuasion. Ankara: Hacettepe University Publications, 1974.

Wiesenfarth, Joseph. *The Errand of Form.* New York: Fordham University Press, 1967.

Wilhelm, Cherry. "*Persuasion:* Time Redeemed." *English Studies in Africa* 22 (1979): 91–98.

Williams, Raymond. *The Country and the City.* New York: Oxford University Press, 1973.

Willis, Lesley H. "Eyes and the Imagery of Sight in *Pride and Prejudice.*" *English Studies in Canada* 2, no. 2 (1976): 156–62.

Wilson, Mona. *Jane Austen and Some Contemporaries.* London: Cresset Press, 1938.

Wilt, Judith. "Jane Austen's Men: Inside/Outside 'the Mystery.'" *Women & Literature* 2 (1982): 59–76.

The Wordsworth Circle 7, no. 4 (1976). Special Jane Austen issue.

Wright, Andrew. *Jane Austen's Novels: A Study in Structure.* New York: Oxford University Press, 1953.

Zelicovici, Dvora. "The Inefficacy of *Lover's Vows*." *ELH* 50, no. 3 (1983): 531–
    40.
Zimmerman, Everett. "Jane Austen and *Mansfield Park:* A Discrimination of Ironies."
    Studies in the Novel 1 (1969): 347–56.

Acknowledgments

"Chance and the Hierarchy of Marriages in *Pride and Prejudice*" by Joel Weinsheimer from *ELH* 39, no. 3 (September 1972), © 1972 by The Johns Hopkins University Press. Reprinted by permission.

"'A Pair of Fine Eyes': Jane Austen's Treatment of Sex" by Alice Chandler from *Studies in the Novel* 7, no. 1 (Spring 1975), © 1975 by North Texas State University. Reprinted by permission.

"*Sense and Sensibility,* or Growing Up Dichotomous" by Ruth apRoberts from *Nineteenth-Century Fiction* 30, no. 3 (December 1975), © 1975 by the Regents of the University of California. Reprinted by permission of the University of California Press.

"Ann Elliot's Dowry: Reflections on the Ending of *Persuasion*" by Gene W. Ruoff from *The Wordsworth Circle* 7, no. 4 (Autumn 1976), © 1976 by Marilyn Gaull. Reprinted by permission.

"Shut Up in Prose: Gender and Genre in Austen's Juvenilia" by Sandra M. Gilbert and Susan Gubar from *The Madwoman in the Attic: The Woman Writer and the Nineteenth-Century Literary Imagination* by Sandra M. Gilbert and Susan Gubar, © 1979 by Yale University. Reprinted by permission of Yale University Press.

"Civilization and the Contentment of *Emma*" by Julia Prewitt Brown from *Jane Austen's Novels: Social Change and Literary Form* by Julia Prewitt Brown, © 1979 by the President and Fellows of Harvard College. Reprinted by permission of Harvard University Press.

"Guessing for Ourselves in *Northanger Abbey*" by Susan Morgan from *In the Meantime: Character and Perception in Jane Austen's Fiction* by Susan Morgan, © 1980 by The University of Chicago. Reprinted by permission of the University of Chicago Press.

"Reading Aloud in *Mansfield Park*" by Gary Kelly from *Nineteenth-Century Fiction* 37, no. 1 (June 1982), © 1982 by the Regents of the University of California. Reprinted by permission of the University of California Press and the author.

233

"Persuasion in *Persuasion*" by Ann Molan from *The Critical Review*, no. 24 (1982), © 1982 by Ann Molan. Reprinted by permission.

"Austen: Manners and Morals" (originally entitled "Manners, Morals, and Jane Austen") by Martin Price from *Nineteenth-Century Fiction* 30, no. 3 (December 1975), © 1975 by the Regents of the University of California. Reprinted by permission of the University of California Press and Yale University Press. This essay also appeared in *Forms of Life: Character and Imagination in the Novel* by Martin Price (Yale University Press, © 1983 by Yale University).

"Austen's Ambiguous Conclusions" by Robin Grove from *The Critical Review*, no. 25 (1983), © 1983 by Robin Grove. Reprinted by permission.

"Jane Austen and the Traditions of Comic Aggression" by Ian Watt from *Persuasions: Journal of the Jane Austen Society of North America*, © 1981 by Ian Watt. Reprinted by permission.

"Achieving Authority: Austen's First Published Novel" by Deborah Kaplan from *Nineteenth-Century Fiction* 37, no. 4 (March 1983), © 1983 by the Regents of the University of California. Reprinted by permission of the University of California Press.

Index

Abstract diction, 43–45, 163–64
Almon, John, 31
Anglicanism, 216–17
Antithesis. *See* Dichotomy
Archer, Isabel (*The Portrait of a Lady*, James), 10, 88
Arnold, Matthew, 45
Assertiveness, 76, 78, 161, 203–18
Auden, W. H., 73–74
Auerbach, Nina, 82
Austen, Jane, 2, 7, 27–28, 151, 179, 206; and Anglicanism, 216–17; anonymity of, 69–70; as asexual writer, 27, 41; and authority, 207, 214–15, 216–17; and characters, 157, 158–59, 187–88; and children, 52–53; class attitudes of, 97–100; complex protagonists of, 155, 191–92; as conservative, 57–58; criticism of, 70–71; and escapist fiction, 76, 81; in historical context, 216–17; and human nature, 102–3, 115, 118, 120, 121–22, 153; irony in works of, 155, 171, 182–83, 186–87, 188; language, criticism of, 145; limitations of, 70–72, 86, 200–201; literalism, 45, 47; literary conventions, attack on, 126–27, 141; love, concept of, 94; as miniaturist, 70–71; as moralist, 103, 169–70, 171, 173; optimism of, 57–58; paradoxical attitudes of, 185; patrilineage, ridicule of, 217–18; on perfection, 109; and poets, 43, 46–47; and reader, 67–68, 130, 137, 145; and realism, 66; and

Romanticism, 110; and society, 5, 28, 31–32, 60, 78; as symbol of culture, 72–74, 79; and use of literary allusion, 29; and women, 36, 216–17; as writer, 71–72, 163, 176, 187–88, 206–7, 215–17, 218; Works: "Catharine, or, The Bower," 76, 81–82, 84; "First Impressions," 206; "Frederic and Elfrida," 86; "History of England," 187; "Jack and Alice," 85; *Lady Susan*, 79, 186; *Love and Freindship*, 69, 75–77, 78–79, 186; *Sanditon*, 79–80; "Susan," 206; *The Watsons*, 76, 84, 85; *See also Emma; Mansfield Park; Northanger Abbey; Persuasion; Pride and Prejudice; Sense and Sensibility*
Authority, 203–18; Austen's attitude toward, 207, 214–15, 216–17; as dependence, 217; illusory vs. real, 215–16; masculine vs. feminine, 207, 208–9, 210, 213–14; modification of, 207–8; narcissism and, 207, 209; patriarchy and, 206–18; reform of, 214–15; and reproduction, 207, 208–9
Authorship, female, 203–6

Bates, Miss (*Emma*), 73, 102, 172
Beginnings (Said), 204, 205
Bennet, Elizabeth (*Pride and Prejudice*), 186; and chance, 20–21, 22–24; as Cinderella, 59; comic aggression and, 194–95; contrast to Darcy,

235